MANAGING RISK IN
HIGH-STAKES FACULTY
EMPLOYMENT DECISIONS

Managing Risk in High-Stakes Faculty Employment Decisions

Julee T. Flood and Terry L. Leap

ILR Press
an imprint of
Cornell University Press
Ithaca and London

First published 2018 by Cornell University Press

Printed in the United States of America

Library of Congress Cataloging-in-Publication Data

Names: Flood, Julee T., author. | Leap, Terry L., 1948– author.
Title: Managing risk in high-stakes faculty employment decisions / Julee
    T. Flood and Terry L. Leap.
Description: 1st edition. | Ithaca [New York] : ILR Press, an imprint of
    Cornell University Press, 2018. | Includes bibliographical references
    and index.
Identifiers: LCCN 2018013448 (print) | LCCN 2018015230 (ebook) |
    ISBN 9781501728969 (pdf) | ISBN 9781501728976 (epub/mobi) |
    ISBN 9781501728952 | ISBN 9781501728952 (pbk. : alk. paper)
Subjects: LCSH: College teachers—Legal status, laws, etc.—United
    States. | College teachers—Selection and appointment—United States. |
    Universities and colleges—Law and legislation—United States. |
    Tort liability of universities and colleges—United States. | College
    teachers—Tenure—United States.
Classification: LCC KF4240 (ebook) | LCC KF4240. F56 2018 (print) |
    DDC 344.7301/01—dc23
LC record available at https://lccn.loc.gov/2018013448

To our families

You may think, at times, that you have reached a correct and final answer. I assure you this is a delusion on your part. You will never, in my classroom, reach the final, correct, and ultimate answer. In my classroom there is always another question. There is always a question to follow your answer.

—CHARLES KINGSFIELD, *The Paper Chase*

CONTENTS

PREFACE

Challenging human resource management issues plague U.S. colleges and universities. In this book, we provide an analysis of how these institutions hire, employ, and evaluate tenure track, non–tenure track, and adjunct faculty members. Our analysis of these important functions is based on the ways that institutions manage risk and try to avoid hiring faculty who turn out to be unproductive, counterproductive, and sometimes even toxic or dangerous. Disputes between faculty members and their institutions often arise over issues associated with contract and constitutional law, often intensifying when the nebulous concept of collegiality is added to the mix. And contracts, constitutional amendments, and collegiality are not isolated. They interact and are superimposed in ways that make academic human resource management decisions especially complex.

Dozens of books and hundreds of articles have been written about the ways institutions of higher learning are run and academic freedom is defined and about the wisdom of granting tenure to academicians, among other issues. Our unique contribution to this literature is to focus on how we might integrate risk management concepts and frameworks into issues that have plagued colleges and universities for decades. We will avoid a lengthy discussion of civil rights laws, most notably Title VII of the 1964 Civil Rights Act, because civil rights statutes have been analyzed in detail in an earlier work, *Tenure, Discrimination, and the Courts* (Leap 1995), and because civil rights cases have largely favored the institution. Instead, we will first provide a description of the academic landscape, including a discussion of academic careers. We will then examine growing concerns about faculty contracts and the constitutional issues associated with free speech and academic freedom. Additionally, we will examine behaviors that raise questions about a faculty member's collegiality. At the same time, we will reinforce the idea that these issues are intertwined and defy simple analysis.

Most administrators, when hired to serve as department heads, deans, provosts, chancellors, and presidents, have little background in or formal instruction on human resource management issues, so they often learn as they go. A few administrators may be lucky enough to avoid suits that create serious public relations problems or expensive litigation. We believe, however, that the vast majority of academic decision-makers need to understand critical academic personnel problems and institutional risk exposures.

Our audience includes attorneys and counsel who have substantial legal knowledge but little knowledge of the culture of academia; faculty who have accepted administrative positions and who understand the culture of academia, but have little knowledge of or training in legal requisites; and faculty members who face or who may face hiring, retention, or promotion issues. Higher education consultants may also find the book valuable, especially those who help their clients to manage the many risks associated with faculty employment decisions.

Acknowledgments

Many have supported this project along the way. We thank Matthew B. Fuller, associate professor of higher education leadership and director of the doctoral program in higher education leadership at Sam Houston State University, and an anonymous reviewer for their helpful comments. To research assistant Janelle Wendorf, thank you for providing additional scrutiny of manuscript drafts. Thanks also go to the talented professionals at Cornell University Press who have helped us convey our message—Meagan Dermody, Karen Hwa, Julia Cook, and Martyn Beeny. Finally, we especially appreciate the guidance of Frances Benson, editorial director of ILR Press, for her continued support of this project as it evolved.

Managing Risk in High-Stakes Faculty Employment Decisions

INTRODUCTION

Recruiting, hiring, and retaining college and university faculty members raises a number of important issues. Where do these institutions look to find the best faculty candidates, and how do these institutions identify the best candidates from the applicant pool while avoiding faculty who may later pose problems? On the one hand, did the University of Illinois hiring committee that extended a job offer to Rosalyn Sussman Yalow in the 1940s have any way of knowing that over three decades later she would win the Nobel Prize? On the other hand, would a more careful vetting have prevented the murderous rampage of biology professor Amy Bishop, who killed three of her colleagues—and wounded six—at the University of Alabama in Huntsville after she had been denied tenure there? Why did a background check not uncover Bishop's erratic and violent history? Likewise, would a more informed screening have identified serial sexual harassers before they had the opportunity to cause disruptions at some of the most prestigious universities in the United States?[1] Or could more prudent risk management have avoided the overeager hiring of a "next academic superstar" faculty member whose research productivity quickly fizzled out? These difficult questions indicate a need for better risk management by colleges and universities. For instance, should colleges and universities do a better job of screening faculty members before they are hired, looking beyond what formal background checks may or may not reveal? Is it possible to dig deeper into a faculty candidate's past than is normally the case with a routine background check? Would Bishop's banishment from campus—perhaps while still paying her for the academic year—have prevented her murderous rampage?

The vast majority of problem faculty members demonstrate considerably less egregious behaviors than those of an Amy Bishop or a serial sexual harasser. Yet the public pronouncements and embarrassing behaviors of faculty members might still discredit the institutions where they work. What risks, for example, did a major medical school take when it unknowingly hired an academically prominent but ill-tempered dean who led a secret double life as a partier who abused drugs and participated in orgies?[2] Could this institution, which had garnered ample warnings about his behavior, have done more to avoid the embarrassing publicity that this dean inflicted upon it?[3] How tempting is it for an institution to look the other way when a rogue faculty member is also a gigantic rainmaker who brings in millions of dollars in research grants? Challenging human resource management issues such as these continue to plague U.S. colleges and universities. How do we avoid hiring faculty who turn out to be nonproductive, counterproductive, and even toxic? Bad faculty hires may exhibit a disappointing level of research productivity, incompetent teaching, disruptive behaviors, a litigious bent, or possibly actions that pose physical threats to themselves and others.

Hiring and retaining the most productive faculty members also requires that institutional decision makers and counsel be mindful of the academic landscape of U.S. higher education. What are the latest trends in tenure, free speech, and collegiality? What about the emerging multitiered system of tenured faculty, tenure track faculty, non–tenure track faculty with contracts, and adjunct faculty? The third group may teach the same classes and work only feet away from their more privileged colleagues, but they might as well be on another planet when it comes to how poorly they are often treated.

Risk management plays an important role in finding answers (or partial answers) to these questions. This book seeks to provide advice on how to prevent, minimize, or avoid issues pertaining to the hiring and management of faculty members. We believe that a better understanding of legal and human resource management practices, framed within the unique culture of academia, may help decrease institutional risk exposure. The audience for whom a discussion of the risks associated with faculty employment may be most useful includes attorneys and counsel who have substantial legal knowledge, but little knowledge of the culture of academia; faculty who have accepted administrative positions and who understand the culture of academia, but have little knowledge of or training in legal requisites; and faculty members who face or who may face hiring, retention, or promotion issues.

Faculty and administrators usually have limited training in human resource management issues (hiring, developing, evaluating, and rewarding staff) or legal issues (equal employment opportunity law, contractual matters, or basic constitutional protections). A newly appointed provost with a professional background in nuclear engineering cannot be expected to understand the intricacies, or even the basics, of employment law. Since colleges and universities provide little or no legal or human resource management training for newly appointed administrators, these administrators are often forced to learn on the job, perhaps with the help of university legal counsel and academic consultants.

This lack of training can become a quite risky and expensive problem for the institution, especially if it leads to an inadvertent violation of civil rights, contract, tort, or constitutional law, resulting in a lawsuit. For the faculty member, litigation costs can be highly variable and potentially financially ruinous. The psychological trauma associated with a civil suit can be devastating as these cases drag on, moving in and out of court over a period of several years. Immersing one's life and financial resources into a highly complex, drawn out, and stressful process where the odds of winning are low takes its toll both personally and professionally. For large institutions that employ full-time in-house legal counsel, the expense of litigation is largely fixed and is viewed simply as another cost of doing business, but the public relations fallout is something that most schools prefer to avoid.

The landscape of U.S. higher education is in a state of flux with many uncertainties on the horizon. Before we address the issue of risk management, we believe it would be helpful to describe the categories of institutions along with some of the major issues and trends affecting U.S. higher education. Readers who work outside academia or who are new to it may find the issues summarized here to be of special interest. We will then delve into some of the salient risks that arise on U.S. campuses.

The Academic Landscape

U.S. colleges and universities are regarded collectively as the best in the world, and many of these schools are steeped in rich traditions of academic excellence. These institutions of higher learning disseminate vast amounts of knowledge, prepare students to become responsible and productive citizens, sponsor major cultural and athletic events, and create knowledge through basic and applied research.

Academia can also be a wonderful place to work. Faculty members often find themselves surrounded by intellectually stimulating colleagues and an internationally diverse student body. An especially attractive feature of academic life is being able to work in an environment that encourages creativity. Professors have traditionally had the academic freedom to pursue their professional interests and to teach their classes the way they want. They also have a great deal of discretion with regard to the research agendas they pursue. Furthermore, many colleges and universities have beautiful architecture and landscapes that enhance the quality of life for those fortunate enough to work and study there.[4]

But, as is the case with every occupation, there are drawbacks. Not everyone is comfortable working in an unstructured environment with little day-to-day supervision and accountability. College and university faculty do not punch time clocks and, with few restrictions, they come and go as they please. Although tenured faculty members have a strong degree of job security, faculty members on the tenure track must eventually face an up-or-out tenure evaluation process that can be contentious and even brutal. Meanwhile faculty salaries, with the possible exception of those in the professional schools of medicine, engineering, business, and law, fall well below the salaries of the corporate world. Roughly measured, the level of education and effort required to secure a university faculty position vastly exceeds the pay and benefits of that position.

The Kaleidoscope of U.S. Colleges and Universities

Most large universities fall into the category of research school. Faculty members at these schools are expected to present the results of their research and creative work in books, academic journals, government scientific reports, exhibits, and concerts. Elite private universities, including the eight Ivy League schools plus the Massachusetts Institute of Technology (MIT), the University of Chicago, Stanford University, and the California Institute of Technology (Cal Tech), along with top-tier public universities such as the University of California, Berkeley, the University of California, Los Angeles (UCLA), the University of North Carolina at Chapel Hill, and the University of Michigan, expect their faculty to produce research of the highest quality. While much of this creative work escapes the public eye, a great deal of it has led to advances in the biological, physical, and social sciences as well as in the arts and humanities. Not surprisingly, the work of Nobel laureates often begins on a college campus.

Faculty members at research institutions typically become experts in a narrow segment of an academic discipline. For example, an entomologist at a major research school may be known worldwide for her expertise on certain species of bees found in the Amazon River basin, a biologist may devote his professional life to the study of fungi, a psychologist may spend her career studying the personality development of children, or a law school professor might be known for her expertise on legal issues in the music industry. Although the top-tier research schools support and pay their faculty well, the standards for promotion and tenure at these schools are often extremely high. In fact, the well-worn phrase "publish or perish" is the norm at nearly all research institutions.

Research schools also expect excellence in graduate teaching. A university that is serious about the research productivity of its faculty, however, usually offers teaching loads of no more than two classes a semester. Most research universities also provide tenured faculty with periodic paid sabbaticals.[5] Sabbaticals allow for uninterrupted time for research, and many faculty members spend their sabbaticals working at other universities, usually with colleagues who share similar research interests.

Teaching schools focus primarily on teaching undergraduate students. Professors at these schools conduct little or no research. Instead, they teach seven or eight classes during an academic year, and their teaching load may cover a wide variety of subjects. A history professor at a teaching school, for example, might teach courses in ancient history, Chinese history, the history of religion, and U.S. Civil War history, all within the span of one or two academic years. Heavy teaching loads and multiple class preparations make it difficult for faculty at these schools to conduct research or to write journal articles and books. Professors in community colleges, small private colleges, and specialized institutions such as technical schools devote their professional lives primarily to sharing existing knowledge and preparing students for the workplace—that is, they typically disseminate rather than create knowledge. Promotion, tenure, and job retention at these schools is based on a faculty member's teaching quality, the demand for his courses, and his participation in school service activities such as student advising.

In reality, the distinction between teaching and research schools is not always clear. Colleges and universities have different teaching and research balances—not only among different institutions, but also within these same institutions. Even within a single department, teaching and research expectations may vary from one faculty member to another. These differences should be carefully explained to each faculty member so that misunderstandings about expectations are avoided. The Carnegie Foundation for the Advancement of Teaching has classified institutions of higher learning. Each of these categories, in turn, contains subcategories that further differentiate these institutions.[6] The classifications are as follows: associate's colleges, baccalaureate colleges, master's colleges and universities, doctorate-granting universities (this category has three subcategories, including schools that awarded at least twenty research doctoral degrees), special focus institutions, and tribal colleges.

The point that we want to make here is that colleges and universities come in all sizes and shapes, which makes it difficult to generalize about their missions and modes of operation. It is the job of an institution's leaders to determine how faculty members are hired, trained, and evaluated as well as the specific tasks, duties, and responsibilities to which they are assigned. A school's board of trustees, along with its president, chancellor, provost, and collegiate deans, is responsible for a school's broad strategic initiatives. Other administrators, such as associate and assistant deans, institute directors, department heads, and nonacademic staff, usually work in the trenches, overseeing a school's day-to-day operations.

Issues Facing U.S. Colleges and Universities in the Early Twenty-First Century

U.S. institutions of higher learning face a complex set of issues. Some of the more prominent ones are: (1) the soaring cost of higher education and the heavy debt loads faced by many college graduates; (2) concerns over eroding standards and less rigor in college classrooms; (3) the growing number of nonacademic administrators who hold positions of increasing power and who are thought to usurp the academic autonomy of the faculty; (4) the zealous pursuit of higher and higher institutional rankings by colleges and universities—especially those published annually by the *U.S. News & World Report*; (5) the controversies about academic freedom, free speech, and political correctness in institutions of higher learning; (6) the long-standing debate surrounding what constitutes the "proper" curriculum and goals of a college education; (7) the growing problem of criminal behaviors on college campuses; (8) the ongoing and sometimes contentious debate about academic tenure; and (9) the plight of adjunct faculty.

The High Cost of a College Education

The cost of higher education in the United States has increased substantially faster than the rate of inflation, and the tuition and fees charged by many colleges and universities place a heavy financial burden on middle-class families. Added to the steep tuitions are the exorbitant costs of textbooks and computer technology. Although most textbook prices fall in the $100 to $200 range, *CBS MoneyWatch* has identified at least two textbooks that have a retail price tag of over $1,000 and at least a dozen others that cost $500 or more.[7] The tab can increase by another $2,000 to $3,000 when a student is required to purchase a laptop computer and course software.

Three quarters of the students graduating from U.S. colleges and universities carry an average indebtedness of $35,051. When the debts are added up for all students, the total reaches an amazing $1.2 trillion.[8] Staggering debt coupled with dim job prospects and meager projected incomes for many students—especially those with degrees in the humanities—means that student loan debt will plague many graduates for years or even decades after they leave campus. Onerous debt loads can create personal financial dilemmas that have serious implications for major life decisions such as marriage, starting a family, purchasing a home, or seeking a postgraduate degree. Even declaring bankruptcy will not erase these debts. Some politicians, however, have advocated legislation that will tailor loan repayments to a debtor's post-graduation income, with the government picking up the tab on any remaining outstanding debt after a defined repayment period such as twenty years.[9]

Eroding Academic Standards

An unacceptably large percentage of undergraduate students who are entering college in the early years of the twenty-first century are taking more than four years to earn their baccalaureate degrees. Students who fail to complete their studies in a timely fashion not only increase the costs of their own education, but they make it more difficult for a college or university to accommodate new students. Delayed graduations are sometimes the result of a student switching majors or losing transfer credits, but this trend also suggests that colleges and universities are admitting students who are either academically unprepared or who are in no hurry to leave the comforts of a college campus and face the workaday world. Highly selective schools, almost without exception, have higher four-year graduation rates than their less selective counterparts. According to the College Board, for example, the highly selective and academically rigorous MIT has a four-year graduation rate of 84 percent, whereas the nearby University of Massachusetts Boston graduates only 13 percent of its students in four years.[10]

All professors—even those with only a modicum of classroom teaching experience—can share stories about students who rarely, if ever, attend class. And when it comes to identifying and correcting irresponsible student behaviors, faculty members and the families of students find themselves hamstrung by federal law. The Family Educational Rights and Privacy Act (FERPA) restricts parents and other interested parties from obtaining academic information about a college student. Thus, parents who are paying huge sums to send their son or daughter to college might have no idea that their investment in tuition, room, and board has been squandered. A cab driver related to one of us that she worked at three jobs to save the $26,000 needed to send her daughter to a state university in

Florida. Months later she discovered to her horror that her daughter had spent her first year of college attending numerous parties but never setting foot in a classroom. Her freshman grade point average was a perfect 0.00. Had the woman inquired, she would have been told by school officials that FERPA would not allow them to disclose her daughter's academic progress (or, in this case, a complete lack of progress).

But even for the diligent student, the road to a college degree may contain obstacles, most notably the need to hold a part-time job to help cover the costs of tuition, food, rent, and other necessities. Employment outside the classroom not only cuts into study time, but a late-night job may lead to chronic sleep deprivation, a further impediment to academic progress.

Although college graduates stand to earn a much larger income over their lifetimes than do people holding only a high school diploma, some critics continue to pursue the argument that college today is not worth the money, claiming that there has been a gradual but significant erosion of the academic core. These critics—members of the media who write for publications such as *The Chronicle of Higher Education* or *Inside Higher Ed* as well as faculty and administrators who follow educational trends and events—bolster their position by pointing to how colleges pamper students by offering them posh dorms, access to gourmet dining, no early-morning classes, and state-of-the art weight rooms and rock climbing walls. Other critics sound off about the distracting emphasis of intercollegiate athletics and the surface appeal of extracurricular functions that contribute little to learning. Many critics cap their argument by citing evidence that college graduates lack the ability to think critically or to communicate effectively, both of which diminish their employability.[11]

Paradoxically, delayed graduations do not seem to be the result of heavier academic demands. To the contrary, there are accusations that courses and curricula have been watered down and are less rigorous than in decades past. College students today spend significantly less time studying than did students of their parents' generation. Baby boomers attending college in the late 1960s and early 1970s regarded the grade of C as an acceptable evaluation of their work. But the Generation Y students, who now live with a grade distribution that has been truncated by years of relaxed standards, view the grade of C as unacceptable.

The conservative columnist and Stanford University professor Thomas Sowell has made reference to the "touchy-feely mush" and "trendy social projects" that have become a part and parcel of K–12 education.[12] Sowell could have easily blamed these same practices for the erosion of academic standards at U.S. colleges and universities. Furthermore, U.S. students are avoiding the rigorous STEM majors (science, technology, engineering, and math) that are now heavily populated by students from outside the United States. In fact, international students—not students from the United States—earn more than half of the advanced STEM degrees that are awarded on U.S. campuses.[13]

We tend to overlook the fact that students spend only about five percent of their life span attending college. So, how should this narrow window of opportunity best be used? Do students benefit more by studying philosophy and calculus or by picking up roadside litter as part of a college-sanctioned public service project? Perhaps academic pursuits should trump social programs since college graduates will still have four or five decades after graduation to do whatever community volunteer work they find rewarding. Given concerns with eroding standards and excessive time spent earning a degree, colleges and universities should take a hard look at extracurricular student activities and decide whether these activities enhance or diminish the core academic mission of an institution of higher learning.

Academic standards may also be lowered by the professor's desire to stay on good terms with students so that his teaching evaluations remain positive. Because promotion and tenure committees scrutinize student assessments of teaching effectiveness, an untenured professor may be especially fearful that a handful of disgruntled students may rate him harshly if he imposes uncomfortably high academic standards or awards too many low grades. Furthermore, an anonymous student can damage a professor's reputation through postings on Internet sites such as RateMyProfessors. com. These sites were originally designed to enable students to exchange useful information about professors and their courses. But these same sites can be used as a tool for cyberbullying.[14]

Administrative Bloat

The public is less aware of a major problem on many U.S. campuses—the rapid growth of campus bureaucracies that divert money from educational endeavors and distract faculty from their scholarly work. The organizational structures at most colleges and universities have become overrun with administrators, and at some schools administrators outnumber faculty members. The Johns Hopkins University political science professor Benjamin Ginsberg has pointed to the multilayered administrative structures where administrators have inserted themselves into faculty hiring, curriculum development, grading, and other academic matters—tasks that have traditionally been the purview of academics.[15] One author has described such administrative creep as a "cancerous disease."[16]

Growing academic bureaucracies and their increasing span of control are forcing institutions of higher learning to spend large sums of money on compliance efforts. Nicholas Zeppos, the chancellor of Vanderbilt University, broke down the compliance costs at his school and claimed that these costs annually amounted to $11,000 per student. Vanderbilt, a highly respected research university that also covets excellence in teaching, had total compliance costs of $146 million in 2014, of which $117 million were for research compliance. Also included in this cost estimate was the $14 million needed to cover the costs of higher education–specific costs, including the costs of accreditation.[17] A *New York Times* article offers this view of administrative bloat:

> By contrast, a major factor driving increasing costs is the constant expansion of university administration. According to the Department of Education data, administrative positions at colleges and universities grew by 60 percent between 1993 and 2009, which Bloomberg reported was 10 times the rate of growth of tenured faculty positions.
>
> Even more strikingly, an analysis by a professor at California Polytechnic University, Pomona, found that, while the total number of full-time faculty members in the C.S.U. system grew from 11,614 to 12,019 between 1975 and 2008, the total number of administrators grew from 3,800 to 12,183—a 221 percent increase.
>
> The rapid increase in college enrollment can be defended by intellectually respectable arguments. Even the explosion in administration personnel is, at least in theory, defensible. On the other hand, there are no valid arguments to support the recent trend toward seven-figure salaries for high-ranking university administrators, unless one considers evidence-free assertions about "the market" to be intellectually rigorous.[18]

Most families are willing to write a tuition check for several thousand dollars, believing that their student will receive a quality education from knowledgeable professors. These same families, however, might be outraged to learn that a huge chunk of their hard-earned dollars has been diverted from their student's learning to cover the salaries of an ever-expanding cadre of administrators, most of whom never teach a class.

The Rankings Game

Brand name and reputation are clearly important to U.S. institutions of higher learning. In the late summer months, academic administrators can be found anxiously awaiting the release of the latest *U.S. News & World Report* rankings of colleges and universities. These rankings have become a driving force in U.S. higher education as administrators develop strategic plans and focus on metrics that they hope will enhance their school's chances of moving up the rankings ladder. And it seems that advancing one or two places in the rankings might trigger a major celebration, even though such progress may be nothing more than random measurement error.

The *U.S. News* uses over a dozen criteria to rank colleges and universities, including admission acceptance rates, alumni giving, graduation rates, the number of small classes offered, expenditures made per student, and peer assessments from other schools. It is certainly not lost on college administrators that these metrics are susceptible to manipulation. Applicant acceptance rates can be lowered—making the school appear to be more selective than it really is—by encouraging unqualified applicants to apply, knowing full well that these students have no chance of being admitted. The *U.S. News* rankings also favor class sizes of fewer than twenty students. So, another way of manipulating the rankings is to create one huge class section of, say, 200 freshman English students and then to schedule several small class sections of the same course. To encourage low enrollments, a university might offer the small sections of the freshman English course at inconvenient times (for instance, at 8:00 a.m. or 6:00 p.m.). As far as we can tell, however, the *U.S News* ranking experts seem to care little about the quality of the instructors who actually teach these class sections, though students enrolled in a class of 100 taught by an award-winning instructor stand to learn much more than students in a class of fifteen taught by an inept one.

The *U.S. News* is not shy about making side-by-side comparisons of schools that are vastly different. An article in *The New Yorker* by

Malcolm Gladwell noted that placing two dissimilar schools—Penn State University and Yeshiva University—under the same ranking system makes little sense because these schools have different missions, locations, and modes of operation.[19] One is large, one is relatively small. One is rural, the other urban. One is public, the other private. One places an extremely heavy emphasis on NCAA Division 1 athletics while the other does not. This example illustrates an apples-and-oranges comparison that is at best meaningless and at worst grossly misleading.

When one looks at the math behind these rankings, the ranking process appears to be even more nonsensical. One public institution that was recently ranked among the *U.S. News* top twenty had no undergraduate colleges with a national top twenty ranking. Equally perplexing was that this institution's administration was accused, when completing their peer assessments, of ranking competing schools as "below average" as a way of elevating their own ranking.

Rankings have long precipitated heated debate, regardless of what (or who) is being ranked. Interestingly, significant increases or declines in institutional rankings are not common, even when highly publicized academic, athletic, or sexual harassment scandals taint the reputation of a campus. Not long ago, one of us was asked to complete a ranking questionnaire that solicited our opinion about schools with which we had little or no familiarity. We were able to assess our own institution (with no biases, of course) and we were able to evaluate—with some semblance of accuracy—a school where one of us recently worked. Beyond that, however, we knew next to nothing about the schools we were being asked to rate.

A question that academic administrators, especially those with social science backgrounds, should ask themselves is this: if a PhD candidate developed a dissertation proposal that ranked business corporations using a methodology that was similar to the *U.S. News* methodology, would any self-respecting social scientist approve this project? We suspect that the answer to this question would be a resounding "no." A corporation is evaluated on end-results measures such as the price of its stock, consumer ratings of its products and services, or its profits. But the *U.S. News* ranks colleges and universities primarily on process measures such as class sizes and expenditures per student rather than on the achievements of their students or the prominence of their faculty. A good measure of student achievement is the percentage of an institution's graduates that later earn a postgraduate degree, and a good measure of the quality of a school's faculty is the number of professors holding fellowships in prestigious academic societies. It can be argued that even these successes are more of a reflection on the caliber of those who are hired or admitted to an institution rather than on what the institution contributed to their achievements. Nevertheless, process measures that are poorly linked to end results tell us little about the true quality of an institution. But, at least in the eyes of the *U.S. News* analysts, processes speak louder than end results.

Academic Freedom and Academic License

Academic freedom is supposed to allow professors to pursue the truth, no matter where that pursuit might lead. Yet, contrary to popular belief, academic freedom is not necessarily synonymous with free speech, and faculty members can no longer count on these ideals to protect their employment at a college or university. At one end of the spectrum, for example, a professor who asserts that Descartes's philosophy is "full of logical flaws" may astound other academics who believe that Descartes's thinking forms the foundation of modern philosophy. Despite the heated rhetoric that might emerge from this debate, academic freedom supports such honorable, but conflicting, views. At the other end of the spectrum is the problem of academic license, where a faculty member engages in unprofessional or irresponsible behavior and expects naively that the principle of academic freedom will serve as a free pass. A professor, for example, cannot use the idea of academic freedom to get away with canceling most of his classes and giving students high grades for doing little or no work. Nor can a professor be allowed to take unfair advantage of a student by requiring him to provide free babysitting or domestic help as part of a research assistantship. Somewhere in the middle of the academic freedom-academic license spectrum is where the protections afforded to certain types of speech become less certain. A state university professor who is tempted to level accusations of incompetence against the central administration on her campus is advised to proceed with extreme caution. Based on recent litigation (to be discussed in chapter 4), such criticisms appear to fall outside the scope of academic freedom and protected speech. Furthermore, faculty members at private colleges cannot rely at all on free speech rights to protect their jobs. A professor at a denominational college who speaks out in support of gay marriage may find himself in a precarious position if the college's president is offended by his speech. A professor at a state university making the same speech, however, could invoke her constitutional free speech rights to protect her job.[20]

Anyone who has spent time on a college campus in recent years is aware of the growing pressures for faculty and students to comport themselves in ways that will ensure conformity with political correctness. One infamous case is the Water Buffalo scandal at the University of Pennsylvania.[21] A dormitory resident at Penn asked a group of African American sorority sisters who were gathered outside his window to be quiet so that he could concentrate on writing a term paper. When they ignored his pleas, he yelled, "Shut up, you water buffalo!" This utterance was construed to be racist and it set off a firestorm on the Penn campus.

More recently, leaders at the flagship campus of the University of Missouri in Columbia were forced to resign amid accusations that they were not doing enough to stifle racism. In the wake of the Missouri debacle, students at Ithaca College, Yale University, Claremont McKenna College, and other small schools demonstrated over racial issues that appear to be far from egregious, citing stray remarks, inappropriate Halloween costumes, and "micro-aggressions" as evidence of "systematic oppression."[22]

While overt racism, sexist behaviors, or ethnic discrimination are to be condemned, some campus protesters are willing to make specious accusations of racism and mistreatment based on evidence that falls well short of the "beyond a reasonable doubt" or "preponderance of evidence" standards of criminal and civil cases, seemingly ignoring the tenets of due process in their haste to censure and punish those whose views they dislike.[23]

The University of New Hampshire's *Bias-Free Language Guide*—an eight-page guide written to inform faculty, staff, and students as to how to make speech more inclusive—provided a glossary of acceptable and unacceptable terminology, as well as a Gender Pronoun Guide and examples of microaggressions and macroaggressions.[24] As reflected in the guide, some members of the university community were apparently offended by the university's use of the terms "mothering" and "fathering," suggesting that "parenting" was the politically correct word of choice.[25] The supposedly neutral term of "parenting" overlooks the fact that mothers and fathers have for centuries served different biological, social, and cultural roles.

Although the university has since distanced itself from the guide, as demonstrated by its removal from the university's website, one has to wonder whether the notion of academic freedom might be in jeopardy if only the most outspoken purveyors of political correctness try to impose their opinions to the exclusion of the free speech rights of others.

The Curriculum Debate

A related concern is the age-old question of whether an ideal college curriculum exists. Academic debates on curriculum matters often address a number of interconnected questions. Does a college education provide a springboard for lifelong learning? Is there an ideal mix between courses in the arts and sciences and courses that are designed to enhance a student's employability after graduation? What is the appropriate level of rigor for an undergraduate education? Should colleges be more assertive in forcing students to take challenging courses in mathematics, the hard sciences (physics or chemistry), and foreign languages, even when these requirements fly in the face of *U. S. News* criteria, lengthening a student's time to graduation and lowering an institution's graduation rate? If so, will students avoid enrolling at colleges that impose heavy academic demands in favor of those that have more modest standards? Discussions of curriculum matters can become extremely heated, especially when those debates threaten the hidden agendas and turf wars of deans, department heads, and faculty who are trying to protect their courses, curricula, and student enrollments.

A critical issue facing institutions in the 2010s is trying to predict how online courses and distance learning will affect higher education over the following decade. Colleges and universities in the United States and beyond are diving headfirst into Internet technology to deliver a variety of courses and educational programs. The edX venture, initially a partnership between MIT and Harvard, has a growing number of prestigious universities on its list of affiliates. The venture provides high-quality courses—known as MOOCs (massive open online courses)—at little or no cost to the learner. Upon completing a course with a passing grade, an edX learner receives a certificate. Businesses may reward employees who complete a series of courses and earn a "micro masters" or equivalent online credential in subjects such as project management, business analytics, supply chain fundamentals, or computer programming.

Another MOOC provider that awards certificates of completion is Coursera. Coursera has teamed with the University of Illinois to provide a quality iMBA degree at a cost that is well below that of most on-campus MBA programs. The proliferation of online courses and degree programs raises the question as to whether traditional on-campus programs will experience declining enrollments as the number of online courses continues to grow and diversify. Earning a degree from a prestigious university program—once a pipe dream for many—may now be within the reach of thousands of talented and motivated students.[26]

Dangers on Campus

From the perspective of a criminologist, college campuses are crime facilitative organizations that provide an ideal climate for robberies, burglaries, and assaults. Institutions of higher learning are easily accessible to the public, and perpetrators from both inside and outside the campus can use classrooms, campus streets, green spaces, walking and hiking trails, dorm rooms, and parking garages as their hunting grounds. Criminals may also target victims at nearby off-campus sites such as bars, apartment complexes, and public parks. In addition, late-night parties that get out of hand, alcohol and drug abuse that lowers inhibitions, broken romances that turn suitors into stalkers, and the abundance of immature and entitled minds easily tempted to engage in acts of sexual harassment are all issues that campus administrators and law enforcement agents must face.

Title IX, which was passed in 1972, prohibits sex discrimination at educational institutions that receive public funds. Although Title IX is best known for addressing gender equity in sports programs, the law has also been applied to cases of sexual violence and harassment. The U.S. Department of Education's Office of Civil Rights (OCR) has issued multiple letters of guidance to colleges and universities describing their responsibilities under the act. Although it is clear that colleges and universities (and their surrounding communities) have social and legal obligations to create a safe campus environment, it is not clear how these institutions should proceed in dealing with the dark side of campus life. Laws regulating college campuses do not exist in isolation. It is a complicated task to develop a campus-wide safety plan that is fair, impartial, and in compliance with a web of federal laws, advisory letters, and reporting policies.

The efforts to control crime and violence, however, require a group effort from administrators, student organizations, health care staff, and even campus clergy. In addition, the support and coordination of local and state law enforcement is critical.

The Tenure Minefield

Perhaps the most hotly debated topic in U.S. higher education is faculty tenure. This debate has generated dozens of books, hundreds of journal articles, and countless editorials. Within these publications and, we suspect, within faculty lounges, professional meetings, and university administrative offices throughout the country, eloquent arguments have been made supporting the retention of tenure and equally eloquent arguments have been made encouraging its abolishment. An examination of both these arguments and current practices in higher education administration suggests that tenure may be on the gradual decline, but it is not going to disappear overnight.

The tenure system is supposed to protect professors from being terminated because of controversies surrounding their research findings, classroom teaching, political views, or public pronouncements. Admittedly, concern has been expressed from some corners that professors are using the classroom as a bully pulpit to indoctrinate students to their political views.[27] But the long-standing rationale behind tenure is that professors should be allowed to pursue the truth through their research and writings no matter where that truth might lead, and they must be able to do so without fear of reprisal.

Suppose that a faculty member at a state university conducts research showing that organized labor has improved the wages, hours, and working conditions of the state's manufacturing workers. These research findings, however, might be at odds with the agenda of politicians who are trying to attract industry and promote economic development. If tenure works as advertised, the faculty member should be protected from those who want her dismissed—even when those calling for her head come from such lofty places as the governor's mansion, the state senate, or the headquarters of a powerful lobbying group.

But even among tenured faculty members themselves, the usefulness of tenure is often questioned. Those supporting tenure point to it as the vehicle for promoting academic freedom and maintaining academic rigor. Yet the terms "academic freedom" and "academic rigor" defy precise definition. Does academic freedom mean the same thing for faculty in civil engineering as it does for faculty in political science? How does one compare the rigor of mathematics with the rigor expected of faculty and students in English or art history? And are there really that many cases where the protections afforded by tenure even need to be invoked?

Those rejecting the tenure system feel that it restricts an institution's ability to allocate resources and control costs as it sees fit. Opponents of tenure argue that the system can slowly, over time, create a faculty group that has a diminished interest in quality teaching or meaningful research. They claim that older professors who refuse to step aside make it difficult for institutions of higher learning to replenish their ranks with younger and, presumably, more engaged teachers and more productive scholars. The vocal and radical opponents of tenure, we believe, have unfairly painted tenured faculty members with a broad brush, characterizing them as overpaid, aging deadwood who add little value to the institution's academic mission. In reality, the vast majority of tenured professors, especially those beyond middle age, do not "retire on the job," and their performance ranges from very solid to monumental, even extending to winning the Nobel Prize.

Every year hundreds of tenure track faculty members fail to clear the tenure bar, usually because their research fails to pass muster or because their teaching is inadequate. In a few cases, a tenure track professor may be derailed because of problems with collegiality—they simply cannot get along with their fellow faculty, staff, or students. In chapter 5, we further explore the difficult concept of collegiality, especially as it pertains to faculty retention, promotion, and tenure. Once a decision is made to deny tenure, a faculty member is usually placed on a one-year terminal contract and is forced to start looking for a job elsewhere. Since the late 1960s, plaintiffs facing tenure denials or other adverse actions have used federal civil rights laws as their primary legal option. These laws, known commonly as equal employment opportunity or EEO laws, include Title VII of the 1964 Civil Rights Act (race, gender, religion, national origin, and skin color), the Age Discrimination in Employment Act (for plaintiffs age 40 and above), and the Americans With Disabilities Act (for plaintiffs with physical or mental disabilities).

Cases may arise where other laws also apply. These laws might include the Family and Medical Leave Act, the Pregnancy Discrimination Act, the National Labor Relations Act (regulating labor activities at private colleges and universities), the Occupational Safety and Health Act and state workers' compensation laws (when faculty are injured on the job), state privacy statutes, and laws regulating employee health care and retirement benefits (such as the Employee Retirement Income Security Act). And, as colleges and universities expand their presence outside of the United States and open campuses abroad, laws such as the Immigration Reform and Control Act may come into play.

We have seen from the extensive litigation of past years that laws prohibiting race and gender discrimination have not, to any significant extent, helped faculty who have been dismissed from their professorships. Judges simply do not want to second-guess the decisions of university faculty and administrators, and jurors have a hard time understanding why anyone is entitled to a lifetime of job security. Although judicial deference to academic decision makers has clearly been the norm over the past three decades, exceptions occasionally do arise where the faculty member prevails with at least a partial settlement. And, most important, we believe that contractual issues—separate from EEO law—will play an increasingly prominent role in the dismissal of tenured faculty.

The Rise of Non–Tenure Track Positions

As noted, the percentage of tenured faculty in U.S. institutions of higher learning appears to be declining—albeit slowly. One projected trend is that the number of tenured faculty will decline and eventually hit a plateau where only a few high profile professors are granted tenure. Dozens of articles lament the decline of tenure, and most of these articles suggest that the only remaining tenured faculty members may be those who are star researchers who are hired into tenured or tenure track faculty slots.[28]

Another current trend, however, is already crystal clear: tenured faculty members, when they quit or retire, are being replaced more and more by non–tenure track faculty who work under renewable contracts. Although non–tenure track faculty members have no job security beyond the life of their contracts, those who competently teach courses with robust enrollments may have their contracts renewed year after year, giving them a degree of job security that is on par with their tenured colleagues.

For colleges and universities, the major benefit of hiring non–tenure track faculty members is their low cost and flexibility. Non–tenure track faculty work for significantly lower pay and fewer benefits, and they usually receive no summer research stipends, graduate assistants, or expensive laboratory or computer equipment. A university may be able to hire two or three non–tenure track faculty members for the price of one tenured faculty member. And, since non–tenure track faculty members are not expected to engage in research, they usually carry teaching loads that are twice as heavy as their tenured counterparts. Furthermore, if enrollments decline or shift toward other disciplines, non–tenure track faculty members who no longer add significant value can be let go as soon as their contracts expire. For these reasons, non–tenure track faculty, with their high teaching loads, low salaries, and promise of flexible staffing, are a resource that many colleges and universities find too good to resist.[29]

The Adjunct Professor Paradox

Historically, tenured and tenure track faculty have enjoyed a middle-class lifestyle with good pay, benefits, and job security. More recently, non–tenure track faculty, including clinical professors and professors of practice, have emerged. Life, in terms of pay, benefits, and security, has also been good for this group, as long as their teaching is of sufficient quality and the demand for their courses remains strong.

The fastest growing groups of professors, however, are adjunct faculty members—graduate assistants and part-timers. According to the U.S. House of Representatives eForum report, adjunct faculty now comprise over half of U.S. college and university faculty, up from 20 percent in 1970. The U.S. report generated 845 responses from adjuncts that were highly educated and willing to take on heavy teaching loads for modest pay—pay that the report described as piece rate because adjuncts are typically paid by the course or credit hour. It is also quite likely that these same faculty members receive zero pay for tasks such as advising students and service activities outside of class, and zero promises of retention beyond the current semester. The eForum respondents had a variety of stories to tell about what it was like to be overworked, underpaid, and completely taken for granted.[30]

The dilemma faced by adjuncts is especially puzzling when one considers the difficulty of earning a postgraduate degree and the growing demand for higher education services in the U.S. economy. Scarce skills along with a high demand for those skills should bode well for an aspiring adjunct faculty member. Instead, this combination seems more likely to lead to stress and its associated health problems as well as a high level of frustration that might even encourage dysfunctional behaviors. The Colby College sociology professor Neil Gross wrote an op-ed piece for the *New York Times* that documented inappropriate and threatening remarks made by some adjunct faculty as well as a feeling of adjunct alienation on the part of frustrated part-time faculty members that have been made to feel like second-class citizens. According to Gross, "Social scientists have found that when aspiring intellectuals face highly restrictive employment opportunities, they often take refuge in extreme politics."[31]

The day-to-day economic plight of adjunct instructors is often nothing short of horrible. Stories abound of adjuncts living in poverty, often homeless and forced to reside in shacks or even in cars that are often old, poorly maintained, and unreliable. There is at least one instance of a female adjunct faculty member who resorted to making money by soliciting customers for sex. Her biggest fear was that one of her customers would turn out to be one of her students. Other adjuncts have had to deal with substandard housing, defaulting on student loans, going without basic healthcare, and hiding their homelessness. To make ends meet, many adjuncts teach at several schools within driving distance of their homes. It is mind boggling to imagine the chronic fatigue that these faculty members must endure while working thirteen-hour days, day after day, to meet their teaching obligations.[32] The treatment of adjunct faculty might be the single most critical issue currently facing U.S. higher education.

Accountability, Assessment, and Deprofessionalism

Throughout the history and development of American higher education, institutions have been held accountable to and influenced by people who work away from campus. These stakeholders include governing boards, taxpayers, politicians, benefactors, and alumni. Ironically, while public institutions have had their budgets cut dramatically by state legislatures, these same bodies are asking for greater accountability and oversight of their state colleges and universities—an emerging doctrine of increasing control with decreasing financial support. On top of the growing amount of regulation by federal and state agencies, regional and professional accrediting agencies are imposing yet another layer of policies and assessment measures on institutions of higher learning.

All of these measures have created an unintended consequence—the deprofessionalization of the professoriate. Faculty members who once had the freedom to teach as they saw fit, assign grades, counsel students, pursue research agendas, and make other academic decisions based on their professional judgments are now challenged—seemingly at every turn—by an arsenal of laws, regulations, and policies. Some faculty are now being forced to adhere to structured syllabi and lesson plans with predetermined "outcome measures." Others, as we have mentioned, are forbidden by federal law from talking to concerned parents about their son or daughter's academic progress without first getting the student's approval. In the past two decades, professors have been called on increasingly to explain their grading methods to academic grievance boards. And, any professor conducting research on human subjects knows that they must have their proposal scrutinized by institutional research offices—a process that requires multiple approvals from various administrators, most of whom know little about the research being conducted.

Accrediting bodies that serve U.S. colleges and universities have become increasingly intrusive.[33] Although accreditation agencies may perform a highly useful quality control function, they are demanding more and more detailed reports and analyses. All of these documents require thousands of personnel hours to produce and at least some of it may be little more than busy work. Assessment measures imposed on faculty may go beyond the usual testing that occurs in a semester-long class, requiring a professor to complete additional assessments and related documentation. Strangely, these same accrediting bodies are content to allow professors to grade often redundant exercises that add little or no value to student learning—something akin to eliminating baseball umpires and allowing players to call their own balls and strikes.

Managing the Risks

The conflicts and controversies described here require administrators and senior faculty members—perhaps without realizing it—to engage in the amorphous exercise of risk management. Providing some context in this chapter will help frame our subsequent discussion of faculty employment and management practices in higher education.

Private industry executives regularly factor risk management principles into the strategic plans of their corporations. In business management parlance, risks may be assumed (litigation is accepted as the cost of doing business), reduced (corporate decisions are reviewed by legal counsel), transferred (another firm is contracted to handle certain business responsibilities), and shared (risks flow to an insurance carrier).

Tasking legal counsel when reviewing the decisions of academics, accepting that litigation is an expected business cost, or passively allowing risks to flow to a well-funded insurance policy does little to promote a sense of academic community. Traditional industry thinking about risk management—as we might see in the financial or insurance sectors—does not necessarily provide a useful set of practices for colleges and universities, whose employment practices are deeply entrenched in the unique cultural and historical contexts described in this chapter. For these institutions, effectively managing risk requires defining what risk is and developing a system that identifies and confronts risks at multiple levels. Poorly managing the risks associated with faculty hiring, retention, or dismissal can lead to unnecessary legal expenditures; divisiveness among faculty, staff, and administrators; and unfavorable media attention.

Baker and Moss delineate several principles of effective government risk management.[34] Although their analysis focuses on the broader aspects of management in the public sector, three of these principles are especially relevant to U.S. colleges and universities:

1. *Shift from loss control to prevention.* Loss control is *ex post*, whereas loss prevention is *ex ante*. Loss control encompasses actions such as severance pay, grievance hearings, legal proceedings, and the skillful use of public relations and media exposure tactics. Loss prevention is preemptive, and it involves actions such as careful hiring practices, fair performance evaluation processes, and equitable pay structures.

2. *Link responsibility with control.* This approach places responsibility on those who are in a position to eliminate or mitigate a risk. Department heads, deans, provosts, and others who are guilty of a perfunctory or slipshod application of human resource management policies should be called upon to explain and justify their actions. Although most litigation in higher education is directed at the institution, plaintiffs often name individual administrators and faculty as defendants in these lawsuits.

3. *Manage moral hazard.* When responsibility is detached from control, moral hazard may arise. The insurance industry takes great care to minimize moral hazard by life and property insurance policy holders. Automobile owners, for example, have a great deal of control over the damage history or theft of their car. If an automobile insurer replaces wrecked clunkers with brand new automobiles, the owners of the clunkers would be strongly tempted to have their nearly worthless automobiles wrecked or stolen. Similarly, tenure committees have a great deal of control over who is granted tenure and who is denied tenure, but the members of the committee are not likely to be punished professionally or be held responsible financially for a lack of due diligence in the event that a tenure or promotion denial results in expensive litigation. For this reason, colleges and universities, along with administrators and senior faculty, must bear some of the liability for the damage they might cause to a faculty member's career. Institutionally, moral hazard might be controlled through insurance deductibles and limited legal expense reimbursements. Individually, decision makers should be held at least partially accountable for their improper actions. This accountability usually does not lead to a liability judgment against a decision maker, but it is likely to force them into enduring long, drawn out, and contentious legal proceedings and it may irreparably damage their professional reputations and careers.

The crux of risk management is that human behavior can be quite unpredictable and, during the campus interview, it is important to take every precaution to vet thoroughly the credentials and background of each faculty candidate. When a hiring or tenure decision is made, the decision makers are actually placing a bet that the new hire will be a productive member of their faculty with tenure being awarded in due time for a tenure track hire. But they cannot be absolutely certain of this outcome. The candidate who seemed so polite, polished, and scholarly when invited to campus for a job interview may, after being hired, turn out to be an academic superstar. Conversely, this seemingly well-qualified candidate may turn out to be a highly dysfunctional wolf in sheep's clothing. Careful hiring, mentoring, and evaluating become key risk management tools.

Drawing on our combined legal and managerial experience in higher education, our goal is to help readers (administrators, faculty, and legal counsel) identify, address, and prevent risks associated with the hiring and retention of faculty members. Although the list is not exhaustive, examples of major risks include:

1. *Litigation costs associated with adverse employment decisions.* Promotion and tenure denials may lead to highly unpleasant, embarrassing, and expensive litigation that forces the institution to pay hundreds of thousands of dollars in litigation expenses and damages.[35]

2. *Human resource management costs associated with faculty turnover and substandard pay and benefits.* Colleges and universities sometimes confuse labor costs and labor rates. By paying higher salaries and by providing superior benefits packages (labor rates), institutions of higher learning may actually reduce total labor costs by shrinking or eliminating recruitment, selection, and training costs. Even when expensive litigation is avoided, faculty and staff turnover that is often traceable to poor hiring, development, and evaluation practices can create hidden, but significant, costs.

3. *Acrimonious relationships among faculty, staff, and administrators that waste time and detract from academic pursuits.* These risks arise as the result of a lack of poor administrative decisions such as the distribution of merit pay or other resources. Whether the injustice is real or perceived, certain administrative decisions may be regarded as personal affronts that lead to morale problems. A toxic work environment is rarely a productive one.

4. *The continued erosion of academic standards.* An erosion of standards diminishes the value of a college degree and generates faculty morale problems and cynicism. The economist Walter Williams contends that the erosion of standards, both in K–12 and in U.S. higher education,

has resulted in the awarding of "fraudulent" diplomas and degrees that, in reality, signify grossly inflated levels of individual achievement.

5. *Adverse media publicity arising from faculty and administrative disputes, athletic scandals, and campus criminal activity.* A notable example is the scandal involving allegations of academic fraud that centered on athletes and the African and Afro-American studies program at the University of North Carolina at Chapel Hill.[36] Not only did a professor fail to hold classes, he relegated the assignment and grading of papers to his administrative assistant. The assistant, in turn, awarded generously high grades for what amounted to be mediocre quality work. The intense media publicity surrounding the UNC scandal not only damaged the reputation of a highly regarded institution of higher learning, but it also tarnished the value of the degrees of thousands of students who were not part of the scandal and who did not cut corners while earning their diplomas.

This chapter provides a view of the landscape and salient features of U.S. higher education, and it will serve as a springboard for the chapters that will follow. The news media are interested in the goings on not only in the highly visible, academically prestigious schools, but also in local community colleges and lesser-known state and private institutions. A lesser-known state university might employ thousands of faculty and staff who often have disparate views and interests, with a budget that might approach or exceed a billion dollars.

We treat issues such as decision making, faculty or union contracts, free speech boundaries, and collegiality in separate chapters, but these topics are frequently intertwined. A professor who is fired for making a controversial speech in a public forum may encounter questions not only about her free speech rights, but also about her contractual rights and about the opinions that fellow faculty members hold regarding her collegiality. Concerns may also arise about the fairness of the decision to fire her. Did she receive due process? Was her case examined carefully with attention paid to avoiding biases that might creep in and distort decisions about her future professional life? This book examines a multitude of issues concerning higher education. We will thus look at the critical interfaces of the phenomena we discuss and, at times, we will use segues to shift back and forth through the chapters.

1

ESTABLISHING A CAREER IN ACADEMIA

Faculty Hiring, Evaluation, and Pay

Faculty hiring is a process that is fraught with uncertainty. And with uncertainty comes risk. We will start this chapter by describing the road to becoming a college professor—a road that almost always starts in graduate or professional school. Individuals aspiring to a faculty position in the arts and sciences or in professions such as business, education, engineering, and many of the health sciences usually hold the PhD degree or its equivalent.[1] Law school professors possess the juris doctor (JD) degree, and may have an advanced degree in law or other discipline. Medical school faculty members hold the MD or PhD, or both.

The highest degree conferred by U.S. universities and the one held by most faculty members is the PhD degree. The degree typically requires two to three years of coursework plus the passing of one or more comprehensive examinations. The most significant requirement of the PhD, however, is writing the dissertation. Doctoral dissertations must represent an original piece of research that creates new knowledge, not simply a reinvention of current knowledge. Unlike most university degree programs, where the completion of a specific set of courses leads to the conferral of a degree, PhD programs are more open ended and often have no set time for completion.

Obtaining a PhD can be an arduous undertaking that involves significant financial hardships and, in some cases, major disruptions to family and social life. Admission to a full-time, on-campus PhD program at a major university is highly competitive, with some programs only admitting one or two applicants a year. The time to complete all requirements for the PhD varies considerably, depending on the school, the discipline, and the motivation and ability of the doctoral student. Furthermore, the dropout rate for PhD candidates is high, with barely half earning the degree.[2] Thus, when one looks at the low admission rates to PhD programs coupled with the low completion rate of those admitted to such programs, it becomes clear that earning a PhD at a highly respected institution can be a monumental task, requiring four to seven years of intense study. The sacrifices involved in earning a terminal degree and finding an academic position, especially at a major research university, represent a huge investment in a person's human capital. From a risk management standpoint, this investment is something that a faculty member wants to defend zealously, and it may prompt him to stand up and fight when a tenure review committee says that his services are no longer needed. For that reason alone, the careful hiring and evaluation of faculty members is paramount.

Faculty Recruitment

Hiring faculty members involves two interrelated processes: obtaining a pool of applicants—the recruitment process—and selecting the best candidates from the applicant pool—the selection process. Active applicants simply learn about a job and apply for it.[3] A passive applicant, however, is not a player on the job market but is approached by the college or university and is asked to apply for an open position. Passive applicants are likely to be established scholars with strong and promising research agendas.

In an attempt to cast a wide net, colleges and universities usually use multiple recruitment sources to search for faculty candidates. The primary external recruitment sources in U.S. higher education are job postings in publications such as the *Chronicle of Higher Education*, private employment agencies that specialize in faculty recruitment, placement services operated by professional associations, and organizations such as the PhD Project that help members of minority groups launch their academic careers. Applicants reached through professional publications, web sites, and professional associations are often a mixed group. Some have superb qualifications, whereas others are clearly not qualified but have applied for the position on the off chance that they might be invited for an interview.

Most academic disciplines are tightly networked—that is, a faculty job candidate is almost always known by the hiring school or is known by someone with connections to the school. Research on recruitment methods outside of academia has shown that informal methods—most notably networking—can provide an inside view of a university. Evidence also indicates that realistic job previews reduce both unpleasant surprises and turnover, especially for people who have been recently hired.[4] Although networking may enable schools to assess the interpersonal fit and collegiality of a faculty candidate, this method may exclude minority candidates, from both inside and outside of academia, who tend to make greater use of formal recruitment methods.[5]

Non–tenure track faculty members are usually hired from local labor markets. Visiting positions, although obviously temporary, may lead to a job offer if the visiting faculty member turns out to be an especially good fit with the host college or university's culture and needs. Universities in or near large cities frequently receive unsolicited applications from people looking for a full- or part-time teaching position. Although some non–tenure track faculty members do not hold a terminal degree, many do. Dual career hires are also becoming more commonplace in U.S. higher education. If a history department wants to hire a renowned medieval scholar, for example, the university may make an offer to hire her "trailing spouse" (who may also hold a PhD degree) as a non–tenure track member of the English department. Academics, it seems, often marry each other.

The Selection Process

Faculty search committees collect information about faculty job candidates from three primary sources: the faculty candidate's curriculum vitae (CV), a series of interviews with the candidate, and a reference or background check. The foundation of the hiring process is the position announcement, which describes what the job is about and the credentials that a job candidate is expected to possess. An announcement may also include broader information about the university and local community. A newly hired faculty member has every right to expect that the announcement under which she was hired will provide a blueprint of the tasks, duties, and responsibilities she will encounter, at least for the first year or two of her employment. Any changes in the initially agreed-upon job duties and performance expectations should be communicated clearly to avoid accusations of misrepresentation during the initial hire. Although most announcements are general, some provide a detailed set of criteria that the hiring institution wants in an applicant, often distinguishing between necessary qualifications, such as an earned doctorate, and preferred qualifications, such as five years of tenure track experience. In theory, there are a large number of selection criteria that can be used in the hiring process. In practice, criteria such as the quality of the program where the faculty candidate obtained her doctorate, her scholarship, and her teaching are the major criteria. Furthermore, the candidate's interpersonal skills and perceived collegiality are important, as well as the degree to which the candidate's research and teaching interests mesh with the needs of the institution. Because hiring and tenure criteria contain a great deal of subjectivity, a significant amount of unexplained variance exists in the predictive value of the selection process. That is our reason for saying that hiring and, later, tenure granting decisions are akin to placing a bet on the outcome of a sporting event; it is impossible to measure every aspect of human behavior and to predict that behavior with certainty.

Reliability and Validity in the Hiring Process

When members of faculty search or tenure review committees are asked to explain their hiring, reappointment, promotion, or tenure decisions to a court or grievance board, the issues of reliability and validity may arise, either explicitly or implicitly. *Reliability* refers to the consistency of a measure. A high school student who takes the SAT several times within the span of a year should receive approximately the same, but not necessarily identical, scores on each testing (known as parallel forms reliability). Likewise, if five members of an interview panel all agree that a faculty candidate is acceptable and warrants a job offer, the panel's assessment is a reliable one because everyone agrees on the candidate's potential (known as interrater reliability).

Validity refers to the extent to which information obtained from a selection process can be used to predict a person's future performance in school or on the job. Students who score in the 90th percentile on the SAT usually do better in college than do students who score in the 10th percentile. In this case, SAT scores are a reasonable, but far from perfect, predictor of a student's success in college. It should be noted that a measure cannot be valid unless it is also reliable. Reliability by itself, however, does not guarantee validity. Faculty hiring depends mainly on criterion-related validity in which various measurements or predictors (such as the number of publications, leadership traits, or communication skills) are thought or shown to be predictive of future job performance.

In a nutshell, faculty and administrators who participate in a faculty search process must be cognizant of whether the information they gather on a job applicant will help them make a better hiring decision than if they did not have this information. That is, if a faculty candidate is hired, will the information gathered from the candidate's CV, interview, background check, or research presentation help a search committee to predict the quality of his performance in the six years leading up to a tenure decision? Most experienced academics have witnessed a "can't-miss" faculty candidate be hired and later fall well short of the tenure threshold. These same academics can probably point to a seemingly marginal candidate who not only achieved tenure, but also became a highly respected researcher or teacher. Reliability and validity clearly matter, but they are sabotaged by the high degree of subjectivity that plagues academic hiring, promotion, and tenure decisions.

Other validity questions might deal with the relationship between a faculty candidate's credit, driving, and criminal history and his performance in an academic setting. Are such measures reliable? The answer to this question is probably yes, because this information is available from public and private sources and, if three equally trained and competent people are sent to do a background check on a faculty candidate, all three should obtain nearly the same information. But are such measures valid? The answer to that question is more difficult to answer because of the subjective assessments that must be made by faculty search and tenure committees. A person with a history of bad credit, irresponsible driving, or criminal convictions may prove to be impulsive or irresponsible—traits that could pose a problem on just about any job.[6] It should be clear that academic searches depend heavily on hard-to-defend assessments of validity. For junior candidates who have recently received their doctorates, the quality of the school and PhD program where the candidate received his degree, the reputation of his dissertation chairperson and mentors, the quality of his limited research productivity, and student evaluations of his teaching effectiveness are all important, but subjective, measures of his competency as an academic. Issues of reliability and validity are usually measured quantitatively using regression analysis.[7] But because the number of candidates who are hired is so small, inferences about the validity of common selection and evaluation tools can be difficult to defend. Standardized measures such as structured interviews, aptitude tests, or psychological assessments are often validated using nonacademic subject samples, making inferences about faculty hiring difficult. Furthermore, search committees must be cognizant of the "false negatives" who were not hired, but who went on to be successful at other schools.[8]

For senior candidates with established research records, a search committee can easily and reliably count the number of refereed journal articles on her CV. But judging the quality of a senior candidate's research record is sometimes subjective and problematic. In recent years, proxies for research quality have emerged. These measures include a faculty member's citation count as well as the impact factor of the journals where the faculty member has published. Numerical ratings, however, may create a false sense of precision. That is, are the forty refereed publications of one candidate better than the thirty refereed publications of another candidate? The answer to that question depends on how the quality and impact of individual journal articles are measured. Top-tier journals gain their reputations primarily through the timeliness, quality, and rigor of their articles. The most elite academic journals in the social sciences have less than a 10 percent acceptance rate, and it is extremely rare for an elite journal to accept a submission on the initial try. The top journals require that an article go through multiple rounds of revisions and often reject submissions even after three or four rounds of editing. Moreover, there is a degree of luck in journal publication. A meticulously researched, conceptually and methodologically sound, and well-written journal article may be summarily rejected if the journal editor does not believe that the topic is timely or does not believe that the article is a good fit for that particular journal. Many otherwise excellent journal articles may go through multiple rounds at several different top-tier journals, never to see the light of day. Academia is clearly not a profession for those who seek immediate gratification.

The Typical Hiring Process

Once a faculty position has been approved, the college or university will advertise the position. Budget approvals, however, may be tentative and not final until shortly before the academic year is scheduled to start. Furthermore, non–tenure track positions may be funded on a contingent basis from one year to the next. For these reasons, it is important for a college or university to be completely transparent about budgets and hiring promises so that candidates are not misled.

At most colleges and universities, faculty search committees are expected to adhere to detailed, multistage procedures under the watchful eye of human resource managers, university legal counsel, and affirmative action officers. Hiring the best faculty, it seems, may depend more on a search committee's ability to navigate byzantine human resource management procedures and policies than it does on a committee's ability to provide a meticulous evaluation of the research and teaching potential of a job candidate.

Some faculty search committees require that a candidate submit all materials by a certain deadline. Others may be willing to accept applications until the position is filled. At some point, however, a search committee will begin screening candidates, eliminating those who clearly do not meet expectations, and deciding which ones to pursue further.

Candidates who are selected to move beyond the initial round of screening may be invited to meet with search committee members at a professional conference or through a Skype or Zoom interview. The emphasis in this round of interviews is to assess whether the candidate's academic qualifications are adequate and whether a candidate fits well with the group of faculty colleagues with whom she will be working.[9] Faculty candidates who are still in contention after the second round of interviews may be invited for an on-campus visit. At this stage, less than a handful of applicants usually remain in contention. The campus interview, especially when it entails extensive travel, can be a grueling experience for the job candidate. A typical visit includes meeting with faculty on an individual basis and meeting with small groups of faculty and graduate students, often over a meal. Candidates can also count on meeting with administrators such as department heads or deans. A critical component of an on-campus interview is the candidate's presentation of a scholarly piece of work. The academic presentation, or "job talk" as it is frequently called, is the rough equivalent of a job knowledge test. For candidates who are in the final stages of their doctoral program, the talk usually centers on the candidate's dissertation and the stream of research that she plans to pursue after the dissertation has been completed. For more senior candidates who may be hired at the associate or full professor level, the talk usually focuses on the candidate's research stream as well as a current research project (or an article that they recently published). This part of the interview provides an important opportunity to assess how well the faculty candidate's research meshes with the research of other departmental colleagues as well as the rigor and relevance of that research. Job talks also provide an indication of how effective the candidate is likely to be in a classroom setting. Most faculty members at a hiring institution are polite in their questions, comments, and criticisms to interviewees. But the way in which candidates respond to these inquiries and criticisms may provide further insights into their knowledge, teaching abilities, and collegiality. An overarching concern is that faculty and administrators must try to predict whether an interviewee has the potential to receive a favorable tenure review several years in the future. This issue is crucial to effective risk management. The pitfall to avoid later is making a controversial and possibly ill-advised reappointment or tenure decision—a concern that applies to both nontenured and tenure track faculty. An unfavorable tenure or promotion decision may not only create divisiveness within a department, but it may also reflect poorly on the institution and sow the seeds of a future lawsuit.

Major Faculty Duties and Expectations

During the hiring process and beyond, it is important to convey clearly the expectations that the institution has for research, teaching, and professional service. Research expectations might include publishing in respected journals, exhibiting art at prestigious venues, performing musical work onstage, obtaining grants from public and private sources, and collaborating on research with private institutes. Applicants for senior positions may be expected to serve as thought leaders and mentors for junior faculty and graduate students.

It is difficult for decision makers to specify the exact quality and quantity of scholarly output that an untenured faculty member must have to achieve tenure. Furthermore, these standards change—usually becoming higher and more restrictive—with the passage of time. For small academic departments, tenure decisions are few and far between, making it more difficult to predict and justify the outcome. Clearly, however, a record that would have warranted a favorable tenure decision ten years ago might be inadequate today.

A statement of teaching expectations might include a statement that details the annual teaching load and the balance between graduate and undergraduate teaching as well as indicating expectations for new course development, leadership in curriculum development, the use of teaching innovations, and the direction of student professional groups and trips. Job candidates may also be requested to present evidence of teaching effectiveness such as prior student evaluations, teaching awards, copies of course syllabi, and evidence of teaching innovations or course development.

Service expectations usually include institutional activities such as committee assignments and professional service activities like participating in academic conferences or holding office in a professional association. As noted, service activities often intrude on the time needed to engage in reading, laboratory work, thinking, and writing. Department heads should insist that tenure track faculty avoid excessive service activities during their first few years of employment and, at the same time, untenured faculty should not be allowed to use the excuse that excessive service activities of their own making impeded their research productivity in the years leading up to their tenure review. Faculty members at research schools rarely get tenure because of their service activities—a point that should be clearly made during the initial interview and reinforced during the early years of a faculty member's career.

The job advertisement for an administrative position usually contains a more detailed list of tasks, duties, and responsibilities than is typically found in an advertisement for a faculty position. This is in part because faculty members usually have a more standardized role than administrators. That is, the expectations of an associate vice provost may vary widely from one school to another, whereas the job of an English professor varies primarily by the genre of literature they teach. Regardless of the position being filled, however, the announcement for a faculty position should create a realistic job preview and establish a set of expectations for both the faculty member and the institution.

Affirmative action policies that have their genesis in federal executive orders also come into play. Faculty and administrators in institutions of higher learning are keenly aware of the emphasis placed on diversity and of the push to hire and retain qualified minorities. Nearly all colleges and universities have established special offices to promote inclusion, equity, and diversity, and these offices must usually approve a hiring decision before an offer is made to the job candidate. Advertisements for faculty positions in the U.S. contain a statement indicating that the institution complies with federal and state equal employment opportunity laws and affirmative action policies. But, beyond those efforts, search committees should be aggressive in identifying and contacting minority candidates who may otherwise not respond to job advertisements, especially if they have little familiarity with the school or its location.

Selection Ratios and Salaries

There is also a great deal of difference in the selection ratios and salaries of PhDs across the various disciplines. The selection ratio is simply the number of hires divided by the number of applicants. Selection ratios range from zero to one. A low selection ratio (closer to zero) favors the hiring institution, whereas a high ratio (closer to one) favors the job applicant.

A candidate holding a PhD degree in accounting or finance from a respected institution may benefit from a high-demand (tight) labor market and a high selection ratio. Such a candidate may be able to select from an array of tenure track positions at major research schools that offer nine-month salaries in the $200,000 range.[10] By contrast, an academic with a PhD in history has a much more difficult battle because candidates for history faculty positions face a low selection ratio in a low-demand (loose) labor market. For some liberal arts faculty searches, the selection ratios can be low with over one hundred applicants vying for a single job. Slightly over half (50.6 percent) of those with a PhD in history are employed in tenure or tenure track positions at schools offering at least a baccalaureate degree, and their salaries are about one-third to one-half of those with degrees in accounting.[11]

When market conditions favor the applicant, schools have to adopt an aggressive recruitment strategy that will likely include pursuing passive applicants. Disciplines with a glut of PhDs, however, may have to spend a great deal of time screening a long list of active applicants—many of whom have sterling credentials—to find the best candidate. Moreover, faculty searches in U.S. institutions of higher education move at a comparative snail's pace, often taking months or even years to conclude. Many university administrators, for example, spend a year or two (or more) with the term "interim" attached to their title, further testimony to the slow-moving world of hiring in academia.

Curriculum Vitae

Candidates for faculty positions usually submit their curriculum vitae early in the recruitment process. Information on the candidate's CV usually includes basic contact information, education history (schools attended and degrees earned), scholarly achievements (articles and books published, academic presentations made), contributions to the development of creative and artistic works, and professional service. Information gleaned from a CV enables search committees to make qualitative judgments about a faculty candidate. Many colleges and universities require faculty candidates to submit statements reflecting their research and teaching philosophies. The time that it takes for a candidate to craft these statements is time well spent. Search committee members read research and teaching statements carefully to determine whether the professional goals of the candidate mesh with the goals of the institution. Such statements may also serve as a writing sample for applicants whose published research is limited.

Interviews

The job interview is the centerpiece of faculty recruiting not only among U.S. institutions of higher learning, but also at schools worldwide.

Employment interviews in general have been the topic of extensive research over the past fifty years by industrial and organizational psychologists.[12] Although a number of self-help articles are available to help aspiring faculty candidates through the interview process, little if any rigorous research has been done using academics as subjects. The interview format varies: interviews may be one-on-one in which the candidate meets with each interviewer, usually in sequence, or the candidate may be interviewed by a panel of interviewers. Furthermore, an interview may be structured, using the same list of questions for each candidate, or unstructured, using off the cuff, impromptu questions that vary from one candidate to the next.

Interviewers must be aware of contrast effects in which one applicant is compared with another. Since faculty applicants are interviewed days or even weeks apart, the contrast effect may be less problematic compared to interviews in nonacademic organizations where job applicants are interviewed only minutes or hours apart. If the misleading contrast effect is not taken into account, an average candidate may get an unexpected boost in his rating if he has the good fortune of being preceded by a candidate who interviewed poorly. When candidates are interviewed weeks apart, however, memories of earlier interviewees might fade, giving an unfair advantage to the more recent interviewees.

Interviewers may be biased. They often place heavier weight on their first impressions of interviewees—either good or bad—and then subsequently look for evidence that reinforces their first impressions. Similarly, negative information about a faculty candidate tends to carry more weight than positive information about that candidate. Failing a PhD comprehensive examination on the first try and barely passing on the second attempt may carry more weight in the minds of some interviewers than if that same candidate later received a prestigious dissertation award. Also, interviewers may harbor biases based on race, national origin, gender, and age. For this reason, questions that stereotype applicants by race, gender, or other protected classes or that hint at a potentially illegal preference or prejudicial attitude toward a certain group should be screened from the hiring process.

Biases go beyond traditional notions of discrimination. A single piece of information or a single characteristic about a faculty candidate may distort the interviewer's judgment. One situation that might work in the candidate's favor is when both the interviewer and interviewee attended the same university—the "similar-to-me" or "halo" effect. Conversely, one interviewer might view a candidate's stint in the Peace Corps as a positive indicator of professionalism and citizenship, whereas another interviewer might regard a Peace Corps volunteer as someone who wasted time on a mission to an impoverished country—time that could have been better spent on building a career.

Robert Gatewood, Hubert Feild, and Murray Barrick, all well-known scholars with strong backgrounds in organizational and industrial psychology, provide eight suggestions for building better interviews.[13] Here are their suggestions and our interpretation of how these suggestions might apply to academic interviews.

1. *Restrict the scope of the interview.* Use the process for selecting, not recruiting. Furthermore, analyze only a few work-related characteristics (WRCs). Do not try to accomplish too much in the interview. For faculty candidates, this could mean focusing questions exclusively on the candidate's research accomplishments and teaching philosophies.

2. *Limit the use of preinterview data about the faculty candidate.* This suggestion might appear to be counterintuitive, but it is supported by research. Gatewood and his coauthors suggest using preinterview information to assess WRCs that will be discussed during the interview. Incomplete or contradictory information on a CV might also merit further investigation. Red flags on the applicant's CV, for example, could include unexplained gaps in the candidate's work and education history or frequent job changes.

3. *Adopt a structured format.* The same list of questions—or core set of questions—should be asked of all job candidates during the initial and on-campus interviews. A structured interview, where a standard set of questions is asked of all candidates, usually yields a higher degree of validity than does an unstructured interview in which the interviewer asks whatever questions come to mind. Despite evidence to the contrary, many interviewers continue to use an unstructured format, relying on their gut feelings about the suitability of a faculty candidate. Interviewers who take a slipshod approach to the interviewing process even include faculty members who are otherwise meticulous

empiricists. Seemingly novel attempts to discover how quickly a faculty candidate can "think on her feet" are likely to be counterproductive. Gimmick questions such as "What type of animal best describes you?" or "What is your favorite color and why?" are best left off the interview question list.

4. *Use job-related questions.* Questions should be confined to topics such as a candidate's relevant work and educational history, research accomplishments and future research path, teaching philosophy and experience, and academic professional service activities. With the possible exception of the phatic ice breaking comments at the beginning of an interview, discussions about the candidate's personal life—families, hobbies, political views—are rarely appropriate.

5. *Use multiple questions for each WRC.* Avoid overly general or leading questions and develop a list of several questions each about a candidate's research, teaching, and professional service. For example, research-related questions might include inquiries about a research stream, the proper methodologies associated with a particular line of research, and the extent to which a candidate's research fits in with the work of other researchers.

6. *Rely on multiple independent interviewers.* Even when using a standard set of questions, different interviewers may have somewhat different observations on a particular candidate. Also, errors such as the contrast effect and allowing assessments of a candidate to be distorted by the biases of an individual interviewer are likely to be reduced when multiple interviewers are asked to evaluate a candidate.

7. *Apply formal scoring that allows for the evaluation of each WRC separately.* A simple 1 to 5 scoring scale for each standard question makes comparison of multiple candidates easier.

8. *Train interviewers in the process of the selection interview.* Interviewers can be taught to avoid hiring decisions based on intuition and gut feelings by making them aware of the biases and mistakes that plague the employment interview process. Since research-minded academics are conducting the interviews, part of this training is to encourage interviewers to understand the lengthy research history that the field of industrial and organizational psychology offers to those who want to improve their interviewing skills.

Personality Assessments

Personality assessments (or tests) are usually not part of the academic hiring process, but they are being used with increasing frequency in corporate settings, especially in large organizations. It makes sense to believe that certain personality traits—and not just a person's pleasantness or social skills—are somehow linked to job performance. Traits such a person's cognitive ability (intelligence) and the widely regarded "Big Five" taxonomy of personality traits—conscientiousness, emotional stability, openness to new ideas, neuroticism, and agreeableness—are, in fact, predictive of good job performance. Conversely, an absence or low level of these personality traits has been linked to bad or counterproductive behaviors.[14] And since personality traits are fairly stable over long periods of time, it is not surprising that employers are interested in assessing the personalities of job candidates. Although the Big Five personality traits can be used to predict the general behaviors of individuals, they may be too broad and not especially predictive of specific forms of job performance. Colin De-Young, Lena Peterson, and Jordan Quilty, psychologists whose research has focused extensively on the Big Five, divided each of the Big Five traits into subtraits or facets. Conscientiousness, probably the most significant of the Big Five traits, was broken down first into industriousness and orderliness, and, in turn, industriousness was divided into achievement striving, competence, and self-discipline, and orderliness was broken down into deliberation, dutifulness, and order. Each of the remaining four major traits was also subdivided into five parts, bringing the total number of facets to thirty. By making the Big Five more finely grained, DeYoung and his coauthors were attempting to focus on more specific job behaviors.[15]

An assessment of personality traits might also include "core self evaluation" that encompasses personality traits such as self-esteem, self-efficacy, locus of control, and emotional stability.[16] Other traits of interest are emotional intelligence and proactive personality. Emotional intelligence has generated considerable debate among psychologists because of its nebulous nature. Proactive personalities, as the name suggests, is an attempt to measure whether someone will take the initiative to complete a task and adapt to workplace changes.[17]

Personality assessments may be administered through self-report measures (paper and pencil tests) that ask questions such as "I tend to trust other people" (a partial measure of agreeableness) or "I tend not to say what I think about things" (a partial measure of extraversion). Some of the better-known self-report measures are the Myers-Briggs Type Indicator, the California Psychological Inventory, and the Hogan Personality Inventory. It is also possible to assess someone's personality simply by observing them, and research indicates that such assessments are fairly reliable and valid. Thus, the comment made by a University of Alabama in Huntsville faculty member about Amy Bishop being "crazy" (not a standard professional term in psychology or psychiatry) was prescient and probably had validity. Deviant (and dangerous) behaviors may also be predicted using psychologist Robert Hare's Psychopathy Checklist-Revised (PCL-R). Hare, a leading authority on psychopaths and antisocial personality disorder, developed the PCL-R to evaluate criminals and others who are prone to dangerous behaviors. The PCL-R should be used only by trained analysts, and we can only speculate as to how Amy Bishop would have fared on this psychological test.

Colleges and universities are not likely to make widespread use of personality assessments when hiring faculty—at least not in the near future. Search committee members probably believe that they have already vetted candidates and noticed no signs of trouble. The candidates themselves might be offended by being asked to submit to an assessment of their personality, and some may be suspicious that these tests are a backdoor way of committing illegal discrimination. Furthermore, personality tests may be viewed by faculty candidates as an invasion of their privacy, especially when the questions drift into areas such as a candidate's religious beliefs, political views, or sexual practices. There are also possible concerns that personality assessments do not really predict job performance because the performance measures themselves are not well defined. Personality assessments also assume—either implicitly or explicitly—that one best personality profile exists for a particular job. Yet, if asked to name the three most influential people in their lives, most readers would probably discover that these individuals had significantly different personalities.

Personality assessments may add little or no value to the selection process for jobs in "strong" situations that must be performed by adhering to a detailed set of rules, regulations, or standardized procedures where there is little room for individual creativity or personality differences. Personality assessments may, however, have more predictive value for unstructured jobs or "weak" situations that place a premium on individual judgment and creativity. College professors would likely fall in the latter category of jobs where structure is minimized and personality assessments are more likely to be useful.

Background and Reference Checks

Background checks are based on the premise that past behaviors are predictive of future behaviors. The use of background and reference checks is a relatively new practice in faculty hiring. Background checks may vary from checking references (whose opinions of a candidate are almost always positive) to a thorough inspection of a candidate's past—work, schooling, credit, and criminal history. Background checks can be used to help verify that the information on a faculty candidate's CV is accurate and truthful. In the past, it was assumed that anyone who was a faculty candidate—especially one who had already worked at another college and university—was above reproach. This assumption is not always safe.

Faculty hiring, as noted, is an information-gathering process and information is sometimes unreliable. In some cases, a faculty candidate may exaggerate accomplishments that are otherwise true. This tactic is known broadly as "puffing." A faculty candidate may, for example, use "creative accounting" to inflate the amount of grant monies that she has received, or she may embellish on her role as a coauthor or coeditor of an edited book. A more serious form of dishonesty is to claim a degree that has not been earned, or to falsify the work history, publications, grants, or awards listed on her CV.

One enterprising professor was fired after it was discovered that he was simultaneously holding two full-time positions—one at the University of Minnesota and the other at the University of North Carolina, Charlotte. During the week, he made the 930-mile trek each way teaching Mondays and Wednesdays in Charlotte before boarding a flight late in the day on Wednesday to make the trip back to Minneapolis to teach the same course on Thursdays. As we noted earlier, academia can be a small world, and the traveling professor's moonlighting was soon discovered. When interviewed, the professor's former doctoral research advisor made the tongue-in-cheek comment that his former student "violated the most severe taboo in the academy: He showed the world what an easy job we have." Between the two institutions, the double-dipping professor was making over $146,000 a year, or the equivalent of almost $250,000 in 2017 dollars.[18] A perfunctory background check may not have prevented this unusual case because both schools were aware of his original employment at Minnesota, and both schools thought he would either stay in Minneapolis or move to Charlotte. Neither school realized that he had said "yes" to both jobs.

A background check can be used to verify an applicant's work history, educational attainments, misdemeanor and felony convictions, and even the candidate's driving record and credit status. With inadequate background checks comes the concern of being sued by an injured party for negligent hiring. Faculty members may use their position of power to take advantage of students or to abuse human research projects. In fields such as medicine, chemistry, chemical engineering, the veterinary sciences, or agriculture, faculty members may have access to controlled substances and toxic chemicals. Furthermore, faculty members have been known to misappropriate grant monies, dragging their institution into an embarrassing and expensive federal investigation. For these reasons, ferreting out dishonest, unstable, or predatory faculty candidates is an important but very difficult duty of search committee members and administrators.

For fear of hiring someone who is dangerous, some state governments refuse to hire people with felony convictions. Such prohibitions, of course, would also apply to public university faculty members. Without a background check, however, a faculty candidate's conviction record may never come to light. This situation appeared to help Amy Bishop secure a faculty position at the University of Alabama in Huntsville (UAH). In the wake of the tragic shootings at UAH and Bishop's sentence of life in prison without the possibility of parole, it seemed inevitable that lawsuits would be filed by the families of the three slain victims as well as by the surviving three victims. The families of Maria Ragland Davis and Adriel Johnson filed wrongful death suits against Bishop and James Anderson (Bishop's husband), seeking medical expenses and damages. The university's provost Vistasp Karbhari was also sued for what appeared to be negligent hiring.

The Madison County circuit judge Ruth Ann Hall, however, granted summary judgment to Karbhari, saying that the plaintiffs had failed to prove that the provost knew Bishop's actions were foreseeable—a major point of contention in negligent hiring cases. An employer cannot be found guilty of negligent hiring simply because an employee commits workplace violence. The injured parties needed to demonstrate that UAH either knew or should have known about Bishop's past dangerous behaviors and chose to ignore them. In addition to foreseeability, the plaintiffs needed to demonstrate a proximate cause between Bishop's erratic past and the shooting deaths and injuries at UAH. Proximate cause is based on the similarity between before and after acts—violent earlier acts followed by subsequent acts of violence—as well as the amount of time between the dangerous acts. Bishop had a history of violent behavior in that she allegedly killed her brother, held hostages at gunpoint, and attacked a stranger in a public place. But Bishop's history was not documented adequately to prove negligent hiring because most of her bad behaviors never found their way into the public domain through police reports or trial proceedings. As long as a prospective employer makes a reasonable effort to uncover bad behavior from an applicant's past, it is less likely that a plaintiff can collect damages for negligent hiring.[19]

Provosts in larger institutions do not interact with faculty members on a daily basis, and Karbhari, according to the court, did not have the specialized knowledge to sufficiently realize the dangers posed by Bishop's presence on the UAH campus. Others closer to Bishop, however, were indignant at the judge's ruling; they felt that her actions were foreseeable and preventable. This situation raises the question as to why she was allowed to continue working in the UAH biology department during the year of her terminal contract and to attend a faculty meeting that she had no business attending. Was UAH culpable for allowing Bishop to remain on the school's faculty and participate in research, teaching, and service activities? Does the fact that one-year terminal contracts in tenure denial cases are a standard industry practice in U.S. higher education provide a mitigating circumstance for the university?

The flip side of negligent hiring is the issue of defamation of character—also known as libel (in the written word) or slander (in the spoken word). If those with a detailed knowledge of Amy Bishop's violent and litigious past had come forward and warned UAH of her unstable and potentially lethal disposition, they would have rightfully feared almost certain legal action from her. The problems encountered by her Massachusetts colleagues and neighbors were now Huntsville, Alabama's problems.

Knowing that she had moved to the South, their reasoning was undoubtedly to leave well enough alone.

Defamation lawsuits are based on the idea that everyone is entitled to protect their personal reputation. The fear of a defamation suit, however, is reason enough to scare former employers or acquaintances from providing an honest letter of recommendation. For this reason, search committees may have to dig beyond the usual materials in a faculty candidate's dossier to uncover the truth. Background checks are best left to experienced human resource management personnel or to private firms and investigators that specialize in this task. The National Crime Information Center (NCIC) maintains a national criminal database, but it can only be accessed by law enforcement officers and a few others. A faculty candidate may have lived in several different locations. Each location will have its own criminal database and rules for using these databases. For this reason, it is best to hire a person who is familiar with how to gain access to a particular criminal database. University human resource management personnel should inform faculty search committee members about the provisions of the Fair Credit Reporting Act (FCRA). The FCRA requires applicant notifications and paperwork in certain circumstances, especially when organizations or personnel from outside the university—such as reference checking agencies, placement firms, or private investigators—are involved in the hiring process.

Once the vetting has been completed, the remaining part of the process is to select the final candidate, make an offer, and negotiate final terms. The offer letter specifies the salary and benefits, teaching load and service expectations, and tenure timeline (if applicable). It almost always stipulates that the faculty member will be employed on a contractual basis (for one or more years) with a tenure decision being set usually in the sixth year after hire. But not all faculty members, as noted earlier, survive to their sixth year. Some may be terminated when it becomes clear that their performance in the next year or two is destined to fall short of a favorable tenure decision.

Moving Through the Academic Ranks

As the title implies, non–tenure track faculty members do not expect to be granted tenure, no matter how long they serve their institution or how well they fulfill their teaching and service obligations. Non–tenure track positions often come with a variety of titles, including instructor, lecturer, adjunct assistant professor, associate clinical professor, and professor of practice. Some colleges and universities provide promotion opportunities for non–tenure track faculty such as a promotion from lecturer to senior lecturer or from senior lecturer to distinguished lecturer, or from assistant clinical professor to associate clinical professor.

The term "tenure track" describes faculty that might in the future be considered for tenure if they demonstrate excellence in scholarship and teaching. Newly minted PhDs have traditionally been hired into tenure track positions at the rank of assistant professor and then begin the process of working their way through the academic ranks. Tenure is frequently granted simultaneously with a promotion to the rank of associate professor, usually after six years in a tenure track position. Beyond the rank of associate professor is the rank of professor. Moving from the rank of assistant professor to associate professor and finally to the rank of full professor may take well over a decade.

Even though academic rank and tenure are not necessarily transferrable from one school to another, senior research faculty with strong records of research and teaching at other schools may be awarded tenure as part of their initial employment offer—that is, they are tenured from the moment they set foot on campus and begin their new job.

In addition, professors who exhibit exemplary scholarly performance may receive an endowed chair or named professorship that includes a salary stipend—sometimes a very generous stipend. The name of the benefactor supporting the professorship is usually attached to the endowed or named professorship (for instance, the Smith Professor of Physics or the Universal Bank Professor of Finance).

Performance Evaluations

During his career, a professor will likely undergo a series of evaluations, which may include a narrative summary of his research, teaching, and service accomplishments during a given period, often accompanied by a numerical rating. These evaluations are usually the responsibility of the department head, but many departments and colleges have retention or reappointment committees that provide an additional assessment of the faculty member's research, teaching, and service contributions. A dean or associate dean usually grants the final approval to reappoint a faculty member. Barring criminal behavior, unethical acts, gross incompetence, or extreme negligence, most recently hired tenure track faculty members survive for at least three years. As noted, however, it is not unusual for a subpar professor to be dismissed prior to his sixth year when the final tenure evaluation usually takes place. Similar to interviews, performance evaluations have potential biases. Here also, biases based on race, skin color, gender, nationality, religion, age, or disability status are always possibilities. In addition, performance evaluations may be distorted by the halo effect (one characteristic distorts the entire evaluation), past-record anchoring (a faculty member's evaluation is tainted by either a good or a bad performance rating during a previous evaluation period), leniency (faculty members receive inflated assessments of their performance), or strictness (faculty members receive harsher assessments than their job performance warrants). Training faculty and administrators seems to be the obvious solution to reducing performance appraisal errors. Contrary to conventional human resources wisdom, however, performance appraisal errors are difficult to eliminate through training.[20]

Performance evaluations that fail to take all major performance criteria into account are said to be deficient, whereas evaluations that include irrelevant dimensions that are not part of the faculty member's job are said to be contaminated. Deficiencies and contamination distort the reliability and validity of the performance appraisal process. Reliability, in the context of a performance appraisal, focuses on the administrative and data-gathering aspects of annual evaluations, whereas validity focuses on how well the performance appraisal reflects the tasks, duties, and responsibilities of the faculty member's job. A number of court cases have arisen that challenge the fairness of an individual performance evaluation or a performance evaluation system. The courts are usually reluctant to challenge the performance criteria used in the evaluation (such as a university performance appraisal system that attaches a greater weight to research than to teaching), but judges and juries are more likely to rule in favor of the plaintiff if the evaluation procedure has been unfairly administered (for instance, when a supervisor with a vendetta holds the disfavored faculty member to a standard that is much higher than the standard imposed on other faculty members).[21]

Faculty performance evaluations become part of the body of work that later determines whether a faculty member is dismissed, retained, tenured, or promoted to a higher academic rank. For those reasons, it is important to provide ample feedback and mentoring to the faculty member as she moves through the pretenure phase of her career. Conscientious and thorough tenure reviews that are conducted during the years leading to a promotion and tenure decision can reduce the suspense, uncertainty, and anxiety faced by a faculty member. H. J. Zoffer, the former University of Pittsburgh business school dean, may have said it best: "Consummate faculty persons are sensitive to the fact that there is always someone more terrified than they about the problems ahead—namely, the group one rank below."[22]

Postappraisal interviews and strong mentoring are excellent ways to manage the risks of avoiding a bad personnel decision. As noted earlier, however, promotion and tenure standards are not static; such standards have become more demanding over time and it is likely that these standards will become even more imposing over the next decade.

Faculty Pay

Pay differentials between the academic ranks within the same discipline can be narrow. Full professors usually have salaries that are larger than the salaries of associate or assistant professors. Salary compression and even salary inversion, however, may occur in some academic pay structures, especially when market forces drive up salaries at the entry-level rank of assistant professor. An up-and-coming assistant professor, especially one with a degree in a high-demand discipline, may command a salary that is higher than the salary of a more senior associate professor who works in a discipline where labor market conditions are less favorable. Faculty pay is not only an important economic issue—more pay means a higher standard of living—it is also an important social psychological issue. Administrators need to be mindful of the three categories of pay equity: external equity (for instance, how does the pay of a full professor of biology at the University of Illinois compare with the pay of a professor of biology at Indiana University?); internal equity (how does the pay of a professor of biology at Indiana University compare with that of a professor of computer science on the same campus? And how does the pay of two associate professors in the same department compare?); and procedural equity (why did a biology professor at Indiana University receive a 5 percent annual pay raise while a computer science professor on the same campus received a 3 percent raise? And why did an associate professor in a department receive a higher annual pay raise than an associate professor colleague in the same department?).

Internal pay equity issues probably create the greatest degree of angst. Many states have sunshine laws that place state university faculty salaries in the public domain, making it easy to see what a particular professor and her colleagues are making. A lack of pay secrecy might make administrators who are charged with setting pay and granting pay raises more mindful of their decisions, but such transparency may also generate accusations of unfairness, which could lead to grievances or lawsuits. Pay inequities can be a major source of trouble that may affect contractual rights and collegial relationships. College and university administrators must be mindful of the social and psychological aspects of pay. One of us remembers our graduate school days when the faculty pay of a large university was published in a statewide newspaper. The edition was sold out during the early morning hours, and people spent the next two or three days dissecting the pay of their colleagues, often noting who was over- or underpaid. To manage the risk of pay discrimination, administrators should be prepared to justify each individual pay decision in adequate detail while at the same time respecting the privacy of other colleagues' performance evaluations. This task is often easier said than done.

2

RISK, BIASES, AND LOGICAL FALLACIES

Bad or ill-advised promotion and tenure decisions are often thought to be the result of an act or acts of illegal discrimination, most notably disparate treatment. But proving disparate treatment requires that the faculty-plaintiff demonstrate illegal intent on the part of the institution's decision makers, something that is difficult to do. In the past, Title VII of the 1964 Civil Rights Act, an equal employment opportunity (EEO) law, was the primary weapon used by faculty legal counsel to adjudicate reappointment, promotion, and tenure disputes. When plaintiffs invoke EEO law and try to prove disparate treatment, they usually try to convince a jury that but for their race, gender, nationality, or skin color, they would have been treated more favorably. Accusing decision makers of harboring such prejudices is easy, but proving illegal discrimination is difficult.

Terry Leap has demonstrated in a previous publication that plaintiffs whose EEO cases go to trial lose more than three quarters of the time.[1]

Furthermore, many if not most cases are settled out of court away from the public eye. But does that mean that the contested cases were adjudicated fairly? In some cases the answer is yes, and in other cases, no. If attorneys and their plaintiffs cannot establish proof of discrimination under EEO law, they may try to make their case by demonstrating biases and flawed thinking in the promotion and tenure process itself. Given the low rate of success by plaintiffs who invoke EEO law in promotion and tenure disputes, we will focus on biases and reasoning fallacies that can create a degree of unfairness in these decisions. Since EEO cases in academic settings have already been examined thoroughly elsewhere, we will not resurrect them here. This chapter discusses instead some basic ideas about risk theory, decision-making biases, and reasoning fallacies that can put one party or the other in an unfair or, possibly, an illegal predicament.

People in power are not always completely rational. At one level, as we have noted, contentious cases may arise from illegal discriminatory actions that are usually based on a decision maker's stereotypical view of a specific group. Suppose that a faculty hiring committee is reluctant to make a job offer to a married woman in her late twenties because she is in the middle of her childbearing years and is likely—at least in the committee's estimation—to require protected leave under the Family and Medical Leave Act (FMLA). This same committee, however, may have no reservations about hiring the male partners of women of childbearing age because of the assumption that the female partner or spouse will assume the child care duties while the father continues to work. This decision represents a classic case of gender discrimination that could violate Title VII as well as the FMLA.

But at another level there may also be more subtle forces at work. Using concepts developed by social scientists, we will try to illustrate two major points regarding reappointment, promotion, and tenure decisions. First, these decisions create legal entanglements and adverse publicity risks—risks that can and should be managed. Second, these decisions may be affected by biases and reasoning fallacies that can lead to unfair promotion and tenure decisions. The possible presence of these biases and reasoning fallacies is not usually sufficient by itself to establish proof of illegal discrimination under the preponderance of evidence standard of civil litigation, but they may be used to bolster a faculty plaintiff's case under tort, contract, or constitutional law.

Risks Faced by Institutions of Higher Learning

Risk is everywhere. The array of risks faced by U.S. colleges and universities includes news coverage that harms the institution's image, program cuts, scandals that exacerbate conflicts between a school's intercollegiate athletics program and its academic mission, expensive litigation, and the loss of revenue as funding sources dry up or enrollments decline. There are also risks that go well beyond the scope of this book, such as risks encountered with campus traffic, food service, laboratories, and livestock arenas. Acting on behalf of their institution's governing body, presidents, chancellors, provosts, deans, department heads, and promotion and tenure committee members all have a hand in shaping the employment prospects of faculty members. These decision makers work at different levels within the institution, and they may be hamstrung by the fact that they do not always talk to each other, setting the stage for misunderstandings and inconsistent decisions. As a result, each level of a school's administrative hierarchy can be viewed as a potential source of risk or liability.

Institutions of higher learning often try to minimize their liability exposure by promulgating a detailed set of administrative procedures that includes strict deadlines, multiple screening committees, and subjective and sometimes nebulous decision-making criteria, all of which must be applied to dozens of dossiers that are replete with massive amounts of information. A detailed and lengthy set of reappointment, promotion, and tenure guidelines may, however, become more of a litigation trap than an aid to sound decision making. One of us served as an expert witness in a case that ultimately hinged on the fact that the candidate was not given proper notice of a tenure committee meeting as stipulated by the school's promotion and tenure guidelines even though there was evidence that the candidate was aware of the time and place of the meeting. This seemingly minor deviation from the timetable forced the judge to rule against the university. Although the plaintiff prevailed in the lower court, and was awarded a very small judgment—a classic "win-lose" outcome—a higher court reversed the decision. The devil is often in the details, and the details are often overwhelming.

Risk Theory

Risk theory is a broad concept that deals with decisions about what people might do when faced with future uncertainties. Probability estimates as a measure of risk range from nearly zero (for instance, the probability that July temperatures will drop below freezing in Miami) to nearly one (for instance, the probability that the sun will rise tomorrow morning). Not surprisingly, events affected by human behavior have probabilities that lie somewhere between these two extremes, approaching neither one nor zero.

Weather forecasters make predictions about rain, temperature, and violent weather events. Sports gamblers try to predict the outcome of football, basketball, and baseball games as well as horse races, soccer matches, and golf tournaments. People with no formal knowledge of risk theory must evaluate the risks associated with whom to marry, what house or car to buy, where to shop for groceries, and whether to leave home without an umbrella. Understanding theories of risk often requires an in-depth knowledge of mathematics and probability theory. In everyday practice, however, the term "risk" usually pertains to a vague idea about the likelihood of a future event occurring. These probability estimates may be based on subjective, "gut" feelings ("There is something about this person that I don't like."), or the decision maker's limited experience in a similar situation ("We denied tenure to a similar candidate several years ago and she moved to a different school where she became an academic superstar.").

Investment bankers, mortgage lenders, traders, and financial advisers working in the financial industry make extensive use of risk theory. One well-known measure of risk for financial instruments such as stocks is the beta.[2] A stock with a beta of less than one means that it is less volatile than the overall market, and a stock with a beta of greater than one indicates that it is more volatile than the market. If a stock's beta is 1.1, for example, it is regarded as being 10 percent more volatile than the market, whereas a stock with a beta of 0.9 is ten percent less volatile than the overall market. Investment managers, for example, not only try to anticipate the general movement of stock prices, but they also often strive to provide their clients with a portfolio of high- and low-risk stocks—some with high betas and others with low betas. In the vast and complicated world of buying stocks and even entire companies, the American business magnate, Warren Buffett, has successfully used his own brand of risk analysis to determine what companies to invest in along with the amount and timing of those investments. Although we have never seen faculty candidates evaluated in this manner, hiring committees could—if they wanted to—view job applicants or promotion and tenure candidates as having a high beta (for instance, someone who is very talented and could be an academic star, but with a personality that is troublesome) or a low beta (for instance, someone with good talent and a stable personality, but not likely to be an academic superstar), or, more likely, somewhere between these two extremes.

Thus, the hiring and retention of faculty is an exercise in risk management. But predicting the likelihood and magnitude of future risks—especially when those risks involve human behavior—can be a daunting task. The global financial crisis in 2007 showed how risk assessments (and economic policy decisions based on these assessments) failed to account for the housing bubble.[3] Economists, the banking industry, and government officials predicted wrongly—and perhaps naively—that home prices would continue to rise in the foreseeable future. This mistaken belief about the housing bubble set off a sequence of catastrophic global events, the magnitude of which had not occurred since the Great Depression. Furthermore, the 2016 U.S. presidential election provided a stark illustration of how pollsters and statisticians underestimated the gap between the popular vote and the Electoral College outcome when predictions indicated that Hillary Clinton would easily win the presidency.

Insurance companies deal with risks that involve such things as the age-adjusted mortality rates of life insurance clients, the amount and likelihood of property damage from an episode of violent weather, or the size and number of automobile accident claims. Automobile insurance companies, for example, understand all too well that male drivers under the age of twenty-five pose higher expected loss values (that is, a high frequency of claims multiplied by the large amounts of money necessary to settle each claim) than the risks posed by forty-five-year old female drivers whose expected claim values are relatively low. These probability estimates are critical to the accurate formulation of automobile, life, and property insurance premiums. The goal of an insurance company is to collect enough premium dollars to cover claims and to provide for a profit or adequate cash flow to ensure that it remains solvent.

At a more subjective level, parole boards must predict whether an inmate is likely to recidivate if released from prison. Parole boards assess the recidivism risk posed by a soon-to-be-released inmate by considering her age, mental stability, marital status, education level, the seriousness of her previous offenses, her apparent degree of remorse for those offenses, the time she has already served, her conduct while incarcerated, and her success in prison-run rehabilitation programs. But even the most diligent parole board member who painstakingly analyzes each case cannot be completely certain as to how the inmate will adjust to life outside of prison.

Large universities typically employ a full-time legal staff that helps them navigate the risks of litigation and select a risk management strategy. Colleges and universities may also use a subjective form of risk management when they make admissions decisions about individual students, decisions about how resources should be allocated, and decisions about whether to promote and grant tenure to a faculty member—the so-called multimillion dollar bet. The value of outcomes from a variety of situations and decisions may be either positive or negative. An example of a very positive outcome would be to grant tenure to a faculty member who later becomes a Nobel laureate or the winner of a Pulitzer Prize or Fields Medal. A negative outcome would be to retain a faculty member who turns out to be an unproductive researcher as well as a poor teacher with few service activities and possibly a disruptive and litigious bent.

Probabilities associated with a particular outcome, such as a promotion, tenure decision, or contract renewal, might be derived from institutional data (if the sample size is adequate) or data derived from a university's peer institutional grouping. For example, one highly prestigious university known to the authors has historically granted tenure to only a very small percentage of its faculty, and it is likely that other prestigious schools have similarly high standards and low percentages of positive tenure reviews. Faculty who accept positions at elite schools should understand that job security beyond their sixth year is highly uncertain unless they are well on their way to becoming an internationally acclaimed scholar. All is not lost, however, because being denied tenure at a top-tier school usually means that a good but slightly lower-tier school will be waiting with open arms to hire a faculty member with several years of experience at the pinnacle of the academic world. It should be noted that the correlation between the prestige of the school where a faculty member received her doctorate and her subsequent publication record is not all that high.[4] That is, when it comes to research output, the reputation of the school where the faculty member earned her doctorate is predictive of her future research productivity, but not by as much as one might think.

The granting or denial of tenure is a selection decision in its own right because it determines whether a faculty member is retained—possibly for decades—or let go. Ideally, a college or university would like to have a mistake-free hiring and promotion process that includes only true positives (the hired person is successful), or true negatives (the person was interviewed, not hired, and went on to have a lackluster career elsewhere). But the hiring process is not perfect and it is subject to two errors: false positives (the person was hired and turned out to be an unacceptable performer) and false negatives (the person was interviewed, not hired, and went on to have a highly productive career at another university). False positives may have significant direct costs such as the expense of hiring a replacement faculty member or the costs of dealing with litigation if things turn sour. False negatives, however, usually generate opportunity costs that are more indirect—"We let an excellent applicant get away and, had we hired her, she would have elevated the reputation of our college." But how do we measure such opportunity costs?

Most colleges and universities hire only those applicants that they believe will perform well enough to achieve tenure—what they hope will be true positives. Colleges and universities might consider developing a data bank or model, possibly with the help of industrial psychologists or business analytics specialists, that could help them to distinguish between potentially successful and potentially unsuccessful promotion candidates. A hiring or retention model might include variables such as the faculty member's quantity and quality of publications, scores from teaching evaluations, a subjective assessment of collegiality, and organizational citizenship behaviors. The major problem of profiling, however, is the base rate issue—faculty who fit into either the "high probability of success" profile or the "low probability of success" profile may fail to perform as predicted (either false positives or false negatives) because such predictions were based on small sample sizes.[5] For this reason, it might behoove a group of similarly situated colleges and universities to pool their data and develop a reliable and valid faculty hiring and evaluation model.

A Foucauldian (power based) framework proposed by Cynthia Hardy and Steve Maguire delineates three risk frameworks: the prospective organization of risk, the real-time organization of risk, and the retrospective organization of risk.[6] The prospective organization of risk focuses on regulatory and risk management issues. It dwells on what may happen in the future and it puts an emphasis on managing risk at a distance by predicting and preventing risk through measures, calculations, and correlations. This approach to risk, according to these authors, encounters difficulties when unexpected events arise. The real-time organization of risk focuses on what is happening in the present. Risk is addressed as it materializes, but it too encounters difficulty when unexpected risks arise. The retrospective organization of risk focuses on what did happen versus what should have happened.

The dominant approach in academic retention, promotion, and tenure decisions seems to be the retrospective organization of risk, something akin to a postmortem investigation. Promotion and tenure decisions in academia usually follow a well-worn path that starts at the faculty member's department and proceeds upward through the collegiate dean, provost, chancellor, president, and institutional board. Most of the critical decision making, however, occurs at the department and college level, so that is where the risk is highest. Occasionally, a favorable decision to promote or grant tenure is reversed at a higher level (usually by the provost). These somewhat surprising—actually rare—decisions may be the result of a campus- or system-wide cascade effect to implement higher standards across the entire university. As discussed earlier, most schools aspire to elevate their position among the various institutional rankings and one possible way to go about this is through a drastic, across-the-board elevation of promotion and tenure standards. The cascade effect can be especially problematic for job applicants or for promotion and tenure candidates who have been denied tenure at another university. Being a victim of a cascade effect can be devastating to a junior faculty member, and getting hung up in this vicious cycle can mark the end of an academic career. The law professor Ward Farnsworth presents the following scenario:

> You have job interviews with two employers and are turned down in both of them. At the next one you are asked if you have had any prior interviews. You recount your unhappy recent history, and the employer concludes that

the two prior rejections probably meant something. This helps him decide to pass on you. The process continues and accelerates from there; the next interviewer finds you have three rejections and has even more cause for concern than the previous one. The process can work in reverse too; a job candidate gets offers, and the offers create interest on the part of others.[7]

Common Ways of Dealing with Risk

Every society, organization, and person faces risk, and, depending on the probability, context, and severity of the risks, their approaches to risk management will vary. One way of dealing with risk is though risk avoidance. Unfortunately, risk avoidance is possible only for a narrow range of activities. For example, to avoid perishing in an aircraft crash, one should avoid riding in airplanes, helicopters, gliders, gyroplanes, or balloons. Similarly, to avoid the risk of being attacked by a grizzly bear, one should stay away from grizzly bear habitats. Because reappointment, promotion, and tenure decisions are part of the fabric of U.S. institutions of higher learning, however, risk avoidance is usually not a viable strategy in academia. The simplest long-run risk avoidance strategy would be for a school to abolish its academic and tenure ranks, possibly by placing all newly hired faculty on renewable contracts. Of course, this strategy might make it difficult for the institution to attract quality faculty and that, in turn, could eventually harm its academic reputation.

A particular risk should be identified, classified, and assessed as to its nature, triggering event, probability of occurrence, and possible impact. Such a structured approach to risk management might lead colleges and universities to adopt a second option, risk assumption. This risk management strategy is one where the decision makers understand the risk and, for economic or political reasons, decide to accept and deal with that risk—perhaps viewing it as another cost of doing business. Large institutions of higher learning know—almost with complete certainty—that they will be sued as the result of a reappointment, promotion, or tenure decision, so they prepare accordingly, deciding how they will assume or manage this risk.

In other instances, however, academic decision makers may simply ignore certain risks, a strategy that is distinct from risk assumption. Being overwhelmed and consumed by too many administrative tasks and teaching duties, an academic department chair may forget to perform timely annual performance appraisals on faculty members in his department, something akin to a "risk ignoring" strategy. Other than possibly being chastised by his dean for neglecting that important task, such inattention to detail is probably of little consequence—at least until a controversial and possibly contentious promotion or tenure decision ends up in litigation. At this juncture, a lack of attention to administrative responsibilities can snowball into a major problem that cannot be easily explained or justified during litigation.

For the most part, tenure track professors with either exemplary or, conversely, lackluster records can usually predict the outcome well before the promotion and tenure process reaches its sixth or penultimate year. A strong researcher who also has excellent teaching evaluations may know that her promotion and tenure prospects are promising. A tenure track professor with meager accomplishments probably has an equally strong reason to believe that he is not going to clear the tenure bar and may take the preemptive approach of finding a job elsewhere, perhaps at a school where performance expectations are more modest. A faculty member facing this predicament should realize that contesting a tenure denial or termination is going to be a time-consuming, emotional, and expensive battle with dim prospects of winning. And even if he prevails in court and is allowed to return to his academic job, it is impossible for a judge to order up a collegial or friendly work environment for the winner of a lawsuit. The alternative route for a faculty member faced with this dilemma might be to get on with his career either at another school or in a job outside of academia.

It is in the middle ground between these two extremes where litigation— and its risks—is most likely to occur. In some instances, risks may be incurred because difficult reappointment, promotion, and tenure decisions are made on the margin. A faculty candidate's expectation about the likelihood of a favorable or unfavorable tenure decision should be shaped by clear and candid performance reviews and conscientious mentoring by senior faculty—measures that serve as a form of risk reduction against lawsuits. But these otherwise honest appraisals may be misunderstood or ignored by a junior faculty member who believes that his body of work deserves a more favorable review.

Just as faculty candidates cannot always be expected to assess their chances of promotion and tenure objectively, promotion and tenure committees do not always make sober judgments about a faculty member's long-term value to the institution. This problem may be compounded when an institution recognizes a risk but decides to bear the brunt of that risk without taking further precautions. That is, the problem associated with ignoring a disgruntled faculty member might add up until he files a discrimination or wrongful termination suit. At that point, the evidentiary impact of inadequate mentoring and annual performance evaluations becomes extremely serious, and the cost to the institution may balloon to thousands of dollars in litigation and settlement expenses. To put it bluntly, slipshod and perfunctory human resources practices coupled with a "risk ignoring" strategy can be a recipe for trouble.

Many risks are handled through some form of liability insurance. All types of insurance involve the same two mechanisms: risk transfer and the sharing of risk on some equitable basis. A casualty insurer might underwrite liability coverage for a number of organizations—both academic and nonacademic—with the expectation that few if any of these organizations will actually face a catastrophic liability judgment. If such a judgment arises, the premium payments received from the large pool of organizations (risk transfer) should be sufficient—if the insurer has accurately tied the premiums to the probability and magnitude of the risk—to cover the few adverse legal judgments that arise (risk sharing). An attractive characteristic of liability insurance is that these policies often cover the institution's defense costs—a major benefit when a school is confronted with long and complicated litigation. In essence, the insurance mechanism can be described as paying a small, certain sum (the premium) to avoid a large but uncertain loss. The cardinal insurance buying rule can be stated as follows: Insurance is best used when the probability of a loss is low and the economic severity of that loss is high. Thus, buying insurance to protect against an unlikely multimillion-dollar judgment is a good use of the insurance-buying dollar. Furthermore, the costs of such insurance can be reduced by incorporating deductibles and cost-sharing (coinsurance) provisions in the policy.

In addition to EEO law violations, which have been discussed elsewhere, institutions of higher learning face several broad risks, including:

Lawsuits that are precipitated by reappointment, promotion, or tenure denials. Such suits might include wrongful discharges that violate administrative law or civil service regulations.

Accusations of defamation of character or negligent hiring.

Disputes arising over the terms of a faculty member's employment
contract.

Challenges affecting a faculty member's constitutional rights.

Such lawsuits and controversies may be the result of mismanaging the faculty hiring and mentoring processes, or the failure of the concerned parties
to understand EEO, contract, and constitutional law, along with the various statutes that cover discrimination based on sexual orientation, family and medical leave, labor unions, and occupational safety and health.
And, if that is not enough, we need to consider procedures prescribed in
faculty handbooks and promotion and tenure policies. The common de-
nominator for these suits is the mismanagement of risk and the failure to
account for the many biases that can affect faculty human resource management decisions.

Legal Risk Management

All organizations, including institutions of higher learning, must manage legal risks, which consist of litigation risks, contract risks, regulatory
risks, and structural risks.[8] Litigation risks relate to the kinds of events
that can lead to lawsuits—for our purposes we refer to the risks associated with reappointment, promotion, or tenure-based lawsuits as an
important source of litigation risk. Contract risks emanate from contract
breaches and arguments regarding the interpretation of contract clauses.
For example, many research universities provide tenure track faculty with
summer research stipends. But what happens if a faculty member is either
dismissed or denied tenure? Are these faculty members still entitled to
summer funds even though they are about to be terminated? A reading
of the faculty member's contract should address this issue, but what if
the contract is vague or silent on this matter? Regulatory risks deal with
the possibility of running afoul of the many statutes, court decisions, and

executive orders that affect human resource management decisions. Complying with the patchwork quilt of human resource management laws imposes significant costs on an organization, but neglecting these regulations may increase litigation risks. Structural risks, although less common, may arise when a college or university alters its mission and strategies, making significant changes to its hiring, promotion, and tenure policies and standards—changes that might derail a faculty member's career.

Mark Little, a risk management expert, describes six steps to legal risk management: (1) select a framework; (2) obtain organizational commitment; (3) identify legal risks; (4) analyze legal risks; (5) evaluate legal risks; and (6) communicate and provide guidance to the proper audience. He views legal risk management on a continuum with no risk management at one end and the use of quantitative models at the other end. At the no risk management end, risks are addressed on an ad hoc basis where the norm is "fire-fighting" unexpected problems as they arise. At the quantitative end, legal risk management entails the use of data-driven predictive analytics, something that few if any colleges and universities are using.

Organizational commitment refers to delineating the type and scope of risks being monitored as well as identifying the intended audience of the legal risk management effort. Little describes the importance of identifying legal risks by examining their sources, along with the need to record risks by name, likelihood, and consequence. The moral and legal risks stemming from wrongful discharge cases can be melded into this scheme, and the approaches to risk discussed earlier can then be fitted into the legal risk management process.[9] Finally, Little emphasizes the importance of communicating the organization's legal risk analysis initiative to a broader audience in the organization, not just to its legal counsel.[10] In an academic setting, providing legal risk management advice to department heads, promotion and tenure committee members, deans, and even provosts, chancellors, and institutional board members is paramount.

In a 2008 survey conducted by the Association of Governing Boards of Universities and Colleges (AGB), 60 percent of respondents said that their institutions did not use a strategic risk assessment to identify major risks faced by their institutions. The AGB's best practices include defining risk broadly, recognizing both the opportunities and downsides of risk, developing a multilevel approach to identifying and evaluating risks, identifying both the monetary aspects and the nonmonetary aspects (such as bad publicity) of risk, and acknowledging the need for institutional boards and presidents to discuss risks collaboratively.[11] PMA Companies, a risk management consulting firm, provides a broad and detailed outline of risks faced by institutions of higher learning that goes well beyond reappointment, promotion, and tenure decisions. The sources of risk identified by PMA Companies include food service, chemical research labs, summer camps, nanotechnology, theater safety, and campus violence.[12] Risk management does not have to be rocket science. These strategies need to have a method for identifying risks, calculating their magnitude and probability (easier said than done), and selecting a risk strategy that will work for a particular college or university.

Biases in the Promotion and Tenure Process

There is a litany of possible biases that can affect a decision maker's ability to fairly assess the promotion and tenure prospects of a faculty member. We may, for example, have a gut feeling about the likelihood of an event or problem without being able to articulate exactly why we believe that an event is either more or less likely to occur. But gut feelings can be unreliable, making rational decisions difficult.

The cognitive biases that decision makers encounter may tip the scales in determining whether a faculty candidate survives the reappointment, promotion, or tenure process, or whether he succumbs to that process. What follows is a discussion of interrelated and sometimes contradictory biases that can distort the thought processes of those tasked with the important responsibility of making potentially career-changing judgments about their colleagues. A description of these biases has two important functions in academic litigation. First, when viewed collectively from the defendant institution's viewpoint, they illustrate that decision makers are human and that no reappointment, promotion, or tenure decision can be expected to be perfect. Second, from the faculty-plaintiff's viewpoint, a possible contention is that academic decision makers should have understood the biases that affect the fairness of the promotion and tenure process. This overview seeks to help identify and reduce the selection errors that might arise in complex promotion or tenure decisions.

Bounded rationality is a term that describes the suboptimal decisions that human beings often make.[13] When a group of academics and administrators participate in a promotion and tenure decision (or, more likely, a series of such decisions during the course of an academic year), they are constrained by the fact that they must sort through a large amount of detailed information, sometimes under tight time constraints. This suboptimal approach to decision making is known as "satisficing," a term coined by Nobel laureate Herbert A. Simon.[14] Thus the concept of bounded rationality suggests that faculty reappointment, promotion, and tenure decisions may, to varying degrees, be incomplete and subjective. Added to this process is the *planning fallacy*, which indicates that people often misjudge the amount of time required to complete a complex task.[15] This fallacy exemplifies the problems that may be encountered with promotion and tenure processes that contain strict timetables and deadlines.

Psychologists and economists have identified a number of cognitive biases that distort the perceived probability and severity of certain outcomes and risks. Such was the case of with Amy Bishop, who shot six of her colleagues—killing three—at the University of Alabama in Huntsville. At least in the minds of UAH faculty and administrators, Bishop's arrogance and unstable personality did not send off adequate danger signals. The default position taken toward Bishop was to ignore her until her terminal contract expired and she finally left campus for good. Two contradictory biases may have been in play here: the *regressive bias*, where low probabilities—such as that of Bishop turning violent—were estimated to be even lower than they actually were.[16] Countering regressive bias, however, is the *hindsight bias*, which could have been used after the fact by some UAH faculty who witnessed Bishop's bizarre behavior and "knew all along" that she was ready to explode.[17] When called to testify in court, witnesses with a hindsight bias might make statements that are extremely damaging to the institution.

Complex evaluation procedures may also lead to an *information bias*. A member of a college promotion and tenure committee may know more about one candidate than another, which causes him to analyze different candidates differently, possibly leading to unrealistic and unfair judgments about a candidate's employability.[18] College-level promotion and tenure committees usually consist of senior faculty from various departments within a college. A large liberal arts and sciences school or college at a major research university may have several hundred faculty spread across a dozen or so departments. Although a college promotion and tenure committee member may know the candidates from her own department well, the candidates for promotion and tenure from other departments may be complete strangers. For this reason, it is difficult to promulgate a uniform set of university or even college-wide promotion and tenure standards. Compounding the decision errors discussed here are the varying interdisciplinary research, teaching, and service expectations that require different performance criteria for different disciplines. Criteria that work for a computer science department may be less appropriate when applied to a sociology department. Furthermore, the *shared information bias* occurs when decision makers focus only on information that everyone else is already familiar with instead of revealing and discussing information that is not known by other group members.[19] Relatedly, the *illusion of validity* is the belief that additional information will somehow be relevant to the decision-making process, even when such evidence contributes little or nothing of value. Simply put, the world of decision making is not a neat, orderly place. According to Daniel Kahneman, a Nobel Prize winner working in psychology,

> The exaggerated expectation of consistency is a common error. We are prone to think that the world is more regular and predictable than it really is, because our memory automatically and continuously maintains a story about what is going on, and because the rules of memory tend to make that story as coherent as possible and to suppress alternatives. Fast thinking is not prone to doubt. The confidence we experience as we make a judgment is not a reasoned evaluation of the probability that it is right. Confidence is a feeling, one determined mostly by the coherence of the story and by the ease with which it comes to mind, even when the evidence for the story is sparse and unreliable. The bias toward coherence favors overconfidence.[20]

A decision maker in the promotion and tenure process may also try to paint a predictable and consistent portrait of the process through *confabulation*. Confabulation occurs when a decision maker fills in the blanks by distorting or changing his memory about an event or sequence of events. Individuals who confabulate actually believe that their recollections are accurate. A person may mistakenly recall discussing the work of a tenure candidate with a colleague from another school even though that specific part of the conversation never took place. In some cases, these distortions are subtle, whereas in other cases the distortions are completely at odds with reality. Confabulation is not done to deceive. Rather, it is an attempt to make sense of a situation that would otherwise make little sense.

Responsible decision makers should be aware of the concepts of *anchoring* and *framing*. A decision maker may anchor her opinion on the first piece of information that she receives about a person, perhaps based on the way information is presented and sequenced in a faculty member's promotion and tenure dossier. Decision makers tend to assign higher values to evidence or events that have emerged more recently and that are at the front of their minds. This phenomenon is known as the *availability heuristic*.[21] Knowledge about three tenure denial lawsuits at three different universities in a given year may lead decision makers into believing that most tenure denials end up in litigation when in fact such litigation is rare. Furthermore, a related concept known as the *recency effect* also plays on the notion that short-term memories trump long-term ones. A decision maker's cognitive limitations may cause her to either overemphasize or underemphasize important data in a faculty dossier that is otherwise bursting at the seams with detail. When faced with examining several dozen dossiers, a rational decision maker may resort to counting the number of a faculty candidate's publications while ignoring the quality of his publications—a convenient heuristic. The use of heuristics may speed up the evaluation process, but may lower its quality.

People have a tendency to make up their minds and then acquire evidence to substantiate their beliefs while discarding other evidence that does not support their beliefs.[22] Furthermore, when the evidence for a certain belief or bias is ambiguous, the ambiguity still favors the initial belief. This well-known cognitive error is known as a *confirmation bias*—and its related error, *past-record anchoring*—a compelling phenomenon that induces people to become overconfident about what they think. For example, one of us knows a state politician who supported Hillary Clinton to the point of aggressively promoting her candidacy and accomplishments while blindly ignoring her transgressions and weaknesses. After Clinton failed to secure the presidency, this same legislator portrayed the election outcome as a gross misunderstanding. And even when confronted with strong contradictory evidence, the bias of *conservatism* creates a tendency for people to begrudgingly alter their beliefs to a lesser extent than the power of the new evidence might suggest. Furthermore, the *trait ascription bias* describes the tendency of people to view others as having more predictable personalities while viewing themselves as being less predictable.[23] The *bias blind spot* may be at work because the decision maker is certain that she is less biased than her colleagues.[24] *System justification* occurs when someone staunchly defends the existing social, economic, and political systems.[25] Even though Clinton received three million more popular votes than Donald Trump, political analysts and commentators generally supported the outcome—despite public demonstrations to the contrary—because that was the outcome that the electoral college system had dictated. The system for our purposes here consists of the faculty guidelines for reappointment, promotion, and tenure. In most cases, university administrators give great deference to an institution's promotion and tenure manuals, even relegating them to Holy Grail status.

The familiar term *sunk cost* and the less familiar term *irrational escalation* also describe why people are reluctant to alter their opinion or abandon their position when new or contrary evidence is presented.[26] Overconfidence, in turn, becomes a problem when erroneous and stubborn beliefs distort important decisions.[27] The *backfire effect* may be at work when contrary evidence is presented about a faculty candidate. Disconfirming evidence about someone may actually strengthen the decision maker's original and possibly erroneous beliefs about this person. That is, contrary evidence may cause the decision maker to dig in and stand even firmer on why she does not believe the candidate deserves promotion or tenure.[28] And, even when the faculty member softens her position in the face of overwhelming evidence, the conservatism (or belief) revision may cause her to change her stance insufficiently.[29] Furthermore, a decision maker's perception of his own expertise can distort his judgments. According to the *curse of knowledge bias*, better-informed people tend to find it difficult to understand or empathize with the viewpoints of less informed people, even when the opinions of the less informed have merit.[30] There is, however, the *Dunning-Kruger effect*, which posits that less skilled individuals tend to overestimate their abilities, whereas experts tend to underestimate their abilities.[31]

In an academic setting, biases are probably less likely to be based on prohibited classifications such as a person's race, gender, ethnic origin, religion, age, or disability status (although there has been no shortage of accusations of discrimination on these grounds). There is, however, the puzzling *moral credential effect* in which a person's track record of nonprejudice can later lead to acts of prejudice.[32] It seems as though some people who behave ethically for long periods of time may build up a sense of entitlement that eventually "allows" them to engage in unethical behavior.

Since promotion and tenure decisions are usually a culmination of a six-year-long process where the decision makers interact frequently with the faculty candidates whom they will eventually be evaluating, the *selection perception bias* (better known as the self-fulfilling prophecy) is problematic.[33] Once a decision maker decides how he feels about another person, he may act in in ways that will channel that person's behavior toward the belief. If a senior faculty member believes that an untenured faculty member is a strong researcher, then he might act in ways—for example, offering coauthorship on a journal submission—to ensure that the junior faculty member is successful. On the contrary, this same faculty member might fail to help another untenured junior faculty member with her research because he believes the junior faculty member lacks the ability to become a strong researcher. That is, she acts in ways to prove that she was right all along about the junior faculty member's lack of research prowess. For faculty decision makers who have been involved in promotion and tenure decisions for many years, the *survivorship bias* may distort a current assessment of a faculty candidate because of the decision maker's tendency to concentrate on those who survived the process—and who may have been an atypical and exceptional crop of scholars.[34]

The way in which someone handles a risk may depend on how a problem or situation is presented or framed. An important aspect of framing is the *contrast effect*.[35] A faculty candidate for promotion and tenure usually knows something about the identity and qualifications of other faculty who are going up for promotion and tenure at the same time. A prospect for promotion or tenure might be either nervous about being in a cohort of highly qualified candidates or confident if surrounded by candidates of lower quality. When included in a high-quality group, a candidate of average merit may face a tenure denial, whereas the same candidate when included in a lower-performing group might be granted tenure.

Note that most schools do not have a tenure quota or limit where only a certain number of candidates will be granted tenure. But when quotas are in effect, the framing bias may be accentuated. Thus, the way in which a promotion or tenure candidate assembles his dossier may exploit the framing bias. Recommendations from prominent scholars, the use of creative artwork, or the order in which a candidate's research, teaching, and service components are presented in a dossier may leverage the use of framing in ways that could tilt a close promotion and tenure decision in either a favorable or unfavorable direction. This problem may be reduced if institutions require faculty to submit promotion and tenure dossiers that adhere to a common format. Past decisions create an anchor for future decisions even when the major decision makers inform aspiring faculty that promotion and tenure standards have become more exacting. That is, anchoring may offset an increase in promotion and tenure standards.

A person's view of the biases associated with risk may take some unexpected twists and turns. *Prospect theory* is the product of the economists Daniel Kahneman and Amos Tversky and is relevant to anchoring and framing.[36] This theory illustrates that people's attitudes toward the risks associated with gains versus the risks associated with losses might be asymmetrical. And, as it turns out, the subjective beliefs that people hold regarding the likelihood of certain risks may deviate markedly from the actual probability of those risks. Tossing a coin and getting nine consecutive heads does not increase the probability of getting a tail on the tenth flip. Yet, it is tempting to overestimate the odds of the tenth flip yielding a tails because of the perfect run of heads that occurred on the previous nine flips.

While each coin flip is an independent trial that does not affect subsequent flips, many risks are, in fact, interdependent and cumulative. The probability of a tenure decision becoming the target of contentious litigation may be low, but small probabilities add up when chances are taken repeatedly over a period of time.[37] The noted Australian wildlife expert and conservationist Steve Irwin repeatedly took risks by handling dangerous reptiles. Because of Irwin's tremendous skill in working with a variety of animals, his single encounter with a stingray did not appear, from his perspective, to be unusually risky. But it was Irwin's increasing confidence and repeated risk taking that eventually led to his being mortally wounded by a stingray during what was for him a routine filming session. Irwin may have been too comfortable and confident around stingrays, which possibly led him to underestimate the danger that these animals posed. This confidence coupled with a highly unusual reaction from the normally calm stingray proved fatal to Irwin.[38] A similar sequence of risk taking might be found in the promotion and tenure committees that get away with making perfunctory and ill-advised tenure decisions year after year until they finally pay a steep price for their negligence in the form of expensive litigation and adverse media publicity.

Given the small number of promotion and tenure decisions as well as the small number of nonreappointment decisions in academia, it is understandable that decision makers and faculty candidates for promotion or tenure would either underestimate or overestimate the risks that they might face. Prospect theory may be behind the "when in doubt, don't" mentality held by many academic administrators when it comes to evaluating—and rejecting—marginal faculty candidates in decisions that come down to a close call.

According to a 2013 article in the *Economist*, "The theory shows that people are in fact terrible at assessing probabilities (they are poor at probability weighting). People feel nervous on planes, and no amount of statistical reasoning will rid them of their anxiety. The theory also shows that people find bad things relatively worse than they find good things good (*"loss aversion"*). People tend to find losing £5 agonising, yet are only mildly happy to find £5 on the floor."[39]

But, importantly, the *negativity effect* (and prospect theory) recognizes that most people regard the absolute value of a "bad" event as more harmful than the same absolute value of a "good" event. This effect might encourage a faculty member into irrationally contesting an adverse promotion and tenure decision even when the chances of her prevailing are low.

Biases in academia may arise because of interpersonal conflicts, a lack of respect for a faculty member's research, or a disdain for the faculty member's choice of discipline. *Naïve realism* holds that rational people believe that their view of reality is completely unbiased and correct, while those who do not have the same viewpoint are biased and irrational.[40] This thinking error is especially prominent in situations described as "groupthink," where a culture of invincibility in an organization—academic or otherwise—dictates that group members either toe the company line or risk being ostracized.[41] In the same vein, the *just-world hypothesis* assumes that the world is fair and good, with injustices being the fault of the victim.[42] But painting people with a broad brush is often unfair. The columnist Walter E. Williams, for example, has contended that collegiate schools of education lack rigor and are the academic slums of U.S. higher education.[43] It is probably safe to say that an applicant for a faculty position with a degree from a school of education might not fare well with Williams and other like-minded people on the hiring committee. Other academics are likely to harbor their own brand of biases that may from time to time color the decisions they make on academic matters.

Over their six-year probationary period, the productivity of most candidates for promotion and tenure follows an uneven course. A year in which a candidate had three journal articles accepted in respected journals might be followed by a year (or more) in which the candidate had no articles accepted for publication. The temporal nature of the promotion and tenure process might be affected by the *clustering illusion*, a tendency to see patterns that do not exist and to overestimate the significance of bursts or streaks of productivity.[44] This particular bias is related to the *hot-hand fallacy*, a reference to gamblers who are on a roll and continue winning with each new bet. But the ebb and flow of faculty productivity over several years may conflict with the thinking error of *declinism*, a bias that occurs when someone views the past as being better than the present—claiming, for instance, that "twenty years ago tenure was much harder to achieve than it is today."[45] Relatedly, the *distinction bias* describes the tendency to see candidates as being more similar when they are evaluated simultaneously rather than sequentially or separately.[46] The distinction bias may be especially important to be aware of because of the assembly-line nature of most promotion and tenure processes at large institutions.[47]

Colleges and universities often spend huge sums of money on tenure track faculty during their first six years of employment. Such expenditures might include expensive laboratory space, generous summer research funding, and an ample travel budget. As noted, sunk costs can lead to an *irrational escalation bias* of sticking with high sunk cost candidates and averting a loss even when it becomes obvious that their body of work does not warrant a favorable tenure decision. Similarly, the *IKEA effect* encourages people to place a higher value on a piece of furniture that they have assembled themselves rather than on a piece of furniture that was assembled by someone else prior to purchase.[48] In this case, the furniture is a junior faculty member who has been mentored by a more senior colleague. Thus, a senior faculty member who is also on a promotion and tenure committee might be more likely to favor a candidate whom he has mentored than one whom he did not mentor. Similarly, the *not-invented-here bias* might result in the assignment of a lower weight to a faculty member's body of work when that work was completed at another institution.[49] And to complicate matters, when an adversary—instead of a friend—publishes a seminal article or receives a major research prize, the bias of *reactive devaluation* may diminish the value of the adversary's work.[50] Envy regarding an adversary might lead someone to say that, for instance, "He would not have the received that honor except for the fact that he had highly competent coresearchers who did most of the work." Faculty making hiring, promotion, and tenure evaluations may also succumb to the *social comparison bias*, which encourages decision makers to avoid hiring or promoting people who compete with the decision maker on the decision maker's own strengths.[51] That is, an expert on high baroque music may be more likely to veto the hiring or the tenure of a faculty candidate who is also a high baroque expert in favor of an expert in music of the early classical period.

Adding to the perception of bias is a possible concern with *rent-seeking behaviors*. "Rent" in this context has nothing to do with apartments or landlords; instead, it pertains to the redistribution of income to the benefit of one party without a concomitant benefit to the rest of society.[52] Opponents of the tenure system might claim that once a faculty member receives the exceptionally strong form of job security provided by tenure and the accompanying assured income stream that could continue flowing for decades, she has benefitted personally, but society has gained little or nothing from her enhanced security. This concern may weigh heavily on a promotion and tenure committee to the point that it becomes biased in favor of denying tenure to all but the most exceptional candidates. Elite colleges and universities, most of which are private, are able to reduce the rent-seeking dilemma by imposing extremely high standards for both hiring and the granting of tenure. This tactic makes sense for the world's most prestigious institutions because hundreds of highly qualified applicants are waiting in the wings, eager for the chance to fill a vacated faculty position at an elite university. Less elite schools, however, may be more likely to be the target of rent-seeking behaviors if they grant tenure to scholars who impose a greater risk of relaxing and lowering their productivity once the security of tenure is granted.

Fallacies and Arguments

Faculty reappointment, promotion, and tenure decisions may sometimes spark heated debates. The book *Understanding Arguments*, authored by Walter Sinnott-Armstrong and Robert Fogelin, describes a number of fallacies that can arise during such deliberations.[53] Although the authors' discussion of these fallacies are not directed specifically at practices in institutions of higher learning, their analyses certainly apply to these organizations.

The *fallacy of vagueness* suggests that the use of unclear language indicates unclear thought. Promotion and tenure committee members may use unclear language for poetic effect, for the purpose of confusing an opponent, or simply with the understanding that the details will be filled in later. Sinnott-Armstrong and Fogelin note that there is no such thing as perfect clarity because the same words can be used to describe different things, depending on the context in which the words are used. The issue of which academic journals are "premier," "excellent," and "good" in a given field has for decades been the subject of lengthy and intense faculty debates, usually among departmental colleagues who seek guidance when making decisions on faculty promotion and tenure. Vagueness can also be exacerbated by using words that have multiple meanings. "Teaching excellence" can be interpreted in a number of ways. This term could apply to the rigor of a professor's teaching (and "rigor" itself is subject to a slippery meaning), a professor's teaching innovations (a similarly vague term—how innovative does a good innovation have to be?), or to a professor's professionalism (another confusing term—is there a standard set of criteria that denotes high or low professionalism, or is it in the eye of the beholder?).

Still another fallacy to consider is the *fallacy of relevance*. The relevance of an argument is usually evaluated on the relationship between its premises and conclusions, and the relevance of something—such as a faculty candidate's professional service—is likely to be debated behind the closed doors of a promotion and tenure committee meeting. But sometimes the wool is pulled over our eyes. "Fallacies of relevance are surprisingly common in everyday life," Sinnott-Armstrong and Fogelin write. "People often introduce irrelevant details or tangents in order to mislead by diverting attention from the real issue. . . . The best strategy for dealing with such tricks is simply to cross out all irrelevant claims and then see what is left. Sometimes nothing is left."[54]

Another major path to trouble is *slippery slope arguments.* One form of this argument is the *fairness* slippery slope. When debating the quality of teaching performance with the need to distinguish between good and bad teaching, a promotion and tenure committee may ask, "Where do we draw the line?" But regardless of where the line is drawn, its precise location can always be attacked on the basis that it is arbitrary, and accusations of arbitrariness may intensify as promotion and tenure standards change from one year to the next.

There is yet another slippery slope argument that may be even more problematic. Suppose that a faculty member who is going up for tenure has a marginal record. In this case, the committee could justifiably argue either to grant or deny tenure to her. Suppose further that a mitigating circumstance is present—the faculty member spent one year on maternity leave and had zero publications during that time, but in the years that she was on the job, her productivity was quite strong. So, based on these facts, a committee member suggests that she be granted tenure. Another committee member disagrees and says, "If we lower our standards for this candidate, we will likely lower our standards even further for the next borderline candidate, and before you know it, even the weakest candidate will be granted tenure." This situation is an example of a *causal* slippery slope argument because it leads to extreme—and often highly unrealistic—conclusions.

Sometimes arguments and claims are *ad hominem.* An *ad hominem* argument shifts attention from a person's claim to the person himself—that is, the argument gets personal. An *ad hominem* argument might strike at the core of a person's motives. A faculty member who is supporting a marginal tenure candidate, for example, might make a strong argument for granting tenure only to be attacked by another committee member who claims that his positive recommendation is based on the faculty member's friendship with the candidate and not on the candidate's academic record. Alternatively, untenured faculty might accuse their tenured colleagues of raising the standards only after they were granted the protection of tenure.

Instead of focusing their angst on the escalation of promotion and tenure standards, they personally attack their tenured colleagues and accuse them of establishing standards that they themselves could not meet.

Most colleges and universities use external reviewers from other institutions to evaluate the research and body of work of a faculty candidate for tenure. This process constitutes an *appeal to authority* that is sometimes helpful in making a complex decision. A cynic might say that it is also a way for a school's promotion and tenure committee to diffuse responsibility for a promotion or tenure denial. The external reviewer's help is usually solicited by the faculty candidate's department head. If the reviewer agrees to serve, she is sent a detailed dossier. Once the reviewer has examined the dossier—no easy task—she writes a lengthy letter that evaluates the candidate's body of work, noting its strengths and weaknesses. Being an external reviewer involves a great deal of time and many well qualified but overburdened potential reviewers reject such requests. Furthermore, some reviewers fear a defamation lawsuit and as a result will not say anything that could be construed as unwarranted damage to a person's reputation. At worst, a candid evaluator may damn with faint praise or provide a left-handed compliment (for instance, "The candidate's record is good considering the pervasive lack of rigor in her discipline").

Appeals to authority, however, can be problematic when the external reviewer is not really a proper authority. A physics professor who is an expert in solid-state physics is probably competent to assess the work of another solid-state physicist who is a tenure candidate at a comparable school, but the same solid-state physicist should not be asked to evaluate the work of tenure candidate who is an economist. But even less obvious is a situation in which an expert in twentieth century British literature is asked to evaluate the work of a faculty member at another university whose expertise happens to be in seventeenth century British literature. Professors at research universities often study highly specialized and esoteric academic areas, and this raises the question as to how we should account for the similarities and differences among scholars from the same general discipline. Relatedly, expert witnesses are used frequently in a variety of court cases, including those involving institutions of higher learning. Such witnesses are hired to render an opinion that is backed by their specific body of knowledge and experience. But expert witnesses may be challenged. The Federal Rules of Evidence, Rule 702, delineates the

requirements that help judges to determine whether the expert is qualified to testify in a particular case. If an opposing attorney challenges an
expert witness's ability to render a sound opinion, a judge may rule that
the expert is qualified or unqualified, or rule that the case does not require
an expert witness.

But it does not necessarily take an expert opinion to make something
believable. *Appeals to popular opinion* can appear to be credible even
when there is little or no evidence to substantiate the belief. Many people,
perhaps the majority of citizens, who are likely to be jurors in a discrimination or wrongful termination suit do not like the idea of awarding
someone tenure with a lifetime guarantee of job security. They seem to
believe that, once tenured, a faculty member will immerse himself in the
so-called leisure class of academia. Since many people believe this problem exists, these citizens say, then it must be true. And, since it is true, the
practice of tenure should be abolished.

Finally, there is the argument of *inconsistency*. In the context of promotion and tenure decisions, a faculty member might argue tongue in
cheek that "standards have become so high that most of the members on
this committee could not achieve tenure if they were subject to a tenure
review today." A comment such as this might sway a jury to side with
the faculty member. If a promotion or tenure denial case contains even
the slightest inconsistency, it is almost certain that the plaintiff's attorney
will vigorously attack it. Inconsistencies might also be traced to statements made during annual performance reviews, mentoring sessions,
or personal conversations away from the workplace. Any conversation
between junior and senior faculty can be potentially problematic. If, for
example, over dinner and a few glasses of wine, a senior faculty member
makes an ill-advised promise or statement to a tenure track faculty member that later turns out to be wrong or untruthful, it is safe to assume that
those offhanded comments may come back to haunt him during a legal
proceeding.

We have attempted to explain a dizzying array of risk assessments, biases,
and fallacies that interact and overlap when reappointment, promotion, or
tenure decisions are made. Three important points should be emphasized.
First, risk is an important but elusive concept to most people—even for
well-trained social scientists who have been tasked with making critical

academic personnel decisions. Second, risks are distorted by biases and reasoning fallacies. Most organizational decisions are complicated and, the more complicated the decision, the more likely these biases will hinder a just or fair outcome. Third, EEO law has repeatedly proven to be an ineffective guide or remedy in resolving academic disputes. Faculty members may be treated unfairly, but the source of such unfairness may reside in distorted perceptions that creep into the thought processes of even the most caring and meticulous decision makers. Even when such biases and thinking fallacies are known and understood, the interaction of the phenomena described here generate problems that are difficult to predict. These biases and fallacies do not exist in isolation. Instead, they interact with how we view contractual, constitutional, and collegial matters.

Our next chapter focuses on academic employment contracts. The long-time Harvard law professor Charles Fried makes an opening statement questioning the role of contracts as contributing to moral principle. We believe that a working knowledge of the risks, biases, and fallacies discussed here may enable academics to use these concepts to better uphold both contractual and moral principles.

3

Faculty Contracts

Contract law is often highly technical; large consequences turn on
what to a nonlawyer may seem to be small differences. Surely this
is why so many, both lawyers and nonlawyers, doubt that contract
law can really be an expression of moral principle. . . . The natural
expression of the promise principle in contract law is the disposition
to hold a promisor to his word, to make him do what he has
promised—or pay the equivalent of the promised performance.

—Charles Fried, *Contracts as Promise: A Theory
of Contractual Obligation*

The Employment Relationship

The employment relationship is a mixture of economic, organizational, psychological, social, contractual, and legal rights and responsibilities that are of importance to both employers and employees. It is an exchange relationship where work gets completed and where power may shift between institutions of higher learning and their faculty members. Although the presence of tenure distinguishes some faculty employment from other forms of employment, all occupations follow a fairly standard set of expectations. For colleges and universities, faculty are expected to:

Perform their job in a safe, reliable, and competent manner while striving for continuous improvement in research, teaching, and service.

Display good organizational citizenship behaviors when dealing with institutional stakeholders—colleagues, students, staff, alumni, research institutes, governmental entities, and business organizations.

Comply with university policies, rules, and directives.

Abide by relevant contract provisions that are germane to the employment relationship.

Adhere to applicable federal and state laws.

Similarly, faculty members expect their institutions to:

Provide the agreed-upon pay and benefits.

Treat faculty members with respect and dignity. This responsibility includes providing safe working conditions that are free from harassment and the potential for workplace violence.

Ensure reasonable job security, depending on a faculty member's contract status, and provide adequate notice of changes in a faculty member's job security.

Abide by applicable individual and group contract provisions that are germane to the employment relationship.

Adhere to relevant federal and state laws.

These expectations seem to be based on old-fashioned common sense. As it turns out and as we will discuss throughout the rest of this book, however, the simplicity of these expectations is a mirage. The parties to an employment relationship keep administrative agencies, mediators and arbitrators, and the state and federal courts busy adjudicating disputes that are precipitated by parties who either violate or ignore the seemingly straightforward expectations surrounding the employment relationship.

The Job Security Hierarchy

As noted earlier, tenure is the strongest form of job security. It applies to a decreasing number of college and university faculty members as well as to certain members of the judiciary such as federal judges. For a faculty member with tenure, the end of her employment could be years or even decades away. If a college or university terminates a faculty member during the life of his written contract, the school may be required to continue paying the dismissed professor's salary until the contract expires. If a faculty member is dismissed because he violated the provisions of his individual contract, he may forfeit his right to further compensation. Although comparatively rare, faculty who accept salary payments from their home institution while on sabbatical may be obligated to reimburse the school if they fail to return.

Beyond the individual contract, the employment rights and responsibilities of some faculty may be controlled by a group contract such as a collective bargaining agreement for unionized faculty members, a set of civil service regulations for government employees, or a faculty handbook that delineates the rights and responsibilities of faculty members and their institutions. An integral part of these contracts is a grievance procedure that ensures due process for faculty who are terminated. Due process generally entails telling a faculty member why and under what circumstances he is being terminated, granting the terminated faculty member access to a formal grievance hearing, giving the faculty member the right to examine evidence pertaining to his termination, and allowing the faculty member to question parties to the grievance. In some institutions of higher learning, group contractual employees may have a degree of job security that is as strong, or almost as strong, as the security enjoyed by tenured faculty members.

The least secure employment arrangement is employment at-will. As the saying goes, at-will employees can be terminated "for good cause, bad cause, or no cause at all." An at-will employee may be terminated for "just cause" (that is, they did something wrong such as testing positive on a drug test or engaging in inappropriate sexual behavior). In addition, a faculty member may be terminated for a reason that is unfair, but legal. Suppose that a sociology professor at a small, private liberal arts college who is neither tenured nor working under a contract is let go so that the college president's son-in-law can have her teaching job. This action is certainly unfair, but probably not illegal. And, of course, an at-will employee may be terminated in violation of civil rights law. For example, if an otherwise competent nontenured faculty member who works without a contract is terminated because he is "too old," the termination may violate the Age Discrimination in Employment Act of 1967. An at-will employee may also enjoy a modicum of job security and protection from an unjust dismissal if she is terminated contrary to public policy (for example, if she is terminated for serving on a jury) or her termination was so egregious and unfair that a state court rescinds the termination (for example, she is terminated after her supervisor plants illegal drugs in her desk with the intent of "setting her up" and getting her fired). A point to remember, however, is that courts' treatment of at-will employees varies from one state to another.

Institutional governing boards of both public and private colleges and universities enter into employment agreements with faculty members—either directly or indirectly—through the authority granted to them through state statutes, institutional charters, or bylaws. The complex and sometimes controversial nature of academia often complicates the contractual relationship, and, when tenure litigation arises, contractual claims are likely to be intertwined with elements from tort, discrimination, and administrative law. Disputes concerning faculty rights have been described as "esoteric."[1] Further complicating contract interpretation is the fact that contract law arises out of state common law, which differs from state to state. Two cases with identical facts (however unlikely this scenario may be), with one being heard in New Hampshire and the other being heard in nearby Vermont, may have significantly different outcomes, depending on the differences in the laws between the two states.

The Contract for Tenure

A grant of tenure establishes a strong contractual right of employment for a faculty member. In contrast to faculty members who serve for a finite period of time, the term of a tenured professor's employment, unless otherwise specified, is generally understood to be for an indefinite term, with dismissal only for cause. Tenure offers professors certain guarantees associated with the contract, including procedures that an institution must follow prior to terminating a professor. In *Haegert v. University of Evansville* (2012), the supreme court of Indiana discussed the legal requisites that the University of Evansville, a private institution, had to comply with before it could terminate a professor who was employed under a tenure contract.[2] The university sought to terminate the professor because he allegedly engaged in sexual harassment. The court noted that it need not rely on cases that applied Title VII of the Civil Rights Act of 1964 or similar state laws because the employment contract specified the procedures, policies, and terms under which a tenured professor could be fired. Examining the employment contract and the Evansville faculty manual, the court found that the act of sexual harassment was clearly defined, and further, that the professor's conduct met the definition of sexual harassment. Because the university had followed established and appropriate procedures for investigating the professor's conduct and for subsequently firing him, the court held that he had received adequate notice and due process.[3]

A grant of tenure can create a multimillion-dollar liability for the institution. A newly tenured PhD in her thirties might remain at the institution that granted her tenure for another three decades. With an average annual salary and benefits package of, say, $100,000, a single tenure decision might create a long-term liability of more than $3 million for her school. The personal prestige, job security, and financial security promised by a tenured appointment can turn a tenure contract dispute into an intense legal battle. A tenure track faculty member who is not granted tenure experiences a loss that has immeasurable career implications. The intensity of such disagreements is magnified by the subjective nature of factors affecting the decision either to grant or deny tenure to a candidate. Knowing that one's own colleagues played a role in her dismissal only magnifies the hurt, regret, and rejection of a negative tenure decision.

Tenure decisions are typically based on three sets of criteria. First, the research, teaching, and service accomplishments of the faculty member who is undergoing the tenure review play a major role, as was previously discussed. Second, the issue of faculty collegiality, which has grown in significance in recent years, and which we will discuss further in chapter 5, is also taken into account. Third, the institution must consider its own needs and strategic initiatives. Institutional needs arise from a multitude of factors and may include financial constraints, the growth or decline of individual academic units and departments, and changes in the program or curriculum offered at the institution.[4]

Following the exhaustion of available administrative remedies such as a university grievance panel hearing, a faculty member who is dissatisfied with an institution's denial of her contract for tenure may file a breach of contract suit against the institution. The suit will likely allege that the institution's faculty handbook and its tenure procedures formed a contract and that the institution deviated from these published procedures and breached the contract. The subjective evidence that institutions of higher learning use to make reappointment, promotion, and tenure decisions is particularly challenging for the courts to review. Being reluctant to function as super-tenure review committees, the judiciary has historically been deferential on such matters, relying instead on the expertise of faculty and administrators to select faculty who are best suited to a school's mission and academic tasks.[5] Such deference is rooted in the belief that those outside of academia do not understand fully what goes on inside the ivory tower.[6] This stance, however, is somewhat puzzling because the courts are frequently called upon to analyze in detail matters such as antitrust violations, cybercrimes, disputes over intellectual property, or accusations of medical malpractice that may be equally unfamiliar to judges and juries.

Traditionally, relationships in colleges and universities have been collegial, with many decisions made through a process known as shared governance. Due to the increasing presence of nonacademic administrators, however, the system of shared governance in U.S. colleges and universities may be eroding. Boards of trustees, comprised of lay representatives, typically oversee and control a school's broad legal, financial, programmatic, and faculty policies. Administrators—both lay and academic credentialed—are involved in the details of managing and implementing the institution's countless fund raising, human resources, budgeting, and curricular tasks. Even so, faculty members continue to play a key role in higher education governance, particularly with regard to academic decisions. Although faculty members are key participants in the educational process, institutions of higher learning are not without their ever-expanding bureaucracies and hierarchies—many of which have expanded because of legal and regulatory mandates placed on institutions. As a result, the bright line that once existed between faculty and administrators has become increasingly blurred.

The Court of Appeals for the Second Circuit in *Lieberman v. Gant* (1976), a case involving claims of disparate treatment under Title VII of the 1964 Civil Rights Act, as amended, expressed frustration over the review of a lengthy, multiyear, fact-intensive tenure battle, and described at length the court's extremely deferential stance.[7] To explain its deference, the court acknowledged the potentially huge financial commitment that a school makes when granting tenure. Citing "rigorous standards," the court quoted a University of Connecticut vice president who echoed what we know to be a piece of conventional wisdom in academia, " 'When in doubt, don't. Since the tenure decision is a commitment by the University to twenty or thirty years of support and several hundred thousand dollars of salary, from which there can be no turning back, we have felt that if we must err, we ought to err on the side of caution; we ought not to gamble widely.' "[8]

Judicial deference, however, is limited.[9] Reviewing courts typically require institutions to give priority to all contractual commitments. To determine procedural fairness and substantive reasonableness in tenure litigation, the courts consider whether reappointment, promotion, and tenure decisions are consistent and fair among candidates, both as individuals and as a group. It is the contract, then, that helps the courts assess whether an institution and its representatives treated a tenure candidate fairly.

Contract Basics and Factors Influencing Judicial Contract Review

In the simplest terms, a contract is an agreement between two or more people that is enforceable by law. Found within that agreement is an offer to do something and an acceptance of that offer. Also vital to the law of contracts is the concept of consideration, which is the benefit or value that each party expects to receive from the contractual deal. Though many contracts are replete with legalese, complex legal terminology is not required to create a valid contract. In fact, many contracts are formed by a simple handshake, letter, or memorandum of understanding. Under common law principles, the courts may construe that an employment contract exists by examining a basic letter of appointment that identifies the title of a position and the salary to be paid, along with other terms to which the parties have agreed.

At its core, then, the contract is a business document that is enforceable by law. The parties to the contract must determine what is desired from the transaction, and the transaction, in turn, is supposed to result in a contract that meets the needs of the parties. Because the expectations of the parties vary, and because each contract is negotiated in its own somewhat unique environment, there is no perfect contract language. Some contracts, however, are better than others. Since contract language reflects the industry in which the contract is drafted, employment contracts made in colleges and universities will contain attributes that are peculiar to higher education, some of which were described in the introductory chapter. The ultimate goal, however, is to choose language that provides clarity so that contract disagreements are minimized or eliminated.

A contract for faculty employment typically refers to the letter of appointment and often makes reference to the institution's faculty handbook as well as its retention, promotion, and tenure policies. Not surprisingly, these policies vary between tenured, tenure track, and non–tenure track faculty. In addition, professional policies, such as those promulgated by the American Association of University Professors (AAUP), may also be referenced in the handbook. Even when there is no written contract between the parties, oral promises made by a person in a supervisory role may be construed to be a contract. A majority of state courts have held that contractual terms can, in certain circumstances, be implied from oral assurances, preemployment statements, or handbooks, with handbooks being the most common source of implied contractual terms.[10]

A faculty member may file a breach of contract suit if she alleges that her college or university broke promises to her or did not treat her fairly. Procedural irregularities are often at the root of breach of contract allegations. When asked to resolve a breach of contract lawsuit, the courts will typically look first to the plain language found in a contract and will resolve a dispute based on what an objective outside observer would interpret the contract to say. Judicial precedent, missing contractual terms, the intent of the parties, academic customs, internal policies, and expert testimony are all factors that are used for guidance when interpreting a contract. Rights germane to the contract may also emanate from statutes, government documents, or administrative regulations.

Judicial Precedent

Judicial or common law precedent is important to contract interpretation. Rooted in the principle of *stare decisis*—interpreted loosely to mean letting the decision stand—courts pursue consistency, stability, and fairness by using past court decisions with similar facts and legal issues as a guide. But this approach has its limitations. Institutions of higher learning are complex entities that change over time. The opportunities and threats described in the introductory chapter may create uncertainties and render the application of previous case law less certain.

The changing composition and cultures of institutional faculty also adds to the complexity of interpreting contract provisions. For example, the label of "faculty" has transitioned from meaning those who, in years gone by, were employed on a full-time basis with tenure (or on the tenure track). Now, the term "faculty" must include part-time, non–tenure track instructors. The changing economic landscape of higher education in the United States has resulted in the hiring of more temporary, adjunct, part-time, clinical, or other types of faculty members who are used primarily to meet a school's teaching needs. A perusal of university catalogues twenty or so years ago would have shown departmental faculties that were almost 100 percent tenured or tenure track. In many academic units today, non–tenure track faculty members often outnumber those who are tenured or on the tenure track. This shift in faculty demographics increases the complexity of interpreting contracts, especially when referencing faculty handbooks that have not been revised for years.

Although contracts can be formal or informal, the courts usually show a preference for formal contracts that are written clearly. Not surprisingly, the courts will turn first to an objective examination of what is within the four corners of the contract. The plain language of the agreement itself is primary and, if clear, the courts will not rely on additional materials or witnesses to reach a decision. In *Mayo v. North Carolina State University* (2005), for example, administrators wanted Robert M. Mayo, a tenured engineering faculty member, to repay his summer salary to the university.[11] The university claimed that Mayo's summer salary was a prepayment for the upcoming academic year. Since Mayo had resigned prior to the forthcoming academic year, the university claimed he had been overpaid. Upon review, the North Carolina Court of Appeals rejected the university's argument and ruled that the written employment agreement prevailed. The written agreement included Mayo's appointment letter, his annual salary letter, the faculty handbook, and additional policies adopted by the trustees—none of which mentioned a repayment policy. Because the court deemed that North Carolina State University's written salary agreement with Mayo was clear, it declined to allow further evidence in the matter.[12]

Appointment Letters

Faculty members are most commonly hired by a letter of appointment, sometimes accompanied by a second document consisting of a written contract. These documents are legal agreements that define the relationship between the faculty member and the institution that has hired him. Appointment letters delineate items such as an academic rank or a position classification, a detailed explanation of the faculty member's pay and benefits, the duration of the appointment, and the conditions under which his appointment can be revoked (for instance, if, as part of the application process, the faculty candidate falsifies information on his CV). Institutional rules and policies as well as a description of employee responsibilities may also be found in an appointment letter. In addition, the letter may make reference to separate documents such a faculty handbook, which is usually available on the institution's web site.

Faculty hiring and retention is also governed by federal and state statutes. All colleges and universities must adhere to a host of federal statutes such as civil rights and occupational safety and health laws as well as affirmative action executive orders. At public institutions, the employment relationship of faculty members, who are state employees, may also be governed by state statutes and civil service policies.[13] In addition, some private institutions may incorporate denominational or doctrinal beliefs into their contract provisions.

Even carefully crafted appointment letters that make detailed reference to a school's faculty handbook and other related documents may not close all possible gaps. To interpret a contract, the courts may consider looking beyond its four corners, including unwritten statements or promises that were made during the hiring process.

Faculty Handbooks

Faculty handbooks define—or attempt to define—the employment relationship between faculty members and their institutions.[14] Provisions in a handbook typically include the rights and responsibilities of the university and its faculty members; criteria for reappointment, promotion, and tenure; and procedures for dismissing faculty.[15] Faculty handbooks may also include general information about the institution such as its history, mission, culture, and vision.

It is uncertain whether the provisions of a faculty handbook must be expressly referenced in an employee's appointment letter in order to be deemed part of the contract. The powers and limitations arising from a handbook may depend on its language and whether it is expressly or implicitly incorporated in the contract or letter of appointment. Also important is whether the handbook mentions applicable state contract law.

Given the proliferation of online and distance learning programs offered by both private and public colleges and universities, institutions may find themselves operating in multiple jurisdictions. Schools such as the University of Phoenix offer courses worldwide, employing faculty from a variety of geographic locations. Thus, for some online educational programs, it might be difficult to know which state has jurisdiction in a specific contractual dispute. And, as noted, each state has somewhat different rules and case precedents when adjudicating contractual disputes.

Particularly newsworthy because of its jury award of $12.7 million in damages—one of the largest awards in a tenure case—is the case of *Craine v. Trinity College* (2002), in which the Connecticut Supreme Court considered the influence of a faculty handbook on a faculty employment relationship.[16] In 1995, two years after she was denied tenure, Leslie Craine brought suit against Trinity College. The college made the adverse tenure decision even though Craine's departmental colleagues gave her continuing and unanimous support. A lower court verdict favored Craine's breach of contract claim, and the case was appealed to a higher state court.

The faculty handbook at Trinity College stated that the school had an obligation to inform a candidate "as clearly as possible" regarding the areas that would require "special attention" in the tenure decision.[17] The handbook explained further that a denial of tenure had to be based on her failure "to meet the standards of improvement," which were to be based on the faculty member's rank and detailed in her last letter of reappointment.[18] Craine's last reappointment letter focused on her need to publish results of her original research, and it also encouraged her to "continue along the lines" of her work at the college.[19] As noted, Craine's own colleagues had judged her to be on track for a tenured appointment. Despite her insistence that she had published an article in a prestigious journal, and that her lengthy article could have been divided into several shorter ones, the appointments and promotions committee voted to deny tenure to Craine.

Upon review, the Connecticut Supreme Court considered the interplay between the publication criteria and the tenure decision. The court unanimously found "that the [college] breached the parties' contract [established by the faculty handbook] by indicating that [Craine] would be evaluated according to one standard by denying tenure because of her failure to meet a different one."[20] While the court ruled favorably on the breach of contract claim, the court did not fully uphold the jury's verdict regarding gender discrimination and, accordingly, reduced her damages. As the court explained: "[A] faculty manual that sets forth terms of employment may be considered a binding employment contract."[21] Because Trinity's requisites for tenure review were provided in the faculty handbook, the court said that the college must "indicate as clearly as possible those areas to which a candidate needs to address special attention" when conducting a second reappointment review.[22] Trinity's failure to specify Craine's inadequacies during the second review (but prior to the denial of tenure) was contrary to the faculty handbook and thus constituted a breach of contract. The court cited Trinity College's apparent "shifting standard" when it emphasized the quantity of publications during her tenure denial, but had failed to emphasize that same standard previously.[23] Noted the court, Craine might have performed differently if she had been provided different notice.

Explicit, Implicit, or Nonexistent References to the Handbook

The express incorporation of the faculty handbook in the appointment letter makes it part of the legal agreement between the faculty member and the institution. When a faculty handbook is not explicitly incorporated in the text of the appointment letter, however, state contract law guides whether the handbook is implicitly incorporated as part of a faculty member's contract. A state court must decide whether to look to academic customs and usage of the handbook, whether the handbook was implicitly incorporated by practices of the institution, or whether any disclaimers can be found in the handbook itself.

In *Black v. Western Carolina University* (1993), the North Carolina Court of Appeals concluded that a faculty member "plaintiff negotiated for and was hired under a fixed-term appointment," and thus "was not entitled to notice of nonreappointment beyond the notice of the date of expiration of her term found in the original contract."[24] Because North Carolina law required handbooks to be expressly included in the employment contract and because the university did not expressly include its policies regarding fixed term appointments in the handbook or faculty member's contract, such policies were deemed not to be a part of the contractual relationship. In *Stanton v. Tulane University* (2001), a court considering a nontenured professor's claim that his termination violated the faculty handbook determined that Tulane had represented the handbook to the professor as "primarily informational in nature," and thus it was not part of the contract.[25]

A state court may rule that even expressly stated terms of a contract may be ambiguous. Such was the situation in *Holland v. Kennedy* (1989), where the court allowed express contract terms to be supplemented by provisions found in the institution's personnel manual.[26] In a caveat, the court explained, "If the handbook or policy statement is intended to supplant or modify the express terms of the contract, however, such intent must also be expressed."[27] With ambiguity in the contract, the court allowed the faculty member, who also performed administrative duties, to provide evidence of past practices, oral representations, and provisions in the handbook to support his claim on an appointment for a definite term.

To complicate matters further, courts in some jurisdictions have ruled that a faculty handbook may be deemed part of the contract even when it is not expressly included in the appointment letter. An online version of the Georgetown University faculty handbook explains that a faculty appointment "carries with it the rights and responsibilities set forth in this Faculty Handbook or in any policies, contracts, or letters of appointment applicable to the faculty member."[28] In New Mexico, the appellate court found in *Hillis v. Meister* (1971) that, although Eastern New Mexico University did not reference its handbook in faculty contracts, the handbook "govern[ed] the relationship between the faculty members and the university's administration."[29] The court ruled that the university had breached its contract by failing to follow its own procedures, as established in the faculty handbook.

A court may incorporate the faculty handbook in a faculty member's contract based on the institution's custom and usage of the handbook. In *Clampitt v. American University* (2008), the court found that American University's employee handbook was obsolete and had not been distributed to its faculty for years.[30] Thus, the court indicated that the handbook was a guiding document only and not the foundation for a contract. To determine whether a faculty handbook was part of an employment contract in *Maas v. Cornell University* (1999), the court looked to the university's intent.[31] Because the university did not expressly intend for the handbook to be part of the contract and because it could be subject to alteration at any time, the court deemed that the handbook was largely informational and was not part of the contract. In *Knowles v. Unity College* (1981), the Maine Supreme Court did not allow an untenured professor to base his argument on the tenure guidelines propounded by the AAUP because the faculty handbook and a study prepared by the college for accreditation stated that the school did not offer tenure to faculty members.[32] Furthermore, the letter of appointment making up the professor's contract did not make a reference to tenure or the faculty handbook.

Overlapping or conflicting institutional policies may complicate contract interpretation. In *Ricioppo v. County of Suffolk* (2009), a personnel handbook explained that "Administrative Officers entering their sixth year of employment with the College shall be granted continuing appointment."[33] Ricioppo, who performed both faculty and administrative tasks at the community college, argued that his appointment reached "continuing" status as of the sixth year of his employment. Upon review of the faculty handbook, the federal district court noted language identifying the handbook as merely a guide that did not replace the institution's practice.

Although culture is important, the facts and proceedings of a case usually control its outcome. The District of Columbia's position on whether a faculty handbook is part of an employee's contract exemplifies the need to pay close attention to both the faculty handbook and the pleadings of a case. In *Brown v. District of Columbia* (2013), the District of Columbia federal court was faced with the question of whether a faculty handbook created a contract between the employee and the employer.[34] The court answered with a resounding "maybe," inserting the caveat that the results depend on the facts and pleadings of the case. The plaintiff, Stephanie Brown, was a former professor who was denied tenure at the University of the District of Columbia David A. Clarke School of Law. She had been employed at the university for some twenty-five years. Having been an associate professor at the institution's law school for many of those years, she applied for tenure. Brown's application for tenure had to proceed through a multilayered tenure review process that is common to most U.S. colleges and universities. The faculty review committee voted affirmatively on her request and forwarded the application to the dean of the law school, who also voted affirmatively. Brown's request was then forwarded to the University's provost and president for final approval. Eighteen months after Brown submitted her tenure application—an inordinately lengthy period of time—the provost and president denied her tenure and notified her that the 2011–12 academic year would conclude her employment at the law school.

In her suit against the university and its officials, Brown alleged that her termination was based on her race and gender and constituted a breach of the faculty handbook. The court disagreed and granted the university's motion to dismiss the complaint, holding that Brown failed to demonstrate whether the faculty handbook was part of her contract.[35] Because Brown did not allege the necessary facts, she did not meet the legal burden needed for her suit to progress. Even if the contract was binding, according to the court, the plaintiff's own pleadings showed that the school had followed the tenure review process as dictated by the handbook. The court also determined that Brown had not presented sufficient evidence of race and gender discrimination.[36]

Brown teaches the importance of adhering to legal requisites. Under District of Columbia law, an employee handbook is a contract enforceable by the courts, and a public university's power to terminate the appointment of a tenured faculty member is subject to faculty handbook provisions.[37] The contractual status of a faculty handbook also depends, however, on a plaintiff's ability to show in the pleadings that the handbook contains an "agreement as to all material terms" and that there is an "intention of the parties to be bound." For some jurisdictions, it appears that the outcome of litigation may depend on whether the handbook says it is part of the contract and on whether the pleadings clearly support that point.

Disclaimers or disavowals may be found at some institutions. Baylor University's handbook, which is posted on its website, states clearly that it is not part of the faculty contract:

> We hope this handbook will serve as a useful reference guide throughout your employment at Baylor. We have endeavored to collect the policies, procedures, and websites that are of common interest to faculty and academic

administrators. Note that this handbook is not intended to be either an official policy and procedures manual or a contractual document. It is thus
not a part of any contractual commitment (expressed or implied), nor is it
intended to create any legally enforceable obligations. The terms and conditions of faculty members' contracts are established by the letter of appointment signed by the President of Baylor University and by the applicable
provisions of the Baylor University Personnel Policy Manual.[38]

Similarly, Auburn University at Montgomery states in a "note" at the beginning of the online faculty handbook, "This Faculty Handbook is not
a contract. It is a collection of policies and procedures that govern action
uniquely pertaining to the Auburn University at Montgomery faculty."[39]

Many faculty handbooks contain disclaimers of various sorts. Inconsistencies are likely to arise when a state court tries to interpret the effect
of a disclaimer on a faculty member's contract. In *Lim v. The Trustees
of Indiana University* (2001), a tenure denial case, a professor brought a
breach of contract claim based on the faculty handbook.[40] Identical disclaimers in the faculty handbook under which the professor was hired and
the faculty handbook existing at the time of the professor's tenure denial
expressed that the "statements and policies in this Handbook do not create a contract and do not create any legal rights."[41] The court found the
disclaimer to be a complete defense to the professor's suit.

If a faculty handbook or policy manual is referenced as part of a faculty
member's contract, it is prudent to consider changing such documents
when contracts or manuals—or both—are updated. An updated faculty
handbook should explicitly state whether it replaces all previously published handbooks and whether it modifies other manuals that address
personnel policies. In *Fenn v. Yale University* (2003), a current contract
controlled the issue.[42] Although a 1975 patent policy in a faculty employment contract was amended during a professor's employment, the district
court held that the university's patent policy was valid and enforceable as
part of the professor's current employment contract. The 1975 policy, as
well as all subsequent policies, provided that the university could—at any
time—revoke or amend the policy.

Interinstitutional arrangements present a challenge to assessing the
currency and flexibility of a faculty handbook. In fact, *Brown* involved
such an arrangement when the University of District Columbia acquired

the Washington, D.C.-based Antioch Law School. These arrangements include mergers (two or more schools join to form a new school), acquisitions (one school buys out another school or schools), and joint programs (two or more schools collaborate, but each school retains its original ownership and identity). As a result, institutions of higher learning are not necessarily constrained by the physical boundaries that once defined most brick-and-mortar institutions. By combining resources, schools can make better use of their resources through economies of scale and scope. For example, North Carolina State University, a public institution, established a joint venture with Campbell University, a private institution, to offer a dual juris doctor and master of public administration degree as well as a dual juris doctor and master of accounting degree.[43] Other mergers involve public-private partnerships such as the merging of Oak Ridge National Laboratory with University of Tennessee, Knoxville, to form the Bredesen Center for Interdisciplinary Research and Graduate Education. Other situations involve acquisitions in which one institution is bought by another. Widener University, with its main campus in Chester, Pennsylvania, acquired the land and buildings of Brandywine College, a now defunct two-year institution in Wilmington, Delaware. Some of the Brandywine faculty members and staff were moved to Widener's Pennsylvania campus, and the Delaware campus was subsequently converted into a law school. Other mergers of significance include Fordham University acquiring Marymount College and Indiana University and Purdue University merging their medical, dentistry, law, and other academic units. Situations such as these raise questions as to which faculty handbook controls, whose contractual and noncontractual employment policies prevail, and whether the handbook can be changed unilaterally to reflect changing conditions brought about by the merger, acquisition, or joint program.

Not only do contractual documents overlap, the contracts themselves can be malleable. As a general principle, the courts allow contracts to be changed. Portions of a contract can be altered, if all parties consent, or voided, if the contract was entered under fraudulent terms. In *Landrum v. Lindsey Wilson College* (2004), Robert Landrum's contract both referenced and incorporated the school's faculty handbook.[44] This particular handbook specified that a faculty member employed on a multiyear contract could be dismissed if given one year of notice and with the consent of the academic division chairs. The handbook also stipulated that misconduct and other conditions could be grounds for dismissal. Then the college threw Landrum—and possibly other faculty members—a curve ball by altering Landrum's contract and by adding a provision stating that the college could terminate his contract for any reason, subject to a thirty-day notice. Upon review of the dispute between Landrum and the college, the court held that an employer could not unilaterally alter the terms of a valid and current contract.[45] Thus, Landrum could only be terminated for cause. Because Landrum was not reappointed when his contract term ended, the court did not have to rule on whether the faculty handbook or the contract applied. A prudent drafting of a faculty handbook, however, should specify whether it forms part of the contract and whether the institution is permitted to make unilateral changes to it.

Contract Law and Institutional Culture

Interpretations of faculty employment contracts using principles of traditional contract law are not always aligned with the traditions or practices of academia. An example of a possible conflict between law and culture arose in *Tuomala v. Regent University* (1996), in which several professors each signed a three-year continuing contract for a "tenured" faculty appointment."[46] The faculty handbook defined the terms of the contracts; subsequent revisions provided that faculty members who were appointed based on continuing contracts were entitled to receive new contracts or to have their existing contracts renewed. Absent specific statements to the contrary, the term "tenured" implies, in an academic culture, a lifetime guarantee of employment. But, using primarily a legal interpretation of the contract, the court found that the professors were entitled to three years of employment after which time they received one-year contracts.[47]

In *Branham v. Thomas M. Cooley Law School* (2012), the Sixth Circuit Court of Appeals declined to define "tenure" as a lifetime guarantee of employment when a law professor's contract was specified to be a one year term, ruling that the terms of the contract trumped the long-term culture and practices of higher education.[48] Lynn Branham, who taught criminal law, had been teaching at the Thomas M. Cooley Law School since 1983. When the law school asked her to teach constitutional law and torts in the spring semester of 2006, Branham first complained, then complied, after which she went on a semester-long leave of absence. Upon her return, she was again asked to teach constitutional law. She refused and was terminated. After the school terminated her employment, Branham sued on multiple counts. She stated that her employment contract incorporated both the American Bar Association's appendix 1 to its "Standards and Rules of Procedure for Approval of Law Schools," and Cooley's Policy 201. According to Branham, both documents confirmed lifetime appointments for tenured faculty.

The American Bar Association's appendix 1, titled "Statements on Academic Freedom and Tenure," provides that "teachers . . . should have permanent or continuous tenure, and their services should be terminated only for adequate cause." Explained further in the ABA's Standard 405 is that appendix 1 "is an example (of a tenure policy) but is not obligatory." Cooley's Policy 201 explained that "no tenured faculty member shall be dismissed . . . prior to the expiration of the term of his appointment, except for good cause shown" and according to appropriate procedures.

A federal district court found that Branham's termination was improper, because her dismissal did not follow the procedures set forth in her employment contract. The law school then followed proper procedures in which the faculty voted to dismiss Branham, a decision that was upheld by Cooley's board of directors. Satisfied with the procedure, the district court then entered judgment for the law school.

Branham appealed after the district court denied her claim to be paid damages. The issue on appeal revolved around the meaning of the term "tenure." The Sixth Circuit affirmed the district court's ruling on the breach of contract issue. Although Branham supposedly had tenure with the Cooley Law School, the Sixth Circuit focused on the contractual issues and on the question of whether the school followed the appropriate procedures to terminate a tenured faculty member. The court's view was that the underlying contract must define the term of employment. Then looking to the contract, the court found that neither the contract nor the additional policies referenced guaranteed permanent employment through tenure. The court explained:

> Branham's contract, including Policy 201, which refers to the concept of tenure but does not go so far as to define tenure as a right to continuous employment, does not create an obligation of continuous employment: her

contract expressly limits its term to a single year. While Branham may have had "tenure" in the sense that she had academic freedom, and that she and Cooley generally expected that they would enter a new employment contract in subsequent years, nothing in her employment contract, or the documents incorporated by reference therein, provides for a term of employment greater than one year.[49]

Although the court acknowledged that the contract incorporated faculty appointment provisions from the ABA's standards, the court viewed these standards to be advisory and not requiring law schools to grant continuous appointments to their faculty. As a result, the Sixth Circuit upheld the district court in its conclusion that Branham was "due only the employment protection and process specified in her contract."[50]

The decision in *Cooley* was perceived in some academic circles as a threat to the cultural interpretations of tenured faculty employment.[51] In most higher education institutions, including private law schools similar to Cooley, tenure has been historically and culturally understood to mean lifetime employment, with terminations occurring only for egregious misconduct. But in the rapidly changing environment of higher education, cultural definitions and interpretations cannot be expected to last forever. In reality, it would be more troubling for the court not to follow the contract, because the contract expressed the will of the parties.

When individual faculty members prefer to negotiate contracts that best suit their individual needs, the broad cultural interpretations of terms such as "tenure" should not be assumed to have a universal meaning. Furthermore, the courts cannot be relied upon to infuse cultural and historical traditions into their decisions. Though perhaps troubling to some in academia, the *Cooley* decision was solidly grounded in contract law. Looking to the contract, the court sought to determine the intent of the parties. It applied deference to the institution in matters of academic concern and it relied on the judgment of faculty members who—either rightly or wrongly—decided that the law school had "good cause" for the termination of Branham.

Most significant, perhaps, is that *Cooley* beckons to those in academia to understand the importance of state contract law when establishing and defining the terms of a faculty appointment. This case also highlights the importance of the four corners of the contract, and it places provisions of the agreement in perspective. It reminds contract drafters to define carefully, clearly, and concisely what it means—and does not mean—to earn tenure. And the case highlights the difference between legal protections that are enforceable by law and the cultural protections that depend on the careful language and watchful eyes of academics and institutional attorneys themselves.[52]

Collective Bargaining

Collective bargaining defines, at least in part, the employment relationship in institutions of higher learning where faculty are represented by labor organizations (unions). In fact, the largest labor organizations in the United States are the teacher's unions. Labor-management relations in private institutions is governed primarily by federal law—most notably the National Labor Relations Act (NLRA), as amended—whereas the collective bargaining arrangements of public colleges and universities are governed by applicable state laws.

The bargaining process requires a community of interest. That is, a bargaining unit is comprised of individuals who share common matters of concern such as similar pay levels, benefits, job duties, and working locations. In a collective bargaining relationship, labor representatives negotiate with management on behalf of unionized workers over wages, hours, and working conditions. The National Labor Relations Board (NLRB) oversees union certification elections and adjudicates unfair labor practice charges that arise under the NLRA. Agreements made by union and management negotiators at the bargaining table determine the rights of both the institution and its employees. As a group contractual arrangement that covers all members of the bargaining unit (and that includes faculty who do not support organized labor), a collective bargaining agreement can have a significant impact on a school's faculty reappointment, promotion, and tenure processes. These agreements may also address in detail faculty pay, benefits, workloads, working conditions, job security, and seniority provisions. When disputes arise over the interpretation and meaning of collective bargaining agreement provisions (for instance, when is a faculty member fired for "just cause?"), a grievance procedure culminating in binding arbitration may be used to resolve the dispute.

Collective bargaining exists to benefit nonsupervisory employees, but not managers. Local union representatives who are involved heavily in contract negotiations and the administration of those contracts can amass enough influence to have significant control over policies affecting wages, hours, and working conditions, making the human resource manager's work difficult. In extreme cases, a human resources manager may have to go to the union to get approval for even the most mundane personnel matters—something that professional administrators and human resource managers clearly do not like and something that can precipitate a monumental tug-of-war between university administrators and union officials.

The National Education Association (NEA), the largest of all U.S. unions with 3.2 million members, advocates collective bargaining for faculty members, touting among its benefits increased involvement in the decision-making process.[53] The NEA supports a very strong degree of faculty influence and job security through the collective advocacy of a faculty union, which goes beyond the advisory role professors often play in campus faculty senate bodies. Similarly, the AAUP also supports the unionization of faculty members.[54] The AAUP promotes collective bargaining as a means of "protecting academic freedom, institutions of faculty governance, fair procedures for resolving grievances, the economic well-being of faculty and other academic professionals, and the advancement of the interests of higher education."[55] Governance issues, according to the AAUP, are enhanced by strengthening the authority and responsibility of faculty members.

In reality, faculty members have attributes of both employees and managers, making collective bargaining rights for faculty members tentative and unclear. The same faculty member who is employed through an appointment letter that explains her rights and responsibilities can also share responsibilities with administrators for interviewing, hiring, supervising, and evaluating university faculty and staff.

Furthermore, professors who perceive themselves as traditional, autonomous scholars can find themselves at odds with the collective view of faculty unions. While unions seek to protect a group's collective interests, tenure serves to protect the individual. And, whether tenured or not, many faculty members are in the position to negotiate individual contracts to their highest benefit—but not necessarily to the highest benefit of the faculty as a group. Star research faculty, especially those who attract large sums of research grant dollars, typically want little to do with the unifying presence of organized labor. These professors want to negotiate individual contracts that are tailored to their specific research and teaching needs. Superstar faculty members may also be able to negotiate salaries that far exceed the structured salary scales that are common to collective bargaining agreements in institutions of higher learning. Individual bargaining situations such as these decrease the community of interest that has long been associated with traditional collective bargaining.

The federal NLRA gives faculty in private but not public institutions the right to organize, form, and assist a labor organization as well as to bargain collectively through a process known broadly as "concerted activity." The right of faculty members to bargain collectively at private institutions of higher education, however, has undergone significant change. Although managers within an organization do not have the right to organize for the purpose of collective bargaining, the NLRB and the courts do not always view faculty as managers, even when their duties include some managerial tasks.

In *National Labor Relations Board v. Yeshiva University* (1980), the Supreme Court focused on the faculty members working at a small, private institution.[56] The faculty duties at Yeshiva were so intertwined with those of management that their interests were often aligned. The Court held that full-time faculty members were exempt from protection under the NLRA because of their status as managers. The Supreme Court identified key responsibilities that contributed to faculty members' managerial status: their "absolute authority" in academic matters, their "significant role" in faculty personnel issues, and their participation on committees from which a majority of their recommendations were adopted by the administration.[57]

In today's changing landscape of higher education, however, the *Yeshiva* court's reasoning may not be as applicable as it was three decades ago. Institutions of higher learning have become increasingly businesslike with bureaucracies, hierarchical structures, and centralized decision making by those whose allegiance is more to administrative than to academic matters. A key position on the administrative side of the institution is that of the department chair, who keeps one foot in the academic trenches and the other foot in the world of administration. Unlike other administrators, department chairs usually anticipate serving for several years and then returning full time to research and teaching. But, department chairs also have significant power when it comes to faculty hiring and retention decisions. Further up the administrative hierarchy, decisions made by nonfaculty administrators significantly affect academic matters that have historically been the purview of nonadministrative faculty members. In some institutions, the increasing prominence of central administrations has reduced traditional faculty governance activities, often to the point of symbolic window dressing.

To bargain collectively on behalf of a faculty group, a union must successfully navigate through the bargaining unit determination and certification election processes as mandated by the NLRA for private institutions or by applicable state law for public institutions. This process not only requires demonstrating a community of interest among bargaining unit faculty members, but the union must also receive a majority of the votes cast in the certification election. The determination of the bargaining unit has historically required that college and university faculties show that their roles and responsibilities are somehow different from the roles and responsibilities of the mixed management and faculty group in *Yeshiva*. Yet there is the distinct possibility that employment relationships in higher education will evolve even further, perhaps in unpredictable ways.

Point Park University v. Newspaper Guild of Pittsburgh (2015) reconsidered *Yeshiva* and placed at stake faculty members' rights to organize, join, and participate in labor union activities.[58] In *Point Park*, the NLRB revisited the factors contributing to the managerial status of faculty members under the NLRA. Faculty members at Point Park University, who were dissatisfied with changes in the faculty handbook, voted in 2003 to form a bargaining unit. The NLRB affirmed the nonmanagerial status of the faculty and determined that they could unionize. On appeal, the D.C. Circuit Court overruled the NLRB's decision and asked the board to explain how the faculty's role was not managerial. The NLRB, through the decision of a regional director, provided a supplemental decision that explained why criteria in *Yeshiva* did not apply to Point Park.

Amicus briefs were submitted by interested parties in 2012. But, in the summer of 2015, before a decision could be reached, Point Park dropped its appeal.[59] In contrast to a perceived lack of power by the faculty, the briefs in support of the university's position advanced the concept of shared governance as the predominant model. The university also criticized the NLRB for ignoring U.S. Supreme Court precedent and the mandate of the D.C. Circuit Court of Appeals on remand. If nothing else, *Point Park* illustrates the shifting landscape of higher education employment in the U.S., and the sometimes painfully slow world of employment law.

The NLRB does not have jurisdiction over faculty or other employees of religious educational institutions.[60] In the case of Saint Xavier University and other pending cases, the NLRB is examining whether its "substantial religious character" test is valid for determining whether an educational institution qualifies as a religious educational institution. In applying this test, the NLRB analyzes the involvement of the affiliated religious group in the institution's daily affairs, the religious mission of the institution, whether indoctrination and proselytizing are included as part of the institution's purpose, and whether faculty are chosen or evaluated based on religious criteria. According to the D.C. Circuit Court of Appeals, however, the NLRB's inquiry is driven by a determination of whether the institution is sufficiently religious. This inquiry is probably in direct violation of the First Amendment's establishment and free exercise clauses.

As noted, collective bargaining and labor relations at private colleges and universities are under the jurisdiction of the federal NLRA and the NLRB. In contrast, each state and the District of Columbia have their own separate laws or executive orders for governing labor relations among public sector employees. The collective bargaining processes at the various state schools are covered by a patchwork quilt of thirty-four public employee labor relations acts. State labor laws have similarities to the NLRA in that they establish requirements for bargaining unit determination, certification elections, and the collective bargaining and dispute resolution processes. Unlike the NLRA, nearly all state laws either ban or severely restrict the rights of public sector employees to engage in economic strikes or other work stoppages.

In the current higher education environment, finding a true community of interest among faculty members has become increasingly difficult. As the interests of the faculty of a particular college or university become more disparate, bargaining to meet significant collective purposes of the faculty is challenging. With the disparity of power and institutional influence between tenured and nontenured faculty members, faculty members who are less empowered may actually have a stronger community of inter-est than do their higher-ranking counterparts. Research professors with strong international reputations behave more like entrepreneurs or sole proprietors than do their more local and less cosmopolitan colleagues. The former have a strong loyalty to their academic disciplines, but they often have little or no loyalty to their institutions. Lower status and less powerful non–tenure track faculty, meanwhile, may be in a better posi-tion to organize and demand that their college or university bargain with them. Roughly one-fourth of the U.S. professoriate is tenured or work-ing in a tenure track position, leaving the other three quarters as nonten-ured, contractual faculty members.[61] The less secure status of the latter faculty group may, by itself, constitute a strong community of interest—an essential ingredient in the collective bargaining and labor relations pro-cesses. A side effect of this trend is to force colleges and universities to draft employment contracts that are exceedingly meticulous at delineating clearly the terms and conditions of individual contracts. At least for the present, the *Yeshiva* case may enable administrators to classify faculty members as managers and avoid encounters with union negotiators who are often both contentious and savvy. But, if future presidential appoin-tees to the NLRB take a view that is contrary to *Yeshiva*, it could open the door to increased collective bargaining and greater job security protec-tions through group-oriented collective bargaining agreements.

Since the courts are willing to review contract decisions, it magnifies the need for institutions to have thorough and crystal clear policies for hiring, performance evaluation, faculty retention, promotion, and tenure deci-sions. It is prudent that all terms and conditions of faculty employment be stated clearly in writing. Human resource management policies should always emphasize merit and eschew bias. To this end, institutions must provide adequate training to the administrators, faculty, and staff mem-bers whose responsibility it is to draft, enact, and enforce the policies. As a means to minimize risk, faculty contracts should be drafted and handled through the human resource departments and under the watchful eye of competent legal counsel. Yet, while it is prudent in terms of legal risk man-agement for universities to govern the employment of faculty members with the same carefully crafted human resource policies that govern other employees, this is not to say that the *academic* aspects of the agreement should also be governed by the human resources department. Senior academic officers must maintain the responsibility to describe and define what the academic agreement is. Academic administrators must not, however, be in the position of promising more than they have the authority to deliver. For example, promises of assisting with work-life balance or spousal relocation should occur through the appropriate human resources channels. Finally, for those who review and manage faculty contracts, it is of paramount significance that no two situations present the same exact facts and circumstances. Each faculty employee's situation is unique and should be addressed accordingly. For this reason, the institution of binding arbitration might be a useful tool for resolving contract disputes.

Risk mitigation should be a key concern for all administrators in institutions of higher learning, and nowhere is risk more heightened than in faculty employment contracts. When interpreting issues of constitutional tenure claims, it is likely that the courts will continue their deferential stance because of the academic and subjective nature of disputes that arise in colleges and universities. But the courts will defer to institutional judgment only as long as reappointment, promotion, and tenure decisions stay within the bounds of civil rights laws and institutional policies and procedures. And it is likely that courts will intervene in contract disputes when institutions clearly violate their own procedures. While courts will continue to recognize that academia involves specialized knowledge such as scholarship quality and teaching expertise, decisions that conflict with contractual agreements and constitute a breach of contract will not likely be tolerated. Thus, the more that institutions adhere to and closely follow their own policies and rules, the more insulated they will be from judicial influence on faculty contractual decisions. Under the law, the principle of contracts will likely be held in higher regard than the more nebulous principles of academic freedom and institutional tradition.

As the culture of higher education becomes more businesslike, faculty employment agreements will increasingly rely on the law of contracts, and these contracts will trend toward greater complexity. As faculty members become renowned researchers in their field, individual contract negotiations for the best salary and facilities will change the focus from the good of the whole to the good of the individual, thus increasing the importance of specialized contracts. We predict that the use of contracts will only grow more important. Managers will necessarily become more involved in the business aspects of higher education, and collegial relationships will continue to transition toward more and more procedure and process. In response, the courts will be called upon increasingly to sort through the quagmire of red tape that accompanies much of the decision making in academia. As institutional norms decrease and as individualized faculty contracts increase, the courts may be more likely to assert their views in contract administration.

It will be interesting to see the extent to which professional arbitrators will evolve in matters pertaining to contract interpretation and administration. Historically, the institution of arbitration and the binding nature of arbitration decisions for both private and the public sector contract rights disputes have been given great deference by the courts. By staying largely outside of the court system, arbitration often provides a much more expedient and less expensive method of resolving a wide variety of disputes. Arbitrators often develop a specialized expertise in a particular industry (such as arbitrators who adjudicate disputes involving professional baseball players). It would be logical to believe that a growing cadre of arbitrators with a specialized knowledge of institutions of higher learning might also emerge.

FROM CONTRACTS TO CONSTITUTIONS

Faculty Free Speech Issues

Academic Freedom

The American Association of University Professors (AAUP) was founded in 1915 and, in that same year, a fifteen-member committee comprised mostly of social scientists from prominent universities promulgated *Appendix 1: 1915 Declaration of Principles on Academic Freedom and Academic Tenure*. This ten-page document addressed academic authority, the academic calling, and the function of academic institutions, along with a set of "practical proposals" designed to safeguard freedom, protect college executives and governing boards from charges of imposing constraints on academic freedom, and ensure that institutions of higher learning could attract men of high quality and character (women, in 1915, were apparently of little concern to the AAUP). The declaration is regarded as the seminal document on academic freedom, with revisions being made to the document in 1925, 1940, and 1970. The AAUP also enacted a faculty governance statement in 1966.

The notion of academic freedom, especially as it pertains to institutions of higher learning, is also bound inextricably to the First Amendment of the U.S. Constitution. The First Amendment, of course, does not make reference to academic freedom directly, but court decisions beginning in the early 1950s have shaped the meaning of academic freedom and its relevance to institutions of higher learning. Most court decisions on academic freedom pertain to disputes between an individual faculty member and her institution of higher learning. These disputes may, however, spill over into the public domain. Lars Maischak, a lecturer in history at the California State University, Fresno, was quoted in February 2017 as saying that "[Donald] Trump must hang."[1] He also reportedly said in the same month that Republicans should be executed for each immigrant deported by Trump's administration. Maischak's statements, not surprisingly, created a stir beyond his campus. His comments may even have caught the attention of the U.S. Secret Service, the Federal Bureau of Investigation, and local law enforcement agencies, all of which take threats of bodily harm—especially when those threats are directed at the president of the United States—very seriously. The university's president, Joseph I. Castro, immediately launched an investigation into what he perceived as potential threats of violence that might violate the law.

In April 2017, the conservative writer and political commentator Ann Coulter was forced to cancel her talk at the University of California after her sponsors feared that her presence could ignite violent demonstrations at the Berkeley campus. Six months after the Coulter debacle, George Ciccariello-Maher, a professor at Drexel University, made a wish for "white genocide" and, earlier, expressed his contempt for an airline passenger who gave up a first class seat to a soldier, saying that the passenger's generosity made him want to vomit.[2] In May of that year, controversy occurred at Duke University when a theologian expressed his disdain for race and diversity training seminars. The utterances of a faculty-member-turned-loose-cannon may have free speech protections, but that does little to help university leaders clean up the mess as benefactors and students threaten to take their donations and tuition payments elsewhere.

Academic freedom concerns have arisen over the issue of mandated student grade changes, the appropriateness of summer reading program selections, religious beliefs and practices, and the use of intercollegiate team mascots that are viewed as disrespectful to Native Americans.

Furthermore, academic freedom cases also touch on a professor's right to use classroom photographs, materials, or language (profanity, sexual remarks, or blasphemy) that might be regarded by some as offensive. Other academic freedom issues may arise over the imposition of a faculty member's academic standards, the role that state legislators play in academic affairs, and a faculty member's right to question and critique institutional matters. Policies affecting faculty privacy and the use of university-provided websites and electronic mail systems have expanded the domain of academic freedom and free speech. An overarching concern in our analysis is the extent to which a dispute over a faculty member's First Amendment rights might jeopardize her prospects for reappointment and tenure.

The seminal 1957 higher education case heard by the U.S. Supreme Court, *Sweezy v. New Hampshire*, offers insight into the meaning of academic freedom.[3] In his decision, Justice Frankfurter summarized four essential academic freedoms: (1) who may teach, (2) what may be taught, (3) how it shall be taught, and (4) who may be admitted to study. University administrators and faculty members usually make the first decision when they hire faculty members and assign them to teach certain classes. The question of what may be taught is also under the control of administrators and faculty who design curricula and who make curriculum changes. In some cases, these decisions result in introducing new programs or abolishing ones that have become outdated or suffer from declining enrollments. Justice Frankfurter's third freedom of how a subject shall be taught usually rests with the individual faculty member once she has been assigned a class to teach—that is, the faculty member decides on the inclusion of course topics and the emphasis that will be placed on certain topics within a course, such as how many class sessions in a world history course should be devoted to the European front of World War II and how many should be devoted to battles in the Pacific. Finally, deciding whom to admit to study—at least at the undergraduate level—is almost always the purview of the college or university admissions office. At the professional and graduate school level, however, departmental faculty often play a more prominent role in admitting PhD students.

A key aspect of academic freedom involves the quest of pursuing the truth, wherever that quest might lead. The importance of academic freedom was expressed in *Sweezy:* "To impose any strait jacket upon the intellectual leaders in our colleges and universities would imperil the future of our Nation. . . . Scholarship cannot flourish in an atmosphere of suspicion and distrust. Teachers and students must always remain free to inquire, to study and to evaluate, to gain new maturity and understanding; otherwise our civilization will stagnate and die."[4]

In more recent times, the chancellor of the University of Wisconsin-Madison, Rebecca Blank, observed:

> Universities are unique places, characterized by their acceptance of people who push the boundaries of perceived truth. Universities frequently employ faculty members whose opinions are considered "out there"—people who embrace alternative ideas and identities that surprise and (and occasionally shock or anger) others . . . I have always thought that universities' greatest value to society is that they are places where any idea is thinkable and debatable . . . even ideas that shock and insult. A university's commitment to academic freedom and free speech is a commitment that allows all ideas to be presented and discussed. Ideas should be dismissed out of hand only after research and debates prove them inadequate, rather than being dismissed out of hand without debate because they challenge perceived wisdom or offend current beliefs.[5]

Earlier U.S. Supreme Court Decisions

The U.S. Supreme Court and, to a lesser extent, the federal circuit courts have generally recognized the legitimacy and benefits of academic freedom not only in U.S. institutions of higher learning, but also in elementary and secondary schools. In *West Virginia Board of Education v. Barnette,* a case that dealt with school children being forced to salute the United States flag, the court noted, "If there is any fixed star in our constitutional constellation, it is that no officials, high or petty, can prescribe what shall be orthodox in politics, nationalism, religion, or other matters of opinion or force citizens to confess by word or act their faith therein."[6] Presumably this 1943 case would also favor institutions of higher learning because the freedoms delineated in *West Virginia Board of Education* clearly touch upon the "orthodox" attributes of academic freedom.

In *Sweezy*, a University of New Hampshire professor, Paul M. Sweezy, was accused of being affiliated with the Communist party, and he refused to answer questions directed to him by the state attorney general. Ruling in favor of *Sweezy*, Justice Frankfurter noted in his concurrence,

> In a university knowledge is its own end, not merely a means to an end. A university ceases to be true to its own nature if it becomes the tool of Church or State or any sectional interest. A university is characterized by the spirit of free inquiry, its ideal being the ideal of Socrates—"to follow the argument where it leads." This implies the right to examine, question, modify or reject traditional ideas and beliefs. Dogma and hypothesis are incompatible, and the concept of an immutable doctrine is repugnant to the spirit of a university. The concern of its scholars is not merely to add and revise facts in relation to an accepted framework, but to be ever examining and modifying the framework itself.[7]

Similarly, in *Keyishian v. Board of Regents* (1967), University of Buffalo professors (state of New York employees) refused to sign an affidavit declaring that they were not and never had been affiliated with the Communist party.[8] The U.S. Supreme Court eventually had to settle the question of whether requiring state employees to renounce Communism was so overly broad and vague as to be unconstitutional. The court answered in the affirmative, stating that the country had an interest in protecting the First Amendment rights of teachers to keep the education system as free and open as possible. Explained the court, the First Amendment "does not tolerate laws that cast a pall of orthodoxy over the classroom."[9]

Tinker v. Des Moines (Iowa) Independent School District was a 1969 case that involved public high school students who peacefully protested the Vietnam War by wearing black armbands.[10] After learning of the planned protest, the school principal warned students that they would be expelled if they demonstrated, a threat that the principal carried out. The dismissals, in turn, precipitated a federal lawsuit by the students' parents that focused on the First Amendment. After the plaintiffs lost their case at the federal district and appellate court levels, the U.S. Supreme Court granted a *writ of certiorari* and subsequently ruled in favor of the protesting students' claims that teachers and students do not relinquish their freedom of speech or expression at the schoolhouse gate.[11]

Academic freedom may conceivably be threatened through the termination of funding if there is a disagreement between the funding source and the recipient. For example, in the wake of several instances of campus speech infringement, the anthropologist Stanley Kurtz has suggested that Congress should take steps to "ensure that taxpayer dollars no longer underwrite campus assaults on freedom of speech."[12] He opines that it is the legislature's duty to protect citizens' "most basic individual rights," and defines "intellectual freedom and free expression" as being "core functions" of the university.[13] Using the Higher Education Act as a basis for his argument, Kurtz proposes a framework through which higher education institutions would be required to protect speech freedoms in order to receive student financial aid and institutional research grants.

The Elements of Academic Freedom

A modern and comprehensive description of academic freedom has been set forth by Cary Nelson, a former president of the AAUP and an emeritus professor of English at the University of Illinois at Urbana-Champagne.[14] Nelson first describes what academic freedom is:

Faculty members have the right to engage in intellectual debate without the fear of censorship.

Faculty members have the right to adhere to their pedagogical philosophy and intellectual commitments.

Faculty and students have the right to compare and contrast the work found in one discipline with the work found in other disciplines.

Academic freedom gives faculty members and students the right to express their views through a broad array of media both on and off campus without fear of sanction unless the manner of expression substantially limits the right of others.

Faculty members and students have the right to study the topics they choose, though it does not impair others from judging the value and soundness of their research. Universities must protect faculty and student research findings from being blocked by government, corporate, or other influential sources.

The political, religious, and philosophical beliefs of politicians, university administrators, and the public cannot be imposed on faculty and students.

Faculty and students must have the right to seek redress if they believe that their rights have been violated.

Faculty and students must be free from reprisals for disagreeing with administrative policies.

Faculty and students have the right to challenge the views of others without fear of reprisal.

Faculty have the right to assign grades and uphold academic standards as long as the imposition of standards and the assignment of grades is fair, being neither capricious nor punitive.

Faculty have substantial latitude with regard to the selection of their teaching methods.

Faculty accused of wrongdoing must receive a full measure of due process.

Nelson also describes what academic freedom does not guarantee:

Faculty do not have the right to harass, threaten, intimidate, ridicule, or impose their views on students.

Student academic freedom does not diminish the obligation of students to master course material and the fundamentals of a discipline.

Academic freedom does not protect an incompetent faculty member's job. Tenure does not guarantee lifetime employment for an incompetent faculty member.

Academic freedom does not put a faculty member in an unassailable position free from challenges to or disagreements with a faculty member's educational philosophy and practices.

Academic freedom does not provide protection for faculty members who break the law, ignore institutional regulations, or face disciplinary action. Faculty are, however, entitled to procedural and substantive due process.

Academic freedom does not necessarily protect a faculty member from adverse administrative actions such as the denial of a merit pay raise, sabbatical, favored office space, or preferred teaching and committee assignments.

Academic freedom does not protect a faculty member from adverse action for failing to meet teaching or service obligations or for disrupting meetings and academic presentations of faculty or invited guests.

Academic freedom does not protect a faculty member from charges of scientific misconduct, the violation of reasonable university policies, or penalties associated with such misconduct.

In a nutshell, academic freedom does not constitute academic license. Faculty members are expected to comply with institutional rules and guidelines, treat colleagues and students with respect and dignity, engage in ethical behaviors and practices, and perform up to institutional expectations with regard to teaching, research, and service obligations.

The Changing World of Academic Communications

With few exceptions, the primary task of a nonadministrative faculty member is to create and disseminate knowledge through research, teaching, and professional service activities. These three major academic functions are, in essence, different forms of communication or speech. Historically, communication about academic matters usually took place through scholarly books and journal articles, papers presented at academic meetings, or private correspondence between faculty members. These older modes of communication were usually person to person (sometimes in confidence) or directed to a very small audience of academic readers, delivered through written publications, private telephone conversations, and handwritten letters. Occasionally, a faculty member might be invited to speak to a nonacademic group such as a local Rotary Club, and a few noteworthy professors such as the late University of Chicago economist and Nobel laureate Milton Friedman have given televised talks or served as guest columnists for major newspapers such as the *New York Times* or the *Wall Street Journal*.

It was not until the 1990s that the world of communications in academia began to change significantly. Books and journal articles were, and still are, a major way of communicating research findings or developing arguments or positions that are of concern to fellow academics and to the public. Unlike the academic world of a quarter of a century ago, however, when finding an article or a book required rummaging through labyrinthine library stacks, electronic copies of academic journal articles and books are now accessible within seconds. Faculty members now communicate through email messages that might be read by hundreds of recipients (a far cry from the handwritten or typed letter sent to one colleague and perhaps shared with one or two more). Many other faculty members have taken their messages to social media channels such as Twitter or Facebook, places where controversial or offensive views may go viral. Prominent news channels such as CNN or Fox News use Skype, Zoom, and other technology to reach millions of viewers. These around-the-clock news media outlets also invite prominent (and sometimes not-so-prominent) academics to air their views about controversial topics such as abortion, immigration reform, affirmative action, global warming, and international affairs. Advanced technology puts free speech issues to the test, especially when academics submit controversial editorials to online columns that are broadcast to millions of viewers, listeners, and readers. With new and expanded channels of communication come new challenges to the concepts of academic freedom and free speech.

The First Amendment

The First Amendment of the U.S. Constitution packs a great deal of freedom—and, sometimes, controversy—into its forty-five words: "Congress shall make no law respecting an establishment of religion, or prohibiting the free exercise thereof; or abridging the freedom of speech, or of the press; or the right of the people peaceably to assemble, and to petition the Government for a redress of grievances."

The presence of the First Amendment raises and will continue to raise a number of delicate issues when it comes to academic freedom. How is academic freedom defined and applied? What effect does the First Amendment have on academic freedom? Does the First Amendment focus primarily on the individual or does it protect group activities? One way to analyze the First Amendment is to examine those forms of speech that have been denied or controlled by the U.S. Supreme Court. In essence, employees working in public entities—notably state colleges and universities—have some free speech rights, whereas faculty, staff, and students in private colleges and universities have few First Amendment rights. Faculty members in state-assisted institutions of higher learning generally have constitutional protections when acting as citizens, but little protection for actions encompassing their official duties.

Two cases that serve as anchors for the discussion of First Amendment rights of public university faculty members and staff are *Pickering v. Board of Education* and *Garcetti v. Ceballos*.[15] Ironically, neither of these cases pertained directly to faculty members in U.S. institutions of higher learning. *Pickering*, a 1968 case, involved an Illinois high school teacher who wrote a letter to the editor of a local newspaper that was critical of school board decisions and operations. The more recent *Garcetti* (2006) case involved an attorney who was employed by the Los Angeles District Attorney's office and who took exception to the way in which a search warrant was obtained and executed.

Pickering focused on the speech of Marvin Pickering, a teacher at West High School in Lockport, Illinois, located in Will County in the southwest suburbs of Chicago. Pickering's letter, which was published in the local Lockport newspaper, leveled scathing criticism at his school board. It criticized the school board for the way that it allocated funds and it cited inadequate teachers' salaries, needed improvements to the physical plant at the district's high schools, and misleading public statements made by the school board. Pickering's letter was especially critical of the favoritism shown to the school district's athletic programs by the board. Debates also arose over the veracity of some of Pickering's accusations. Pickering signed the letter "as a citizen, taxpayer and voter, not as a teacher, since that freedom has been taken from the teachers by the administration. Do you really know what goes on beyond those stone walls at the high school?"[16]

The board claimed that the statements by Pickering, which they alleged were false, were detrimental to the interests of the school system, and as a result of his speech he was fired. Pickering claimed that his termination violated his rights under the U.S. Constitution First and Fourteenth Amendments. Both the Circuit Court of Will County and the Illinois Supreme Court upheld his dismissal. The U.S. Supreme Court agreed to hear the case and reversed the Illinois courts' decision to uphold Pickering's firing.

Justice Thurgood Marshall wrote the 8–1 majority opinion, which ruled that Pickering's dismissal violated his First Amendment free speech rights. The court indicated that similar speech is not necessarily protected if such speech contains statements that were knowingly false or reckless. But, the court held, Pickering's letter contained no evidence of such statements.[17] This case gave birth to the *Pickering* balancing test, in which the court balanced the employee's interest as a citizen speaking on matters of public concern with the government's interest as an employer providing services to the public.

In *Arnett v. Kennedy*, the balancing act differed from that in *Pickering*.[18] Wayne Kennedy, an employee working in the U.S. Office of Economic Opportunity, forfeited his First Amendment protections because his speech falsely accused the director of his agency of bribery. The case before the U.S. Supreme Court hinged on whether the federal government could fire a nonprobationary federal employee for recklessly false and defamatory statements about his fellow employees without specific rules to guide the decision and without a preremoval hearing. The Supreme Court upheld the constitutionality and procedural due process of the federal grievance mechanism.[19]

Connick v Myers (1983) distinguished between speech that is protected and speech that is not protected by the First Amendment.[20] Sheila Myers worked as an assistant district attorney for over five years when her supervisor transferred her to a different section of the criminal court. Myers publically objected to the transfer that was being forced on her and, before it took effect, she prepared an employee questionnaire that included items about the court's transfer policy, office morale, and confidence in the court's supervisors. When Myers's supervisor learned of her objections and the questionnaire, he terminated her for insubordination.

Myers sued, saying that her termination violated her First Amendment rights. Both the federal district and appellate courts ruled in her favor. By a 5–4 margin, however, the U.S. Supreme Court reversed the lower court decisions. Writing for the majority, Justice Byron White stated that Myers's speech pertained only to personal and internal office issues, and thus was not protected by the First Amendment. Speech in the same vein as Myers's speech may also be disruptive to the running of an administrative office. According to the Supreme Court, however, the federal district court placed too high a burden on showing whether Myers's speech substantially interfered with the operation of the office. The court instead stated it is sufficient to show that the employer reasonably believed her speech would interfere with office operations.[21]

Abcarian v. McDonald (2010) involved a University of Illinois medical school faculty member's pronouncements, which fell almost entirely within the realm of unprotected employee speech.[22] The faculty member, a professor and head of the institution's Department of Surgery, spoke out about risk management issues, fees paid to physicians, and the staff abuse of prescription medications, which the circuit court found to be concerned with administrative policies having little to do with academic issues. Compare *Abcarian* with *Kerr v. Hurd* (2010), where a medical school faculty member's academic freedom argument centered on his favoring vaginal deliveries over Caesarean section deliveries. A federal district court in Ohio ruled that Kerr's espousing the differences between the two delivery methods was a matter of public concern and, hence, protected under the First Amendment.[23]

In *Garcetti v. Ceballos*, Richard Ceballos, an attorney, discovered in the course of his duties that a sheriff had misrepresented facts in a search warrant. He contacted attorneys who were prosecuting the case, and they agreed that the warrant raised serious questions. Even so, the district attorney refused to dismiss the case, and Ceballos took the unusual step of telling the defense about the false statements in the warrant. This revelation, in turn, led the defense to subpoena Ceballos to testify. Ceballos subsequently claimed that the district attorney's office (his employer) retaliated against him for cooperating with the defense in violation of his First Amendment rights. Siding with the employer, the federal district court ruled that Ceballos was not entitled to First Amendment protection for the contents of his memo, and that even if Ceballos's speech was constitutionally protected, the attorneys were protected by qualified immunity and not subject to liability for civil damages. The Ninth Circuit Court of Appeals, however, reversed the federal district court's decision and ruled that Ceballos had engaged in speech over matters of public concern (the questionable handling of the search warrant) and that such speech was protected by the First Amendment.[24]

The U.S. Supreme Court agreed to hear the case and granted a writ of certiorari. The question before the court was "whether the First Amendment protects a government employee from discipline based on speech made pursuant to the employee's official duties."[25] In a 5–4 decision, the U.S. Supreme Court held that speech by a public official is protected only if a person's speech is delivered when that person is acting as a private citizen. Speech may not be protected, however, if it is expressed as part of the government official's public duties.[26] Based on *Garcetti*, a faculty or staff member working at a public university should feel free to speak in a public forum about important social issues. But these same faculty and staff should tread carefully when making critical pronouncements about the internal workings and administration of the public college or university where they work.

Waters v. Churchill (1994), a nonacademic case, addressed issues surrounding the firing for insubordination of Cheryl Churchill, an obstetrics nurse who worked in a public hospital.[27] Churchill complained about her superiors as well as about practices associated with the cross-training and staffing decisions in her nursing ward—actions that hospital management regarded as insubordination. The U.S. Supreme Court, by a four-justice plurality, held that government workers cannot be fired or otherwise punished for their speech unless the employer has a reasonable belief that the speech was disruptive or was a matter that was purely private and outside the protection of the First Amendment. The court held that the employer need not conduct a full investigation on such matters as long as the employer's conclusions are reasonable.[28]

Along the same lines, in *Isenalumhe v. McDuffie* (2010), two faculty members at the City University of New York criticized their department chairperson for bypassing committee processes and for the supposedly inept administration of faculty performance evaluations. A New York federal district court concluded that these matters were employment related and not protected speech under the First Amendment.[29] Similarly, a Michigan elementary school teacher was fired after she complained about a number of issues associated with her job and the operation of the school where she worked. The Sixth Circuit Court noted that the teacher's free speech complaints were weakened based on the fact that her comments were directed solely to her supervisor and not the public in general.[30]

Eight years after *Garcetti*, the Supreme Court held in *Lane v. Franks* (2014) that a public employee's speech concerning the employee's job, but not ordinarily within the scope of his duties, is subject to First Amendment protection.[31] Edward Lane was hired by an Alabama community college as a training manager. Lane was still on a probationary status with his job when he was subpoenaed to testify in a criminal case involving an Alabama state representative and a former employee at the community college. Lane had fired the employee for not doing any work yet drawing a salary. Soon thereafter, Steve Franks, the community college president, fired Lane, and Lane subsequently sued claiming illegal retaliation. The court reasoned that although Lane learned part of the subject matter of his testimony through the course of his employment, that alone was insufficient to make the testimony part of Lane's employment responsibilities.[32]

Lane addressed the dichotomy between concerned citizen and concerned employee. An employee may acquire information about his employer and employment relationship that is directly within his scope of duties. The same employee may also be in a position to acquire information about his employer and employment context when that information falls outside the scope of his employment. In *Lane*, the court held that he was acting as a concerned citizen in a critical role by testifying in court regarding a matter of public concern—the corruption of a public official.[33]

A similar case, *Whitfield v. Chartiers Valley School District* (2010), arose when an assistant school district superintendent, Tammy Whitfield, faced the nonrenewal of her contract based on the testimony that she gave at the disciplinary hearing of another teacher.[34] The beginning of the end occurred for Whitfield when two school board members took exception to her testimony, and Whitfield filed a federal suit against the school district, claiming that her free speech rights had been violated.

The federal district court applied what has become known as the *Pickering-Connick* test, a two-prong analysis. First, the court had to determine whether she spoke as a citizen on a matter of public concern. This inquiry raises two sub-questions: (1) whether the subject of the employee's speech was a matter of public concern, and (2) whether the employee spoke as a citizen rather than solely as an employee. If the answer to either question is no, then the case goes no further. If the answer to both questions is "yes," however, then the court proceeds to the second prong. This analysis poses the question of whether the government entity was justified in treating the employee differently from how a member of the public would be treated based on the government's position as an employer.[35]

Using this balancing test, the court said first that Whitfield's testimony in court was a matter of public concern that had generated a local controversy. Furthermore, the test favored Whitfield because the school board failed to show that her testimony damaged any government interest.[36]

Unlike most other post-2006 cases, *Demers v. Austin* (2014) did not originally center on the analysis in *Garcetti* and instead focused more explicitly on the *Pickering* balancing test.[37] David Demers, a tenured Washington State University communications professor, published a two-page pamphlet criticizing his institution's practices and policies. The Ninth Circuit—the same court that heard *Garcetti*—affirmed the district court's finding that the plaintiff had prepared and circulated the plan pursuant to his official duties. The court held that "*Garcetti* does not apply to 'speech related to scholarship or teaching.' "[38]Using strong language affirming the importance of academic freedom under the First Amendment, the Ninth Circuit concluded that if applied to teaching and academic writing, *Garcetti* would directly conflict with the important First Amendment values previously articulated by the Supreme Court. Instead, faculty speech should be governed by *Pickering*.[39] That is, the faculty member must show that the speech addressed a matter of public concern, as opposed to a mere private grievance. If the case is of public concern, then the court will balance the employee's free speech interests against the state's interest of efficiently providing public services.[40]

In rejecting the application of *Garcetti* to teaching and academic writing, the Ninth Circuit noted,

> Under *Garcetti*, statements made by public employees "pursuant to their official duties" are not protected by the First Amendment. But teaching and academic writing are at the core of the official duties of teachers and professors. Such teaching and writing are "a special concern of the First Amendment." We conclude that if applied to teaching and academic writing, *Garcetti* would directly conflict with the important First Amendment values previously articulated by the Supreme Court. One of our sister circuits agrees.[41] (citations omitted)

The Ninth Circuit concluded that in the wake of *Garcetti*, the state of the law remained "uncertain."[42]

Other Free Speech Issues

Free speech issues and related restrictions go well beyond *Pickering*, *Garcetti*, and *Demers*, however. Free speech protections do not include speech that is harmful to children, false or misleading commercial speech, or loud music that disturbs the peace of a residential area.[43] The production and possession of obscene works has long been a point of contention. With the exception of child pornography, a person can possess most obscene materials in the privacy of his home. University faculty and staff members have been prosecuted for the production, possession, and sale of child pornography and, of course, they do so with no First Amendment protections.[44] But a faculty or staff member working in a private college, especially one with a religious affiliation, may be fired simply for possessing pornographic materials—possibly even "soft" pornography—whereas a faculty or staff member working in a public institution would have First Amendment protections for such possession.

Fighting words are another free speech issue. It has long been held that yelling "Fire!" in a crowded theater enjoys no First Amendment protection and such an outburst may be grounds for charging the guilty party with a criminal offense, especially if the ensuing stampede results in injuries or death to theater patrons. Fighting words on college or university campuses today might be uttered during the emotional heat of a campus demonstration. Shouting racial epithets, cat calling, or directing obscene gestures at a specific person or group of people—especially in a public place—might incite retaliation that could balloon into violence. The spark of a malicious racist or ethnic slur could escalate into serious injuries, the loss of life, and widespread damage and looting.

Barring a strong or compelling governmental interest, content-based restrictions on speech are rare. As a result, incidents of repugnant but protected speech may arise. James Tracy, a then tenured associate professor at Florida Atlantic University (FAU), a public institution, was fired in the wake of his outspoken views surrounding the mass murder shooting of twenty children at Sandy Hook Elementary School in Newtown, Connecticut. Tracy, who taught courses about the media at FAU, claimed that the horrific crime was a media ploy directed by gun control advocates. His pronouncements about the established news media focused on discrepancies in their reporting, their concerns with political correctness, and the appearance of carefully managing a narrative that he claimed sacrificed rigorous journalistic investigation. Tracy was eventually fired for failing to fill out an "outside activity" report, a common requirement for faculty and staff in institutions of higher learning. These reports are commonly used to ensure that a faculty or staff member's personal business interests do not conflict with their position at a college or university. But despite the acrimonious timbre of Tracy's speech, free speech and academic freedom supporters—most notably the union United Faculty of Florida—hurried to his aid.

An equally contentious free speech case arose at the University of Colorado's flagship campus in Boulder. Ward Churchill, a professor of ethnic studies and an expert on poverty among Native Americans, described some of the financial industry victims who perished in the 9/11 attacks as "little Eichmanns," a reference to the despised Nazi war criminal, Adolph Eichmann. Churchill described the deaths of bankers and stock traders as a "penalty befitting their participation in the . . . 'mighty engine of profit' to which the military dimension of U.S. policy has always been enslaved."[45] Not surprisingly, Churchill's pronouncements on the Boulder campus created a commotion as he was forced to step down from his position as department chair.[46]

Although university officials eventually concluded that Churchill's remarks were protected by the First Amendment, he was fired by the university in the summer of 2007 for research plagiarism and falsification along with other misconduct. The allegations against Churchill included misrepresenting facts, fabricating evidence, and claiming the work of others as his own—all cardinal sins of academic research.[47]

Another noteworthy free speech case arose in *Adams v. University of North Carolina-Wilmington* (2011).[48] Michael Adams, a tenured associate professor of criminology and self-described Christian conservative, was denied promotion to the rank of full professor at the University of North Carolina-Wilmington (UNC-W). Adams was outspoken both verbally and in his written work regarding his religious beliefs. He also believed that the university was intolerant of religious views in general. Adams claimed that his promotion request was rejected in retaliation for his beliefs and speech. Sidestepping *Garcetti*, the Fourth Circuit stated that the 2006 case could exclude from the First Amendment protection many forms of public speech, including those of faculty members. The Fourth Circuit concluded that Adams's speech was explicitly protected by the First Amendment, and the fact that Adams included some of his opinionated publications in his promotion dossier was not sufficient to convert protected speech into unprotected speech.[49]

Academic freedom controversies may arise when a faculty member's work is supposedly taken out of context. Jonathon A.C. Brown, the director of Georgetown University's Saudi-financed Center for Muslim-Christian Understanding, came under fire when critics inferred that his eighty-minute talk at the International Institute of Islamic Thought supported slavery and rape.[50] Brown, both a Muslim and a tenured Georgetown professor, denied this interpretation, stating that "scholars are at risk if some de-contextualized quote of theirs is taken out and prompts a feeding frenzy that calls for them to be fired."[51] Perhaps the most controversial part of the lecture in question was this statement: "I don't think it is morally evil to own somebody because we own lots of people all around us and we're owned by people and this obsession about thinking of slavery as property."[52] Brown noted, for example, that a concubine's autonomy in early Islamic civilizations was not that much different from a wife's in the same period because women married whom their family wanted. Brown's controversial speech may hinge in part on semantics as he concluded by saying that "slavery" can mean many things, depending on the historical and social context in which the term is used.[53]

In response to Brown's talk, Rachel Pugh, a Georgetown spokeswoman, provided this statement: "As an academic community, we are committed to academic freedom and the ability of faculty members to freely pursue their research and express their analysis. While we will defend this academic freedom, the body of a faculty member's work does not necessarily represent the University's position. The views of any faculty member are their own and not the views of the University."[54]

Sometimes, however, the context of an academic freedom case is well defined. In *Van Heerden v. Board of Supervisors of LSU* (2011), Ivor van Heerden, a full-time faculty member at Louisiana State University (LSU) and cofounder of the LSU Hurricane Center, became the center of a highly public and contentious lawsuit surrounding the catastrophic flooding of New Orleans in the summer of 2005.[55] Van Heerden was serving as the center's deputy director when Hurricane Katrina hit the Louisiana and

Mississippi Gulf Coasts. In the wake of a levee collapse and the widespread flooding in New Orleans, van Heerden launched a scathing criticism of the U.S. Army Corps of Engineers, claiming that the corps had failed to properly engineer the levees that were supposed to protect the low-lying city. The LSU administration tried to silence van Heerden to no avail, and he was subsequently removed from the team that was tasked with researching the New Orleans floods. The following year (2006), van Heerden published *The Storm*, which described the poorly designed levees and exposed the university's attempt to silence him. LSU eventually terminated van Heerden by not renewing his contract.

Van Heerden filed a lawsuit against LSU for a variety of claims, including defamation, retaliation with respect to his First Amendment rights, and breach of contract. The case made its way into the federal district court where some of van Heerden's claims against LSU were dismissed, but the court allowed him to proceed with the retaliation claim. The court noted the perceived disconnect between *Garcetti* and academic free speech. The court claimed that *Garcetti* could, in the years ahead, eventually erode a faculty member's ability to express opinions that are unpopular or unorthodox. In early 2013, LSU and van Heerden settled the dispute out of court after the university agreed to pay him $435,000.[56]

The broad free speech protections of the First Amendment do not necessarily insulate people from adverse legal action if they make damaging statements about others. The basic assumption that underlies defamation of character lawsuits is that a person's reputation is an asset. If someone utters a false and malicious statement about another person and causes damage to the reputation of that person then, under tort law, the target of the statement may be entitled to recover damages. Defamation has two parts: libel (if the statement is made in the written word) or slander (if the statement is made in the spoken word). Defamation lawsuits are usually adjudicated in a state court and the legal contours of this tort and the damages to which a defendant may be entitled can vary significantly from one jurisdiction to another.

In most states, establishing defamation requires that several conditions be met. First, the defamation must be about a specific person, not a group. Second, the statement must be reasonably specific. Accusing a college administrator by name of being "clueless" or "out in left field" is not specific enough to warrant a defamation claim. Accusing that same administrator of misappropriating funds from a departmental travel expense account, however, is a specific accusation. Third, the statement must be false (or substantially false). The key defense in a defamation suit is the truth, no matter how unpalatable and sordid that truth may be. Fourth, the statement must be published (communicated) to another party. A department head who confronts a faculty member, telling her that he believes she has falsified data on a research project, has not engaged in defamation as long as the two-person conversation is conducted in private and cannot be overheard by others. Even if it is overheard, unauthorized eavesdropping by a third party usually does not constitute publication. Fifth, a reasonable person must be likely to find the statement believable. A preposterous false statement does not constitute defamation because no reasonable person would believe it. Such was the case in a U.S. Supreme Court decision in which the evangelist Jerry Falwell sued Larry Flynt, the publisher of *Hustler Magazine*, for the magazine's portrayal of Falwell as an incestuous drunk. The court held that a reasonable person would not believe the published story.[57] Sixth, the malicious statement must damage a person's reputation—something that may be difficult to prove. "Damage" might include the pain and suffering from embarrassing media coverage, the loss of a business opportunity, or the denial of an employment opportunity. Seventh, a defamation lawsuit may be dismissed if it involves privileged statements. A person called upon to testify in court is expected to tell the truth under oath without being worried about a potential defamation lawsuit if her testimony damages someone's reputation (absolute privilege). Organizations often exchange information about former employees who are job applicants. Providing truthful information for a relevant business reason is not usually defamation as long as the information is exchanged in good faith through legitimate business channels (qualified business privilege). Public figures, however, often find it difficult to win defamation lawsuits. The fact that Jerry Falwell had thrust himself in to the public eye through his evangelical work hurt his chances in the *Hustler Magazine* lawsuit because of his status as a public figure.

Based on our analysis, we can draw several inferences about academic freedom and free speech.

First, the AAUP serves as a good starting point for understanding these interrelated topics. The federal courts, however, have historically ignored the AAUP's definitions and positions on academic freedom and speech issues, resorting instead to constitutional protections and judicial decisions on these matters.

Second, insofar as employment rights are concerned, employees of a nongovernmental (private sector) institution have limited free speech protections under the First Amendment. These organizations have the right to discipline or fire employees for speech that the organization deems unacceptable. Although the speech *per se* is not forbidden, a nongovernmental employer is free to fire at-will, contractual, or quasi-contractual employees for speech that the employer finds unsuitable, although contractual and quasi-contractual employees may be entitled to restitution or due process. Academic freedom in private colleges and universities may depend more on a faculty member's contract provisions than on the protections offered by the Constitution. Instead, it must be written into faculty employment contracts or handbooks or inferred from past practices or academic tradition at a particular institution. A useful guide for drafting such contract language might be the elements of academic freedom delineated by the AAUP and discussed earlier in this chapter. In short, the line is still blurred between speech by someone who is acting in her capacity as a public employee and speech by someone who is acting in her capacity as a concerned citizen. The line is equally blurred between topics of public concern and topics that are relevant only to the internal workings of a governmental entity.

Third, although private citizens have constitutional rights to engage in speech both in verbal and physical forms, protections apply to certain types of speech—even speech that offends the sensibilities of a reasonable person, as might have been the case with the Tracy, Churchill, and Brown incidents. Speech content and the location of where the speech is made may be suppressed only when there is a compelling government interest for doing so. For example, when the State of Florida conducts an execution of a death row inmate, both supporters and opponents of capital punishment—some of whom might be faculty from the nearby universities—are allowed to gather in a field directly across from the prison compound. To allow advocates and protesters inside the maximum security prison (even though it is public property) could greatly compromise security and safety—a compelling government interest. Time and place restrictions may also be imposed on demonstrations in protected areas, such as abortion clinics.

Fourth, faculty members do not necessarily have the complete freedom to establish course content and pedagogical methods, and faculty decisions on such matters may be subject to intervention.[58] Similarly, the selection of summer readings for incoming students may be challenged, especially on religious or moral grounds, but such challenges will likely fail in litigation.[59]

Fifth, faculty members do not have complete authority to assign grades. That is, an administrator may have the right to unilaterally change a grade that was given arbitrarily or with malicious intent. To avoid First Amendment arguments, colleges and universities should not force a faculty member to change a student's grade. There is judicial support, however, for allowing administrators to change a grade unilaterally without involving the faculty member who assigned the grade.[60] This suggestion may seem unpalatable to most faculty members, including the authors, but it is a method that can be used to avoid problems under the First Amendment.

Sixth, journal editors and reviewers have the authority to accept or reject the submission of scholarly papers. Similarly, funding agencies have the authority to disperse funds as they see fit. The fate of an academic journal submission or a grant proposal may depend, at least in part, on the timeliness of a topic being researched as well as biases that might affect an editorial decision to publish or reject the proposed work. It is doubtful that the author of a rejected manuscript or an unsuccessful grant applicant could successfully claim that such a rejection violated a scholar's First Amendment rights. As an aside, a 2017 article in the *Economist* points to the lengthy and terribly inefficient process surrounding the submission, review, and acceptance or rejection of medical academic journal articles.[61] The same criticisms can be leveled at academic journals in the social sciences.

Seventh, faculty members whose speech is profane or unnecessarily offensive generally do not have free speech protections under the First Amendment.[62] Offensive speech is often thought to be protected in the classroom environment, but such speech is also regulated through the Federal Communications Commission (FCC) indecency policy that frowns upon the use of expletives or potentially tasteless fleeting images. Threats to commit bodily harm are usually regarded as a form of assault that is regulated by state and local governments. Not only are threats of bodily harm not protected by the First Amendment, but such speech may lead to criminal charges against the person uttering the threat, if they are in a position to act on it. In *Rankin v. McPherson* (1987), Ardith McPherson, an employee in a Harris County (Texas) constable's office, remarked in the wake of John Hinckley's 1981 assassination attempt on President Reagan, "If they go for him again, I hope they get him."[63] McPherson thought she was making the comment in private to a fellow employee, but later learned that her speech had been overheard and reported to the constable, who fired her for making the threatening remark. The U.S. Supreme Court considered the issue of whether McPherson's ill-advised comment was a matter of public concern, but concluded that it did not amount to a real threat to kill the president and did not discredit the law enforcement office.[64] McPherson eventually won her job back with back pay.[65] In the wake of a close loss in the 2017 NCAA basketball tournament to the University of North Carolina, angry University of Kentucky fans targeted referee John Higgins through 450 telephone calls and 200 to 300 social media and email messages, constituting what law enforcement believed was harassment of "a threatening nature."[66] The Facebook page of Higgins's Omaha, Nebraska, roofing business was also attacked by the irate fans. Free speech First Amendment protections to avoid possible criminal prosecution would certainly seem out of place here.

Eighth, faculty members must also link privacy concerns to the issues of free speech and academic freedom. The Fourth and Fourteenth Amendments to the U.S. Constitution protect faculty members in state schools from certain searches and seizures. As was the case with the words "academic freedom," it should be noted that nowhere in the 4,553-word Constitution is the word "privacy" mentioned. Colleges and universities that provide computers, cell phones, and websites to faculty members may decide that it is appropriate to monitor faculty usage of these electronic devices to track both the content of faculty communications as well as the amount of time spent on communications that fall outside of the scope of routine university business. Not surprisingly, private institutions would seem to have more latitude in monitoring communications than would public institutions. Several laws, however, may reduce even a private institution's access to employee communications. The Safe Streets Act and the Electronic Communications Privacy Act (1986), for example, prohibit the intentional intercepting of any wire, oral, or electronic communication, including electronic mail and eavesdropping on private conversations. In addition, state and local tort laws may regulate privacy concerns affecting faculty members working in private institutions.

Ninth, exceptions to *Garcetti*, both judicial and perhaps also legislative, should recognize the unique importance of institutions of higher learning and their need to have unrestricted pursuit of "the truth." Exceptions should separate the free speech rights of government and private sector workers from those of academics, giving the latter more latitude to inquire about and explore issues that may be viewed as controversial and even offensive.

Tenth, colleges and universities need to manage risk—a recurrent theme in this book—in order to accommodate free speech and academic freedom issues. Public university faculty members need to understand the fallacy of stating, "I have my rights." Such rights are nonexistent when criticizing the internal operations and administration of their institution—issues that cover a myriad of issues from the use of university email systems to curriculum issues, from individual privacy rights to making their concerns known to governing boards and legislatures. Faculty handbooks are a good place to make these points understood. In addition, private college and university administrators can define academic freedom and free speech restrictions on employment contracts. A safe assumption is for employees of state assisted colleges to think in terms of having essentially the same rights as their private college counterparts, with the extra protections enjoyed by public college employees being viewed as icing on the cake rather than as a major privilege.

Faculty matters affecting hiring, promotion, and tenure decisions are complex because they involve complicated contractual and constitutional questions. Thus far, we have addressed questions such as: What is a contract? Are contracts supposed to exist as a single document or as a collection of documents? What are the differences between individual and group contracts (unionized faculty)? How do the courts deal with ambiguous language? What are the consequences of contract alterations?

Our discussion of constitutional free speech concerns raises questions about the differences between protected and unprotected speech. Our examination of the First Amendment indicates that free speech protects faculty members at public institutions much more than it helps faculty in private institutions. But even so, constitutional issues remain complicated. At this writing, a tenured professor at a midwestern university is fighting his dismissal, claiming that his school terminated him because he spoke about how officials allegedly inflated rankings. The fate of this case remains undecided, but it clearly involves both contractual (tenure as a contract) and constitutional (First Amendment) rights of a state university employee. And this case leads us to yet a third major concern—collegiality. It remains to be seen whether this professor will be accused of not being a team player or will be criticized as being overly contentious. If this case makes its way into the federal courts, we may gain further insight into the contract, constitutional, and collegiality triangle. The next chapter addresses this third puzzling issue and suggests a new way of viewing collegiality.

5

COLLEGIALITY

An Enigma

Collegiality as a Criterion in Academic Hiring and Promotion

As noted in earlier chapters, faculty members striving for promotion and tenure have historically been evaluated on three pillars of academic merit: teaching, scholarship, and service to the profession, institution, and community. More recently, however, a fourth and more nebulous criterion has emerged: collegiality. Praised by some and disliked by others, collegiality is a topic that has received increasing attention in decisions affecting higher education. Both job advertisements and promotion and tenure guidelines seem to recognize that the concept of collegiality is important, but these same guidelines provide little guidance on what the term means.

One of us served on a search committee for a tenure track faculty position. The job posting first listed required and preferred qualifications, such as the appropriate degrees and the number of years and type of experience in teaching, research, and service—all criteria that have been used through decades of academic hiring. In addition, the successful candidate

was expected to demonstrate "a commitment to professional collaboration and collegiality." Following the list of the criteria was an instruction
to the applicant to submit a letter that would speak "directly" to the specified criteria. A straightforward response to such a posting would be to list
courses taught, graduate students advised, committees served, and articles published. More challenging, however, would be the task of directly
addressing collegiality. That is, how should one identify direct ways in
which she has been collegial? Without giving guidance to the job applicant regarding the elements of collegiality, this task seems to be asking
the impossible. Furthermore, attempted definitions of collegiality seem to
depend on who is doing the defining. According to Perry Zirkel, an expert
in education law, "Evidence of personality or collegiality is not subject to
precise measurement because personality itself is intangible; it is seen only
indirectly in the form of behavior and its infringement."[1] The American
Association of University Professors (AAUP) discusses collegiality in terms
of "collaboration and constructive cooperation."[2] The *American Heritage
Dictionary* defines collegiality as a "shared power and authority vested
among colleagues."[3] Wikipedia describes collegiality as "the relationship
between colleagues."[4] In an online platform inviting participants to consider the topic of collegiality and its influence on public life, the Society
for Phenomenology and Existential Philosophy explains, based on the
term's Latin roots, that "to be collegial means to choose together with one
another."[5] From a religious perspective, collegiality has roots in Catholi-
cism, relating to unity that exists among bishops or apostolic succession.

"Collegiality" might be regarded by educational and organizational
scholars as a "multi-dimensional construct" that describes the coopera-
tive interaction among colleagues.[6] Dennis Organ, a professor of personnel and organizational behavior, has promoted an inclusive definition of
collegiality that refers to extra-role behaviors that are discretionary, not
recognized by the formal reward system, and yet important to the effective
functioning of the organization.[7] His definition of collegiality fits nicely
with the concept of "organizational citizenship behaviors," a concept
used widely by organizational behavior scholars and one that we believe
is relevant to our analysis of collegiality.

Regardless of the definition of collegiality chosen by the job applicant
in the situation described above, responding directly to the collegiality
criterion would be a challenge. The applicant for this faculty position

would have to self assess as to how she has shared time, authority, and financial resources with colleagues—no easy task. She might ask herself questions such as: "In what ways have I chosen to be with colleagues?" "Have I interacted cooperatively with them?" "Do I have a good relationship with my peers?" "Have I contributed to the effective functioning of the organization?" The seemingly overlapping terms "cooperatively interacted," "good relationship," and "effective functioning of the organization" are as vague as the term that we are trying to clarify. As nebulous as collegiality might be, it is nonetheless important that we define the term if we are going to use it in hiring, promotion, and tenure decisions.

We might also describe a case, *Barding v. Board of Curators of Lincoln University* (1980) that appears to exemplify the antithesis of collegiality.[8] During the early 1970s, Ronald G. Barding worked as an assistant professor of sociology at Lincoln University, a historically black college located in Jefferson City, Missouri. Barding, who was Caucasian, was terminated at the end of 1975 for his contentious behavior toward faculty, staff, and students. He claimed that his dismissal was based on his race in violation of Title VII of the 1964 Civil Rights Act. Barding lost on all the issues that he presented.

Insofar as his collegiality was concerned, Barding's supervisors claimed that he refused to take graduate courses to improve his knowledge of sociology and that he generated a large number of student complaints about his intimidating teaching methods and personal questions about their sex life. Barding, it was claimed, used an overly brief and inadequate syllabus, failed to update his teaching materials and examinations, used crude and indecent language in his classes, gave grades using methods that violated university policy, and made it clear to his department chairperson that he was not going to change his ways regardless of university policy. At one point, Barding referred to his colleagues as "ass lickers" and "sycophants," and threatened his chairperson with physical violence.[9] The Board of Curators, which consisted of "several outstanding lawyers and one state court judge," found that Mr. Barding was "incompetent, unprofessional . . . and that his actions were such that his termination was fully justified on the grounds of unprofessional conduct."[10] A reading of the case indicates that Barding's behavior over the span of several years was clearly not collegial.

One of us recently shared an elevator ride with a highly respected economist. During our thirty-second conversation, he remarked that he put collegiality in the same category with pornography—impossible to define, but easily recognized when observed. Psychologists have for decades developed and used constructs to measure attributes of human behavior and to use these attributes in diagnosing and treating patients. Probably the most developed psychological construct is intelligence. Psychologists have refined the concept of intelligence (sometimes referred to as "g" for general intelligence) and the ways in which it is measured and used. In its current state, constructs of collegiality range from referring to tangible behaviors such as agreeing to read and critique a fellow faculty member's working paper to fluid things such as speech, civility, congeniality, professionalism, one's belief system, and the ability to be friends with colleagues. Compared to intelligence, however, the construct of collegiality is in its very early stages of development, and may remain that way for the foreseeable future.

Definitions of collegiality are usually abstract or general. Since a person's behavior is determined by their personality traits, it is probably best to define collegiality based on observable behaviors—unless a college or university decides to require that job applicants for a faculty position or candidates for promotion and tenure submit to psychological testing.[11] But collegiality varies over time and place. Collegiality can mean one set of ideals or measurements at one higher education institution, while another school might use very different metrics. One prestigious university, the University of Chicago, is notorious for the heated debates of its faculty members—the Socratic method on steroids. Aggressive and sometimes contentious arguments are the norm at this institution. Does that mean that there is a lack of collegiality there? Probably not, because the scathing criticisms are not taken personally. Heated debate at this school is regarded as a method for seeking the truth, not declaring a debate winner. Collegiality may also change over time. What might have been viewed as an honorable difference of opinion among colleagues thirty years ago may now be construed in politically correct corners as racist or sexist. Suffice it to say, the more a hiring or promotion committee tries to develop a working definition of collegiality, the more frustrating the task becomes.

Faculty members are nonetheless expected to be collegial by fostering positive working relationships with colleagues and students. Generally, colleagues are those who unite in and work toward a common purpose. But, as a construct, collegiality is an unstable and often unreliable fourth criterion that can have a profound impact on a faculty member's career and politicize the promotion and tenure process.

In this chapter, we set forth a construct of collegiality that can be used in major human resource decisions. Our definition is flexible enough to cover a wide range of circumstances, yet specific enough to be realistic and useful in making decisions regarding a particular individual. It focuses on behaviors rather than on personality assessments. And, importantly, we look to the courts to examine legal perspectives on collegiality.

A Working Definition of Collegiality

Table 1 presents an overview of our conception of collegiality. As the diagram suggests, collegiality is not an either/or proposition. Instead, it exists as a continuum of behaviors. The most admirable of these behaviors are those designated as "extra-role" or "prosocial," in which a faculty member is willing to go above and beyond his job description to do whatever is necessary to help his college or university. Extra-role behaviors focus of the interaction of a group or team of faculty, staff, and students, with individual needs being subordinate to the needs of the institution and the academy.

Neutral behaviors (table 1) are neither overly good nor bad. Faculty members who display neutral behaviors come to work, display punctuality, meet the basic expectations of the job, collect their paychecks, and remove themselves from the organization as soon as the workday is over. Faculty who are in the neutral segment of the continuum may describe their work at the university—usually with a deadpan expression—as "it's a job." Our combined experience with faculty members of this sort has indicated that it is not likely that they will achieve tenure or, if they do, they will probably never get promoted beyond the rank of associate professor. That failure, however, may not stop them from complaining about their lack of merit pay raises or their disenchantment over the widening gap between their pay and the pay of more productive colleagues. This situation could cause the neutral faculty member to eventually cross the line into the "dysfunctional" category, and it is a good illustration of why hiring, promotion, and tenure decisions are so important and require so much attention.

TABLE 1. A Range of Faculty Behaviors

Extra-role behaviors	*Neutral behaviors*	*Dysfunctional behaviors*
Will "go the extra mile"	Adheres to basic job duties	Ignores job duties, excessive absenteeism
Sacrifices to help others	Takes care of own needs first, then helps	"Me first" attitude, never willing to help others
Reputational asset to institution	Does not harm institutional reputation	Harms institutional reputation
Diplomatic, always supportive	Polite and courteous to faculty, staff, students	Abusive, arrogant, and disruptive
Obeys laws and regulations	Obeys laws, but not all regulations	Violates criminal, civil, or administrative laws or institutional policies 1. Negligence 2. Sabotage 3. Embezzlement 4. Assault 5. Plagiarism and falsification of research 6. Substance abuse 7. Multiple arrests

At the right extreme of table 1, openly dysfunctional faculty members may be easy to identify and dismiss—usually long before their tenure review occurs. Collegiality never becomes a point of contention in these cases because the faculty member's aberrant behavior, possibly the result of drug abuse or mental illness, overshadows all else. But even dysfunctional and potentially dangerous faculty members such as Amy Bishop may initially display a modicum of normalcy. Student comments about Bishop on RateMyProfessors.com reveal that she was a competent but lackluster teacher. There were the faculty comments noted earlier, about her lack of stability and arrogance—certainly signifying a lack of collegiality—but none portended the tragedy to come. Definitional arguments aside, however, faculty members who commit the acts shown on the right side of table 1 will almost always be regarded as displaying a lack of collegiality. But there is an interesting twist, which is that some faculty members may simultaneously exhibit both extra-role behaviors and dysfunctional behaviors. A faculty member who secretly pilfers grant monies or falsifies data on a research project may also be a pillar of the academic community because of her extra-role behaviors. Once discovered, however, the dysfunctional behaviors described in table 1 will likely lead to termination of the faculty member even when the extra-role behaviors are compelling. That is, in these situations, the "bad" outweighs the "good."

Collegiality as a Positive Force

Behaviors that are traditionally thought of as collegial promote the functioning of an educational institution. Being a team player and contributing to teaching, research, and service activities are all aligned with the traditional notions of collegial behavior. An overarching goal of institutional leaders is to create a productive environment while minimizing strife. To this end, collegial faculty aspire to work well within their departments and, at the same time, ensure that their work is aligned with their academic department as well as the larger institution. For example, an English professor is mindful of his department's expectations as well as those of the liberal arts college. The dean of the liberal arts college, in turn, wants to align her strategic initiatives with those of the greater university.

Collegiality and Civility

Civility is a necessary, but not sufficient, component of collegiality. A lack of civility encompasses dysfunctional behaviors such as professional misconduct, bullying, harassment, retaliation, profanity, and other unsavory behaviors. As explained by the AAUP, "Professional misconduct or malfeasance should constitute an independently relevant matter for faculty evaluation. So, too, should efforts to obstruct the ability of colleagues to carry out their normal functions, to engage in personal attacks, or to violate ethical standards."[12] The book *Professors Behaving Badly* is replete with examples of faculty members mistreating colleagues and graduate students.[13]

Consider the case of the hypothetical Professor Pompous, a tenure track professor at a major research university. On the traditional, more objective measures of success in her role, she scores well. Student evaluations indicate that the professor is effective in the classroom. Likewise, her funding for groundbreaking research is solid, the results of which she publishes prolifically. Understanding the promotion and tenure process, Professor Pompous knows that her body of work must include service to her institution, profession, and community, so she has made certain that all of the boxes have been checked in her promotion dossier for these activities. Unfortunately, Professor Pompous is a legend in her own mind only. She is quick to drop the name of a high profile academic she "knows," based in reality on a thirty-second superficial conversation she once had with an academic superstar who in all likelihood has no recollection of Professor Pompous. The clueless Professor Pompous fails to realize that the famous academic with whom she is star struck has people skills that she totally lacks. Professor Pompous's narcissistic self-importance rears its head almost daily as she glares at colleagues and responds to their comments and questions flippantly and dismissively. Her problematic personality is also on display in the contemptuous way she deals with students and staff.

How should Professor Pompous be assessed for measures of collegiality? If collegiality is assessed as "getting along"—clearly a problem for Professor Pompous—her evaluation does not hold promise. But if collegiality is assessed as a measure of meeting professional responsibilities, Professor Pompous seemingly has no problem. Sooner or later every hiring, promotion, and tenure committee will encounter a Professor Pompous. If our experience is any indication, Professor Pompous's attitude and behavior will only worsen with time.

We might also describe a lack of collegiality by describing the equally hypothetical Professor Reticent. Professor Reticent is withdrawn and unfriendly. Psychologists might diagnose him as having a schizoid personality disorder. When he arrives at work—and he is only on campus for classes or for a mandatory meeting—Professor Reticent does not speak to faculty, staff, or students and, upon arrival, he quickly makes a beeline to his office, shutting the door behind him. Intellectually he is on solid ground. Interpersonally he is a self-absorbed dud. If his colleagues happen to see him outside of the office area or on the street, Professor Reticent looks right past them, ignoring their courteous greetings. Asking Professor Reticent an easy question evokes reactions of mild paranoia. He will respond to the question, "What time is it, Professor Reticent?" with either a curt "I don't know" or an evasive "You want to know what time it is right now?" Professor Reticent would never think of asking a faculty colleague or graduate student to work with him on a paper or research project and he is unwilling to participate in a departmental social function unless forced to do so.

So, how does a promotion and tenure committee evaluate Professor Reticent? His research productivity might meet institutional standards, and his students might regard him as effective but aloof. Professor Reticent is not a team player, and he has no desire to work with colleagues for a common cause or for the betterment of the institution. Without psychological intervention, Professor Reticent will not likely change his withdrawn and unfriendly ways. Referring to a faculty member in the Professor Reticent family, a former colleague commented, "Even if we were immortal and could work on the same floor with [Professor Reticent] for the next million years, there would never be an occasion where he would speak to us."[14] As in the case of Professor Pompous, Professor Reticent's fate may hinge on the culture of his institution. As long as Professor Reticent continues to publish quality journal articles, his cold, unfriendly demeanor may be overlooked at many universities. If his institution holds interdisciplinary research in high regard and expects faculty members to engage in collaborative efforts, however, Professor Reticent and faculty like him may be in danger of not clearing the tenure bar. Collegiality may play a role in the fate of both professors if their research or teaching (or both) are marginal.

Collegiality and Socialization

So how does a faculty member become either collegial or not collegial? Inborn personality traits may provide a partial answer, but closely aligned with collegiality is the process of socialization. Generally, the process of socialization encompasses acquiring a set of skills, developing work habits, adopting values and ethics, and fostering attitudes and beliefs that a new faculty member needs to work effectively within an organization.

Most colleges and universities have formal faculty mentoring programs in which senior faculty such as department or dissertation chairs serve as role models and assist junior faculty in launching their careers. Academic careers start in postgraduate programs—usually doctoral programs—and it is there that a future faculty member begins to learn about the culture of higher education.[15] During the socialization process, a new academic learns about the skills and processes of teaching, conducting quality research, and serving the institution in meaningful capacities. Ideally, it is through the tutelage of exemplars that the ethics, traditions, and mores of the professoriate will be passed along to a new scholar.

According to John Van Maanen and Edgar H. Schein, both MIT organizational theorists, formal socialization entails involvement in activities
aimed at teaching individuals the expectations of their role.[16] Socialization entails narrowing the gap between the newcomers and the long-term,
more experienced members of the organization. Newcomers gradually
learn expectations and role requirements through either structured or
unstructured socialization processes. Regardless of whether the process
is formal or informal, it is critical that newcomers are socialized into the
fold, and it is usually here that the notion of collegiality begins to take
hold, a commitment to the profession begins to emerge, and the newly
minted degree holder begins to fit in.[17]

Collegiality and Academic Freedom

Autonomy is highly valued in the professoriate. Collegiality, with its focus
on professional relationships and common purposes, can seem to run
counter to autonomy—most notably academic freedom and free speech.
Thus, professors and their collective representatives have sometimes
viewed collegiality as a threat to the cultural value of these expectations.
In its 1999 position statement (revised in 2016), "On Collegiality as a Criterion for Faculty Evaluation," the AAUP explained the underlying reasons for its opposition:

> The current tendency to isolate collegiality as a distinct dimension of eval-
> uation . . . poses several dangers. Historically, "collegiality" has not infre-
> quently been associated with ensuring homogeneity and hence with practices
> that exclude persons on the basis of their difference from a perceived norm.
> The invocation of "collegiality" may also threaten academic freedom. In the
> heat of important decisions regarding promotion or tenure, as well as other
> matters involving such traditional areas of faculty responsibility as curricu-
> lum or academic hiring, collegiality may be confused with the expectation
> that a faculty member display "enthusiasm" or "dedication," evince "a con-
> structive attitude" that will "foster harmony," or display an excessive defer-
> ence to administrative or faculty decisions where these may require reasoned
> discussion. Such expectations are flatly contrary to elementary principles of
> academic freedom, which protect a faculty member's right to dissent from
> the judgments of colleagues and administrators.[18]

The AAUP went on to say, "Certainly a college or university replete with genial Babbitts is not the place to which society is likely to look for leadership. . . . The very real potential for a distinct criterion of 'collegiality' to cast a pall of stale uniformity places it in direct tension with the value of faculty diversity in all its contemporary manifestations."[19]

Collegiality was further criticized by the late Michael Seigel, a former University of Florida law professor, in a 2004 paper in which he asserted that collegiality is more about one faculty member's personal assessment of the behaviors and beliefs of another. When a faculty member accuses a colleague of lacking collegiality, the comment is usually a criticism of the colleague's professional behavior.[20] Seigel also characterized the term collegiality as over-inclusive, something that can lead to a homogenized faculty in what one might call an echo chamber environment that stifles academic freedom and kills enlightened debate and the exchange of ideas—the essence of higher education.

The quest for collegiality, unfortunately, may encourage self-censorship. Differing opinions that are supposedly valued in an environment of the open exchange of ideas are suppressed as a result of self-censoring, leading to an atmosphere of having to play along in order to get along. This pretense of collegiality can then create a false sense of unanimity on academic content and institutional decisions.

Collegiality and Discriminatory Behavior

Attempting to assess a faculty candidate's collegiality—especially a minority candidate—could lead to accusations of illegal discrimination.[21] An emphasis on collegiality or fit may also foster an atmosphere of ideological purity—a condition that seems contrary to the current diversity efforts of U.S. colleges and universities. In effect, the subjectivity of determining collegial behavior potentially threatens academic freedom and runs the risk of creating the dark corners where discrimination could hide. Although nearly all U.S. colleges and universities claim to hold diversity in high regard, it is often difficult to determine what they actually mean when promoting this goal. It might be wise to stipulate what a diverse faculty, staff, and student body would look like. For example, is this strictly limited to racial, gender, and ethnic diversity? If so, are some ethnic groups more deserving of attention than others? As the Baby Boomer generation of professors ages, how will diversity programs view them? How does a person's political leaning fit? For example, social science departments have sometimes been accused of hiring faculty members whose philosophical and political leanings are to the left—often the far left.[22] How does this accusation mesh with concerns about ideological purity?

In an article titled "The Happy Hour Test," Jeffrey A. Johnson, a history professor at Providence College, likens choosing a colleague to marriage and states, rather starkly: "More often than not, collegiality proves a, if not the, deciding factor in searches."[23] In that vein, collegiality can be seen as synonymous with conformity where critical thinking is discouraged. As the DePaul University law professor Sumi Cho cautions, "The traditional concept of workplace 'collegiality,' popularly understood as the ability to get along well with others, clearly lacks substance. 'Collegial' is what those in power happen to define it as at the time. As such, it absorbs the normative values of the dominant culture. Thus, the utter malleability of the term poses the same dangers to particular identity."[24]

Collegiality may be intertwined with the emerging concept of microaggressions. The Equal Employment Opportunity Commission (EEOC) and the state and federal courts are cracking down on individuals who engage in harassment or retaliation against parties who have filed a discrimination suit. Harassment and retaliation may occur, at least in part, through microaggressions. In fact, some incidents of microaggression might be viewed simply as another form of passive-aggressive behavior.

Microaggressions could be construed as a form of illegal harassment or retaliation when directed at individuals or groups that have a history of being marginalized. Wearing the wrong Halloween costume, asking someone where they are from—a common question among strangers at a social event—making comments about a person's shoes, using "Hi guys" as a greeting, paying too much attention to one gender during a class session, using a gender-neutral pronoun incorrectly when conversing with a student, or referring to undocumented immigrants as "illegals" might all be regarded as microaggressions. Even emojis can be a cause for concern according to one law firm's recent blog post, which cautioned that such digital images that increasingly show up in the workplace could be "used as evidence of discrimination and harassment in employment cases" if used in offensive or inappropriate ways.[25] Not surprisingly, the use or perceived use of microaggressions may damage an otherwise collegial environment. According to the UCLA law professor Eugene Volokh, microaggressions "can lead to a 'hostile learning environment,' which (an institution)—and the federal government—views as legally actionable . . . stuff you could get disciplined or fired for, especially if you aren't a tenured faculty member."[26]

In 2016, Roy Baroff, North Carolina State University's Faculty Ombuds, published a "microaggression tool."[27] This tool defined microaggressions as "the everyday verbal, nonverbal, and environmental slights, snubs, or insults, whether intentional or unintentional, that communicate hostile, derogatory, or negative messages to target people based solely upon their marginalized group membership."[28] In a blog post about the tool, Baroff writes that microaggression tools are important "to build a more collegial environment and based on the concerns that faculty members bring to the NC State Faculty Ombuds Office."[29] One of the many examples of microaggressions listed in the tool document includes the statement, "I think the most qualified person should get the job."[30] This statement is a microaggression, according to the tool, because it implies that "people of color are given extra unfair benefits because of their race."[31] In short, when someone says that an applicant should get a job because she is qualified, this or a similar tool is used by the arbiters of "social justice"—a term that is as nebulous as "collegiality"—to unlock and identify the real meaning of the statement. The tool, at least as it is used by Baroff, appears to encourage inferences that are just short of mind reading. Once accused, the person who uttered the statement is put in the position of having to defend how someone else might interpret it. Such a social dynamic smacks of "guilty until proven innocent"—a situation that bears no resemblance to social justice.

Collegiality and the Courts

As previously discussed in our chapter on contracts, institutions are well served by clearly establishing—and adhering to—contractual expectations, processes, and procedures. An arguable concern, then, is that using collegiality as a separate criterion in hiring or promotion decisions could be deemed a breach of contract if the criterion was conceived and considered by a review committee, but not specifically identified as a component for such decisions. And even if the term itself is identified as a criterion, its meaning may be too amorphous as an evaluative tool—again, exposing the institution to the risk of legal claims.

In *Romer v. Board of Trustees of Hobart and William Smith Colleges* (1994), Frank E. Romer, a tenure track classics professor, brought breach of contract, equitable estoppel (an issue regarding the facts of the case), and intention infliction of emotional distress claims against the colleges resulting from his denial of tenure.[32] The crux of his claim was that that his tenure review process was improper. For his employment, Romer had no formal, written contract; rather, the agreement was established through correspondence with the school's provost and dean. Romer received a copy of the faculty handbook and other documents that set forth the tenure criteria and evaluation process. And, as is the case in most colleges and universities, the bylaws noted the criteria of teaching, scholarship, and service. During Romer's tenure review, a dean expressed—in her "private, personal opinion"—concern about Romer's problematic relationships, especially a volatile relationship with another professor.[33] Departmental reviewers did not find the dean's letter related to tenure because it did not deal with teaching, scholarship, or service. A tenure review committee subsequently did not recommend tenure for Romer, but did not elaborate on its findings. Romer alleged that information was considered that went beyond the tenure review procedures in the faculty handbook. The court ruled, however, that Romer had failed on his claims.

Even if it is not specified as a criterion, collegiality may be viewed by the courts as an implied covenant that is crucial in the employment relationship. In *Mayberry v. Dees* (1981), the Fourth Circuit court applied what it deemed "generally applicable, nationwide principles" when considering an institution's relationship with a professor.[34] Robert J. Mayberry, a tenure track assistant professor in romance languages at East Carolina University, brought suit pursuant to section 1983, an 1871 act designed to protect the rights of former slaves, claiming that his denial of tenure was retaliatory as a punishment for the exercise of his First Amendment rights of free expression. In addition to the criteria of teaching, scholarship, and service, the court considered collegiality as a criterion for use in tenure and promotion decisions. The court defined collegiality as "the capacity to relate well and constructively to the comparatively small bank of scholars on whom the ultimate fate of the university rests."[35] It then held that the professor failed to establish that his tenure denial was in retaliation for his exercise of free expression.

Since *Mayberry*, most courts that have addressed working relationships among colleagues have upheld the use of collegiality as a factor in faculty employment decisions.[36] Foundational to the courts' reasoning is the fact that collegiality plays an important role in the ability of higher education institutions to fulfill their missions. Denise M. Rousseau, a professor of organizational behavior and public policy at Carnegie Mellon University, suggests that collegial behaviors may be embedded in psychological contracts.[37] Psychological contracts include the subtle expectations between an individual and the organization. Rather than being governed by expressly written contractual expectations, evaluative practices may be employing theories of implied contracts under which mutual agreements and expectations of behavior are assumed based on tradition, past practice, or industry norms. In cases that employ alternative dispute resolution procedures instead of taking a case to court, arbitrators may tailor their decisions to tradition or past practice in the absence of specific contract language. But, as noted by Charles J. Muhl, a National Labor Relations Board judge who previously worked as an attorney and economist, courts have warned that employment decisions based on implied contracts put institutions in a vulnerable situation.[38]

The Problems of Noncontractual Evaluative Criteria

A case that demonstrates the dangers of using collegiality in a tenure decision when it is not a contractual criterion is *Nelson v. University of Maine System* (1996).[39] Richard Nelson, an untenured professor with two PhD degrees—one in history and one in education—brought a Title IX claim for retaliation in a tenure denial. Prior to litigation before an arbitrator, Nelson claimed that the university's actions had violated his rights under the institution's collective bargaining agreement. Agreeing with Nelson, the arbitrator determined that the university violated the agreement by considering the noncontractual criterion of collegiality in its denial of Nelson's tenure.

Similar reasoning was expressed in the unpublished case, *Kaplan v. State University of N.Y. at Geneseo* (1998).[40] Randy Kaplan, an assistant professor, was terminated from her teaching position with the university. She filed a gender discrimination suit against the institution and the former chair of her department. Upon review, the court found that Kaplan's evaluation was biased and not based on criteria that were required for evaluating a contract renewal application. Complaints lodged against Kaplan included that she had not been collegial, although attempts to have collegiality included as a specific criterion for reappointment at the university had been rejected by the college senate as lacking objectivity. According to college senate minutes cited by the court, such a lack of objectivity could "reduce tenure or promotion decisions to 'popularity contests.' "[41] Considering testimony that "Kaplan's lack of collegiality was a major reason for the non-renewal of her contract," the court determined that collegiality was not part of the "official criteria" for evaluating contract renewal applicants.[42] The court reasoned that other criteria were included in the written policies and procedures of the university, such as a professor's instructional and professional contributions as well as academic and service activities. Accordingly, the court found the university's assertion of Kaplan's lack of collegiality to be a pretext for discriminatory behavior.

Acceptance of the Criterion of Collegiality

Despite legal risks that could arise when using collegiality as an unspecified criterion for promotional decisions, and limited slaps on institutional hands for doing so, the courts have largely supported its use—even when the criterion is not specifically identified—with a few cautionary guidelines. An early case in which the judiciary noted collegiality as a legitimate criterion in tenure decisions is *Watts v. Board of Curators, University of Missouri* (1974).[43] In *Watts*, the employment contract of a nontenured assistant professor of history at the University of Missouri–Kansas City was not renewed, which resulted in his claiming a deprivation of his constitutional rights. Quoting an earlier case, *Chitwood v. Feaster* (1972), the *Watts* court noted that "a College has a right to expect a teacher to follow instructions and to work cooperatively and harmoniously with the head of the department."[44] The court said that, when judging a candidate's suitability for a permanent position in a faculty, it was "proper" for faculty to consider whether a candidate was "a good colleague to other members of the faculty."[45]

An early Ninth Circuit case in which the judiciary gave its attention to collegial behavior was *Mabey v. Reagan* (1976).[46] Rooted in a First Amendment claim, *Mabey* involved a philosophy professor who worked at what is now known as the California State University at Fresno. Rendell Noel Mabey sought, but was not granted, a renewal of his teaching contract. During an academic senate meeting, Mabey referred to certain colleagues as "older punks," "jerks," and "damned liars."[47] The college asserted that Mabey's unprofessional conduct displayed at the meeting was one reason for his nonretention. The court explained that while "conduct of various kinds in schools and universities has long been a subject for First Amendment protection . . . the problem has been to mark out the boundaries of protection, keeping in mind the specialized needs of the academic environment."[48] Recognizing that "some degree of coherence is necessary for the proper functioning of the institution," and that "collective activity requires at least some mutual regard to fulfill its missions," the court acknowledged that the district court had to consider Mabey's "effect on the meeting itself" as well as "his subsequent relations with the College's administration and those faculty with whom Mabey had to work closely."[49] Further expressing concern for collegial behavior, the court discussed "academic community" and Mabey's "relations with his closest colleagues" and with "senior administrators."[50]

Yackshaw v. John Carroll University (1993) involved a breach of contract claim in which Robert Yackshaw, a tenured English professor at John Carroll University, was dismissed.[51] Yackshaw had written an anonymous letter charging several members of his department with sexual harassment, mental illness, improper sexual conduct, and homosexuality. Although the professor denied having written the letter, university administrators decided he was probably the author based on past, similar behavior. The Faculty Board of Review ruled that Yackshaw authored the letter and that it was "moral turpitude" for him to have sent it.[52] The court rejected Yackshaw's argument that he was entitled to a review of the board's determination.

Collegiality as Inherent in Other Criteria

Instead of considering collegiality as a separate criterion, some courts view collegiality as inherent within another more accepted or measurable criterion. *Bresnick v. Manhattanville College* (1994) represented another challenge to tenure denial for which judicial review was sought.[53] In a breach of contract action that also included a claim for breach of the duty of good faith and fair dealing, Robert Bresnick, a full time faculty member in Dance and Theater, claimed that the college had not made its decision based on the criteria listed in institutional documents. The college's bylaws listed teaching excellence, scholarship, and service to the college as pertinent to a tenure award. A review of Bresnick's behavior pointed to his "unwillingness to work with colleagues 'in a sufficiently collegial and collaborative manner,' raising 'doubts about his ability to offer the necessary leadership.' "[54] Bresnick argued that collegiality and collaboration were not listed in the college's documents, and should not be used in his evaluation. The court, however, viewed cooperation and collegiality as "essential," cautioned against language that was too literal, and expressed reluctance in substituting its judgment for the judgment of institutional decision makers.[55] While recognizing that the AAUP preferred putting in writing the "precise terms and conditions of every appointment," the court cautioned that "overly detailed written criteria can act as a straitjacket preventing consideration of sometimes critical but more subjective factors."[56] The court effectively held collegiality to be an appropriate measure of evaluation that was an aspect of service to the institution.

Similar to *Bresnick*, *University of Baltimore v. Iz* (1997) also concerned a breach of contract action in which the court considered whether collegiality was "an appropriate consideration for tenure and promotion, when . . . it is not specifically listed as a criterion in the contract or policy provisions incorporated in the contract."[57] The *Iz* court deemed collegiality a "valid consideration for tenure review."[58] The court reasoned, however, that collegiality was "impliedly embodied within the criteria that are specified" and further explained collegiality's "essential role in the categories of both teaching and service."[59] Even with its acceptance of collegiality, the court also cautioned against using it "as a pretext for discrimination."[60] Dr. Iz, a business professor, had failed to prove that her tenure denial was based upon discrimination, and the court accordingly held that her contract claims also failed.

In *Fisher v. Vassar College* (1995), a Second Circuit case based in Title VII, Age Discrimination in Employment Act, and Equal Pay Act claims, an analysis of collegiality was subsumed within an expressed leadership criterion of tenure evaluation.[61] Cynthia J. Fisher was denied tenure in the college's biology department. A report assessing her performance showed "generally positive" student evaluations, but also revealed some problems with teaching clarity and research supervision, as well as unsatisfactory institutional service.[62] Leadership, the final "formal criterion" for the report, was deemed to be "a great disappointment."[63] The review committee detailed that Fisher "has difficulty in establishing straightforward, open, trusting, collegial relationships with others in the department."[64] Her claims were rejected.

Additional state court decisions demonstrate the wide discretion inherent in the tenure process, and either directly or indirectly, the approval of collegiality as a criterion for an academic institution's promotion decisions. In *Stein v. Kent State University Board of Trustees* (1998), the court explained, "The ability to get along with co-workers, when not a subterfuge for sex discrimination, is a legitimate consideration for tenure decisions."[65] In *Schalow v. Loyola University* (1994), the court held that faculty handbook's provision for "evaluating the suitability of the faculty member as a professional colleague" was "certainly broad enough to include collegiality."[66] The court in *Baker v. Lafayette College* (1986) noted that "the evaluation of the performance of a college professor and of his or her suitability to the educational needs, goals and philosophies of a particular institution necessarily involves many subjective, non-quantifiable factors."[67] Such factors, the court said, should be assessed by institutional decision makers rather than by the court. Similarly, in *Beitzell v. Jeffrey* (1981), the court observed that a tenure decision "typically calls for the exercise of subjective judgment, confidential deliberation, and personal knowledge of both the candidate and the university community."[68]

Collegiality's Value: The Enigma of Opposing Views

The usefulness of collegiality in hiring, promotion, or tenure decisions remains intensely debated in the academic community. The University of Arkansas has considered allowing a faculty member's poor collegiality to be used as the sole reason for an adverse retention, promotion, or tenure decision.[69] In the past, Arkansas has considered patterns of behavior, but the proposed changes have raised concerns regarding using a lack of collegiality alone as grounds for termination. Collegiality-related incidents sometimes receive attention even in the popular media. A 2002 article in the *New York Times* revealed that in November of 2002, history professors at Brooklyn College protested in a letter to the chancellor the college's decision against renewing the contract of Robert David "K.C." Johnson.[70] Johnson's stellar scholarship and commendable teaching were not enough to outweigh apprehensions about his collegiality. The contrast between his public persona and his behavior toward colleagues was described as a shift "from a brilliant scholar into someone so consumed by arrogance that he disdained colleagues' opinions, disparaged them to students and broke college rules about who could take his classes."[71] In the letter to the chancellor, the history professors deemed the criterion of collegiality as "invented," a "redundant category," and a "threat to academic freedom." Johnson's annual contract was renewed, but his request for an early promotion and tenure decision was deferred.[72]

Summarily, the AAUP asserts that collegiality should not be the sole cause of a denial of reappointment or tenure, or the sole cause of dismissal. Since collegiality is insufficient as the sole cause for denial, the argument is that collegiality should not be treated as a discrete category. As demonstrated in the court cases, however, a lack of collegial behavior, even when identified as a sole criterion for such dismissals or denials, has been used and predominantly upheld.

The courts continue to be reluctant to insert judicial decisions into the affairs of higher education institutions, following the approach they have taken with antidiscrimination laws such as Title VII of the 1964 Civil Rights Act and the Age Discrimination in Employment Act. For this reason, the courts give wide berth to institutional discretion for including collegiality—or not including it—in employment-related decisions. But even when courts give legal validation to the appropriateness of institutional decisions to consider collegiality, they also often recommend that the expectations of candidates be clearly, specifically, and formally stated. Contributing to the ongoing debate is the fact that neither those who support using the criterion nor those who are against using it know fully what it means. While laudable, aims to properly define collegiality through concepts like "pillars of Academia," "shared power," and "the Spirit of Academic Freedom and Shared Governance" fall short of any notions of objectivity.[73]

Scholars have suggested varied ways to improve on measures of collegiality. Pattie Johnston, Tammy Schimmel, and Hunter O'Hara proposed a model of collegiality that would help identify and validate behavioral indicators as a tool for effective job descriptions and faculty reviews.[74] Through the model, expectations could be better communicated, which would help address academic freedom concerns raised by the AAUP. Similarly, Zirkel suggested that any adoption of collegiality as a criterion should include clear definitions and narrow interpretations so as not to impede the flow of ideas.[75] Gregory Heiser, a University of Oklahoma law professor, argued that "collegiality should be considered not a personality trait of individuals, but [rather] . . . a structural quality of organizations. . . ."[76] Through this organizational view of collegiality, benefits to the organization would be valued and professorial collegiality would be understood "as a species of professionalism."[77]

A working definition of collegiality is clearly lacking. Years ago, Terry Leap coauthored an article on humor in the workplace. In trying to define and analyze this elusive construct, he discovered that humor simply disappeared the closer he tried to analyze it! Defining collegiality and understanding the risks of misusing collegiality as a criterion in hiring and promotion decisions is a quagmire of multiple terms, definitions, court decisions, legal rules, and institutional policies. Within the mosaic of institutional culture, socialization, professionalism, and citizenship, certain behaviors will be viewed as being collegial, and certain behaviors will be viewed as not being collegial. Table 1 provides a listing—albeit an incomplete one—of specific behaviors that are clearly on one side of the line or the other. Between the two ends lies rich fodder for continuing debate.

Risks arise when institutions are forced to walk the line and make judgments among extra-role, neutral, and dysfunctional behaviors. To minimize such risks, we offer the following suggestions gleaned from our review of cultural and legal perspectives as well as our experience of working in academia and in the federal and state court systems.

Create collegial climates that are supportive, nurturing, and productive, yet remain vigilant for behaviors that might be dysfunctional and, potentially, dangerous.

Articulate with specificity all hiring and promotion criteria. Faculty members who are denied tenure or promotion may be more likely to bring a claim against an institution if they are frustrated that collegial expectations were not clearly articulated and if they believe a decision was rendered against them based on uncertain expectations. A careful listing of what constitutes collegiality using specific examples from table 1 may be helpful as long as it is understood that the list is not necessarily complete.

If using collegiality as a hiring or promotion criterion, define expected actions for collegial behavior in academic rather than behavioral terms.

If using collegiality as a hiring or promotion criterion that includes any mention of personality-related traits, define and interpret acceptable and unacceptable traits narrowly. The focus for hiring, promotion, and tenure decisions should be on behaviors, not psychological traits. For this reason, we discourage the use of privacy-invading psychological testing in human resource management decisions.

Provide training to faculty and administrators who are charged with making employment decisions that may involve, either explicitly or impliedly, the use of collegiality as a criterion. Any notion of discrimination or infringement on a candidate's rights may ignite tempers and result in litigation, thus relinquishing the rights of academic freedom to the determination of the judiciary.

A lack of collegiality should be addressed early in the promotion and tenure process. Allowing a faculty member to get away with boorish behavior will only worsen the problem. Accusations of sexual harassment are especially problematic. Unfortunately such accusations are often generated against senior faculty who are not only tenured but also highly respected in their professional fields. In the case of serial harassers, a college or university must act swiftly and decisively to protect the victims.

Conclusion

Colleges and universities are dynamic places, and risk-inducing controversies that have either a direct or indirect influence on faculty employment are never far away, especially on campuses that are large and diverse. In effect, these institutions are moving targets that have the attention of a large group of stakeholders, including administrators, faculty, staff, students, sports fans, benefactors, and alumni, not to mention taxpayers and all three branches of the state and federal governments. The phrase "never a dull moment" is apropos to U.S. institutions of higher learning.

Stakeholder Scrutiny

Even beyond the occasional shocking pronouncements of a faculty member, external stakeholder scrutiny and intrusions may be reaching an all-time high. Those devoting their time and money to a school expect accountability. Egregious free speech infractions and heavily weighted partisanship on campuses garners the attention of many, particularly those who hold the free exchange of ideas to be a sacred function of higher education. The ivory tower's walls have been criticized as mere facades where "free inquiry and unfettered learning" are akin to "proverbial Potemkin fake buildings put up to convince the traveling Russian czarina Catherine II that her impoverished provinces were prosperous."[1]

Controversies and canceled speeches—such as one at Middlebury College where Charles Murray, a scholar from the conservative think tank American Enterprise Institute, was attacked and intimidated, thus shutting down his lecture—have called into question notions of a civilized free exchange of ideas. Allison Stranger, the Democratic faculty member who had invited Murray to campus, wrote that as the event was planned, she "was genuinely surprised and troubled to learn that some of [her] faculty colleagues had rendered judgment on Dr. Murray's work and character without ever having read anything he has written."[2]

Faculty who hold unpopular views are ever aware of what speech should be avoided based on endangering career advancement and what speech will be accepted by their peers. One of us attended a faculty meeting shortly following the November 2016 presidential election only to hear open disdain for the newly elected President Trump, criticism of the results of the election, and a battle cry commitment to doing everything possible to restore justice. At another university event shortly following the May French presidential election, a major collective discussion ensued heralding the lessons learned from the disaster that was the Trump election, culminating in the proclamation that France had made an immeasurably better decision than the voters in the United States. We are only left to wonder, then, how faculty members who viewed either of the above discussed results differently may have felt at these events.

Even outside the realm of contentious discussions of election-based politics, crossing the boundaries of expected political views can have ramifications. A recent example is the reported smear campaign against a Cornell professor who opposed graduate student unionization.[3] David B. Collum, a world-renowned chemistry professor at Cornell University and self-identified Libertarian, circulated an email among faculty explaining his view that the unionization of graduate students was not good for graduate programs. "Vicious accusations" were reportedly made against him in a letter to the editor of the *Cornell Daily Sun*, along with a demand that he should be removed as department chair. Many chemistry graduate students came to his defense, as did William Jacobsen, a Cornell law professor who submitted his own letter to the *Sun* detailing research that countered accusations against Collum and arguing that he was owed an apology and a retraction.

In the face of intensifying debate and declining institutional enrollments, many state political leaders are demanding greater transparency from colleges and universities. Often driven by constituent outcry, political entities seem to want to maintain control even though the financial support they are offering has diminished steadily over the past two decades. One such example can be found in North Carolina, where as of this writing Lieutenant Governor Dan Forest is addressing head on the issue of perceived suppression of free speech on college campuses by lending his support to legislation entitled Restore/Preserve Campus Free Speech.[4] The bill would require the University of North Carolina Board of Governors to create and adopt free speech policies. Among many speech-protecting requisites of the bill, it includes disciplinary sanctions for anyone who disrupts the free speech or expression of others, requirements to create a committee to monitor free speech on campuses and report to the legislature, and provisions allowing suit against institutions that fail to follow the law. Free speech debates may go in different directions. In 2016, administrators at the University of Tennessee, Knoxville, were put on the defensive when the education committee of the Tennessee General Assembly led an effort to withdraw funding from the university's Office for Diversity and Inclusion. This controversy was sparked by the fact that the campus diversity office promoted the use of gender-neutral pronouns—something that many Tennesseans viewed as frivolous and divisive—and suppressed religious holiday parties—something that many viewed as an affront to the conservative and religious culture of the state.[5] The General Assembly eventually voted to divert funding for the office for one year. State lawmakers then proposed setting up an intellectual diversity office at the university, earmarking funds to encourage conservative students and faculty to speak out.[6]

External stakeholders, including accreditation bodies, often join the chorus of those who want a say in curriculum matters, diversity issues, and athletics. Tensions may also arise between the academic world and the "real" world of business as stakeholders exert pressures to offer programs and majors that focus on the careers and salaries of graduates instead of placing emphasis on liberal arts and lifelong learning. The shift in accountability, then, has moved from internal to external stakeholders: Chicago-based freelance writer Kristina Cowan has commented on the accountability issues faced by those working in higher education, writing, "It's an irony that's difficult for many in the higher education world to swallow. As policymakers, think tankers, and pundits clamor for more higher education accountability, presidents are often left battling misperceptions that their institutions are asleep at the wheel. Yet higher education has been holding itself accountable—at the institutional, system, and association levels—since long before 'accountability' became a buzzword."[7]

The threat of misperceptions and public backlash did not seem to deter administrators at the University of Chicago—also dubbed the "University of Common Sense"—when it sent a letter to incoming students warning them that the institution would not coddle students and would not protect them from ideas that they might find unduly harsh.[8] The Chicago administration also declared that the school would not support "trigger warnings" that encouraged professors to preface their remarks before discussing a potentially offensive topic or "safe spaces" where students could retreat to avoid being exposed to ideas that they might find repugnant.[9] Admittedly, the University of Chicago is one of the world's most influential institutions of higher learning. Will lesser colleges and universities be as brave?

Stakeholder Concerns—Looking Ahead

Beyond the campus unrest of the early part of the twenty-first century, there are risks and challenges that U.S. colleges and universities will face over the next decade. These risks can be boiled down to two major, interrelated concerns: first, the reputation of a college or university, and second, its ability to remain financially strong. The specifics of these overriding concerns differ from one school to another, and the interrelationship of both will influence faculty employment in myriad ways.

Declining Enrollments and Institutional Closures

Except for at the major four-year public universities and elite private schools, college and university student applications and enrollments are declining. This trend appears to be especially harmful to smaller liberal arts colleges, and as enrollments decline, the need for the services of certain faculty members may also decline, raising contractual questions about the security of their jobs.[10] There was a time when established colleges and universities operating on the margin tended to survive—a trend that may be beginning to change. According to a Moody Investor Service report, the number of college closings may triple as the pool of potential applicants dwindles and the costs of higher education continue to rise.[11] Most of the schools faced with closures are hardly household names and are usually known only in the institution's local community. But included in the growing list of casualties is the for-profit institution ITT Tech, which announced its closure in the fall of 2016. ITT Tech's demise affected some 40,000 students and 8,000 employees.[12]

Professional schools are likewise at risk. A drastic example of recent vintage is the closure of the Whittier College Law School. Citing the institution's financial difficulties and the sagging bar examination passage rates of its graduates, the Whittier College's Board of Trustees announced that it would cease admitting students to the law school, but would continue to operate until the current group of students completed their legal studies.[13] Whittier Law is hardly an exception. Economic troubles similar to those at Whittier may result in other closures.[14] Institutions subsidizing professional schools that have become a drain on finances may choose to pull the plug, particularly when facing financial pressures from multiple directions, poor performance measures, and reputational challenges.

The Persistence of Hierarchies in Academia

Many in academia tout progressive ideals, yet societal inequality is ever present on higher education campuses, particularly in the realm of faculty employment practices. For example, a 2017 press release from the Legal Writing Institute, a nonprofit organization dedicated to improving legal communication, announced the "Full Citizenship Project for Law Faculty."[15] According to the release, the initiative was "aimed at correcting gender and related disparities among U.S. law faculty . . . because of the professional status challenges that continue to plague skills-based and academic support law faculty, who are predominantly women."[16] Further emphasizing the gender disparity, the release stated, "As law faculty status and salaries decrease, the percentage of women faculty increases. Based on available data, roughly—and only—36 percent of tenured or tenure track faculty are female, whereas 63 percent of clinical faculty and 70 percent of legal writing faculty are female. This disparity is due to faculty teaching in skills-based areas often being denied the opportunity to earn the same security of position and academic freedom that traditional law faculty enjoy."[17] Summarily, the project accentuated a lack of justification for faculty subordination among groups, based on course or teaching method.

Hierarchies and gender disparities are common. Across higher education, as noted earlier, adjunct, part-time, and short-term contract employees are compensated far less than tenured professors, often for teaching the same courses. Titles such as teaching assistant, fellow, instructor, and visitor disguise the inexpensive labor force crucial to front-line teaching and to managing top-heavy budgets. Budgets are increasing rapidly, often reflecting the expectations of top-of-the-hierarchy tenure track faculty for added compensation in the form of stipends for research, summer scholarship, travel, and sabbaticals—little of which guarantees increased student interaction or quality of learning. Administrative bloat, including the cadre of academics who are promoted to administrative roles, further increases the need for cheap labor to cover the classroom. Surely, those of us in higher education should look introspectively before espousing supposed ideals to others.

The Declining Institution of Tenure

As budgetary demands increase, the number of tenured faculty lines that open will decrease, and tenure will likely decline; but tenure as a prominent part of U.S. higher education will not disappear. It is possible in the future that tenured faculty will consist primarily of endowed chairs and named professors. These high-achieving individuals may have little loyalty to their current institutions, and they will likely be ready to move quickly to another institution for a better salary and increased support. Concomitant with the decline in the number of tenure track positions is the fact that the number of lower-paying non–tenure track faculty positions will continue to grow.

The Need for Better Evaluative Criteria

The evaluative criteria of research, teaching, and service and the decisions they generate are interdependent and shift in ways that are hard to predict. Part of the unpredictability of these measures is that they are often poorly defined and are subject to disagreement as to how they should be measured and used. One source of seemingly endless debate over the past three decades, for example, is that of qualitative journal lists. Journal impact scores and article acceptance rates, along with liberal amounts of subjectivity, have all been part of the varied attempts to decide which journals are "best" or "better."

Student evaluations of teaching, while numerical and seemingly objective, are another cause for consternation as to how measures are used. Questions arise as to whether "fun" classes get better evaluations than those that are necessarily more dry or quantitative. New teachers chasing good evaluations, particularly those competing for less available tenured positions, whose advancement partially depends on teaching evaluations, may be more inclined to give easy grades—contributing to grade inflation. A more challenging teacher may contribute more to students' learning and yet may receive poorer student evaluations.

Collegiality, both as a subjective evaluative criterion and as a contributor to the culture of an institution, remains a puzzle, although that does not necessarily stop hiring, promotion, and tenure committees from using it in their assessments of a candidate. As with other evaluative criteria, developing reliable and valid measures of collegiality is critical. Otherwise, collegiality may be cited as a pretext for invidious discrimination.

Our point is that no perfectly objective evaluative criteria exist. Bad measurements lead to bad decisions, and bad decisions harm the culture of the institution and leave it open to litigation. Prudent risk management—careful measurements, clear expectations, and fairness in administration of the criteria—is key.

The Prospect of Litigation

Suits involving defamation, reappointment, promotion, and tenure appear to be shifting from EEO law to contractual and constitutional law. Most academic cases are settled out of court, however, which makes it difficult to analyze the salient features of faculty lawsuits. Although most cases do not receive widespread publicity, occasionally a highly visible one will arise, such as the James Tracy case at Florida Atlantic University and *Waters v. Churchill* at the University of Colorado, as discussed in chapter 4. Furthermore, nonacademic cases—most notably *Pickering v. Board of Education*, *Garcetti v. Ceballos*, and their progeny—may have an important impact on higher education cases. Insofar as risk management is concerned, legal counsel can help to avoid lawsuits through the use of clear language in employment contracts, faculty handbooks, and policy manuals. In short, the language of these documents must be understandable to those who lack legal training, and those drafting contracts should be especially concerned with job security, mentoring, pay and benefits, faculty evaluation, and circumstances under which a faculty member's contract may not be renewed.

Beyond the Risks of Major Human Resource Management Decisions

Our discussion of risk management has focused on hiring, reappointment, promotion, and tenure decisions. But colleges and universities consist of a network of risks, issues, relationships, and individuals. That is, the component parts of an institution are related. Sometimes the relationships are strong and direct, and in other cases they are more indirect and oblique. For that reason, we want to mention several other concerns that need to be addressed as institutions of higher learning plot their future strategies.

More Attention to Business Models and Continued Attention to Assessment

There is a perception among many that the business model for higher education is flawed—or even broken. Those making statements about "business models," however, rarely define or explain what that term actually means. Is there a universal business model for institutions of higher learning? If so, what is its structure and what metrics are used to measure its functioning? Should the business model of a large publicly held corporation such as Exxon Mobile or JP Morgan Chase be compared to the business model of large public institutions such as the University of Texas at Austin or the University of Michigan? Does the business model of a small liberal arts college differ from the one used by a technical institute? Regardless of the business models used—if any are used at all—colleges and universities either explicitly or implicitly formulate and implement strategies. Some of these strategies are good and some are not so good. One prominent element of a good strategy, however, is the careful management of risk.

If conversations at faculty and professional meetings are to be believed, "assessment" is a seemingly important function among administrators in institutions of higher learning. Yet the metrics of assessment are often off target and poorly conceived—something that is not conducive to sound risk management. If we cannot define or measure it, we cannot use it as a tool to manage risk. Academic leaders—presidents, chancellors, provosts, faculty senate presidents—as well as institutional board members must take a leadership role by insisting that institutions of higher learning develop performance metrics that are linked directly to quality.

The Expanding Role of Higher Education in Innovation for Economic Growth

Colleges and universities, especially those with large business, engineering, health care, and science departments and institutes, will become more involved in the activities of innovation and economic development. This trend will blur the line between the academic and business worlds, and it will generate increased concerns over intellectual property rights, how a faculty member allocates her time between the academic and business domains, how a faculty member is evaluated for such allocation of time, and the impact of academic and business interests on the curricula in institutions of higher learning. As innovation and economic development increase in importance, faculty roles and their relevant importance in the traditional hierarchy may undergo significant change.

The Increasing Role of Communications Networks

The Web, social media, and around-the-clock news media coverage will continue to increase the visibility of higher education. Texting and tweeting have provided the current president of the United States with a global audience, and the same can be said for faculty members who want to weigh in on political or religious matters that they deem are important. Steven Salaita found himself in a major career bind when his tweets were regarded in some corners as being anti-Semitic. Salaita resigned his faculty position at Virginia Tech and prepared to move to the University of Illinois, Urbana Champagne (UIUC). His career plans were put on hold when the then-chancellor at UIUC got wind of his tweets and rescinded the offer to Salaita before the institution's board of trustees had a chance to endorse it. Salaita eventually received a large settlement from UIUC, but he now believes that his chances of finding a faculty position at a school in the United States are dim.[18] Similarly, George Ciccariello-Maher, a professor at Drexel University, was suspended from his job after the university decided that his tweets about "white supremacist patriarchy" could incite acts of violence against students, faculty, and staff.[19] Both of these cases raise joint concerns about constitutional and contractual protections for university faculty members. Controversial statements by faculty, staff, and students will be less likely to go unnoticed and unchallenged, creating the opportunity for heightened tensions on campus. This trend will also increase the importance of college and university media and communications directors. Furthermore, upper-level administrators such as presidents, chancellors, provosts, and athletic directors will have to become savvy in dealing with the sudden and unexpected news events that can damage an institution's reputation and relationships. Trying to handle the adverse publicity that sometimes befalls institutions of higher learning requires a risk-based public relations strategy that is both transparent and part of a well-designed process that satisfies institutional stakeholders—or, at least, does not add to their embarrassment.

Diversity and Inclusion

In recent years, the goals of diversity and inclusion have become a part of the fabric of U.S. higher education. The benefits of diverse teams for solving complex problems, for example, are well documented. Furthermore, the presence of international students—primarily students who are Hispanic or Asian—enhance the prospects for diversity, although the future of international students in U.S. colleges and universities may be in doubt if the Trump administration imposes stricter sanctions on student visas. A related concern is whether minority students will be able to afford to attend college, especially if state support declines. Furthermore, international programs are becoming increasingly popular as a means of exposing students to cultural and economic differences. As any university international programs coordinator will tell you, sponsoring faculty-student trips abroad creates significant risks that must be managed carefully.

MOOCs and the Democratization of Higher Education

As of this writing, one of us has earned over sixty-five massive open online course (MOOC) certificates. The public view that colleges and universities are enclaves for the intellectual elite may be changing rapidly due to the proliferation of MOOCs emanating from the world's most prestigious universities. Coursera and edX, two major MOOC providers, currently offer courses from all eight Ivy League universities; from such schools as the Massachusetts Institute of Technology, the California Institute of Technology, Stanford University, and the University of Chicago; and from highly rated public universities such as the University of Michigan, the University of California, Berkeley, the University of North Carolina at Chapel Hill, and the University of Virginia. MOOCs are also available through major international universities such as Oxford University, McGill University, the University of British Columbia, and top-tier schools in Australia and Asia. Online courses enhance access to otherwise unavailable educational opportunities, and they provide a flexible learning environment to students facing barriers created by work and family obligations. MOOCs provide forums that students may use to communicate with a highly diverse and geographically dispersed student body.

While learning opportunities through MOOCs abound, the influence on the professoriate remains uncertain. On a larger scale, the expansion of online and distance education may create unique challenges for employment negotiations, the use of evaluative criteria, and changes in institutional structures.

Increasing Threats to Governance

Faculty governance may have reached its peak. The AAUP *Statement on Government of Colleges and Universities* provides a well thought out set of governance principles on general education policy, internal operations of the institution, external relations, governing boards, presidents, faculty, and students.[20] Faculty concerns about institutional governance are three-fold: the abdication of governance responsibilities to the growing cadre of administrators in institutions of higher learning, the increasing pressures from external groups who want to be involved in the operation of colleges and universities, and the attitude of high-achieving professors who increasingly believe that self advocacy and independent benefit is more valuable than institutional commitment.

The Undergraduate Experience

The value of the undergraduate experience will in the future be the subject of greater scrutiny. Questions surrounding the relative value of professional and liberal arts degrees are likely to continue, perhaps increasing tensions between these two faculty groups. A similar set of questions concerns the socialization of college students—that is, do students benefit from entering a college or university immediately after high school or should they be required or encouraged to engage in military or public service for a year or two before moving on to an institution of higher learning? Relatedly, does entering college at the age of eighteen extend the period of adolescence for some students and delay their ability to behave as responsible adults? If so, it is possible that the money spent on students who are free to go about their business without the constraints of adult supervision may be an extremely poor investment. Making the undergraduate experience more academic may become a major challenge for college and university administrators, especially if academic standards continue to erode. Managing risks associated with the adolescent behaviors of some students—binge drinking, risky sexual practices, and violence—is also critical.

Collegiate Rankings

There will likely be a continued interest in collegiate rankings. A high institutional ranking provides an opportunity for college administrators and media personnel to publicize the successes of their institution. A move up the rankings ladder creates a sense of satisfaction among administrators, faculty, staff, and students. The rise, especially if it is a meteoric one, may also generate a stronger applicant pool and other amenities such as increased donations by alumni. And such a success may open up career opportunities for administrators who helped the institution to raise its academic profile. Unfortunately, it is often difficult to identify the people who are responsible for the upward movement of a school's rankings. Furthermore, all of the hyperbole surrounding an upward move in the collegiate rankings could be diminished if a closer look is taken to the methodological flaws that underlie some rankings.

The Clash between Technology and Civility

A less sinister trend is also affecting the collegiate learning environment: the distractions associated with the growing concern of Internet addiction. There appear to be tensions between technology and the behaviors that affect campus civility. Many students live their lives through their smart phones or laptop computers. These individuals arrive in class, set up their electronics, and proceed to text and surf the Web, totally oblivious to the intellectual activities that surround them. Internet addiction not only impairs educational achievement by causing distractions in educational settings, but it also impairs social and physical functioning.[21] The psychology and psychiatric communities are becoming more aware and fearful that Internet addiction is a growing public health concern.

Title IX Concerns

One of the most controversial issues affecting U.S. higher education is the presence of Title IX of the Education Amendments of 1972. Title IX prohibits sex discrimination by colleges and universities that receive funds from the federal government. For all practical purposes, the receipt of federal funding means that nearly all colleges and universities are covered by the law. Furthermore, the U.S. Supreme Court has made it clear that Title IX coverage includes accusations of sexual harassment and sexual assault.

The most egregious Title IX cases have arisen over accusations of gang rape, allegedly occurring at parties where the victim has been rendered unconscious or defenseless from alcohol or drugs. Equally egregious are the cases in which prominent university athletes have been accused of rape. Both categories of assault receive nightmarish publicity that is damning to the reputation of the institution. But, more important, the victims of these brutal assaults are scarred for life. Even worse, psychologically fragile victims may suffer ostracism and attempted censorship at the hands of the perpetrators and, sometimes, from coaches or university administrators who want to sweep the incident under the rug.

Trying to adjudicate a criminal act like sexual assault through an internal procedure (a university hearing) is grossly inadequate. In April of 2011, the U.S. Department of Education issued a "Dear Colleague Letter" that appeared to encourage colleges and universities to deal with sexual assaults internally rather than through the criminal justice system.[22] The Department of Education encouraged the internal resolution of campus sexual assault cases and favored the more lenient "preponderance of evidence" standard of proof used in civil cases to the more stringent "beyond a reasonable doubt" standard of proof used in criminal cases. Whether this confusing mix of standards worked to the advantage of the victim or the perpetrator was unclear. But universities cannot incarcerate those accused of sexual offenses nor do they always have access to the forensic tools and techniques of law enforcement personnel. The approach was criticized by many, including law professors, policy scholars, and Congress.[23] Betsy DeVos, the Education Secretary, has proposed changes that would remove the responsibility from colleges and universities for handling serious crimes such as sexual assaults and rapes and would have such charges prosecuted in criminal court.[24]

Title IX also prohibits sexual harassment. But a broad definition of what constitutes hostile environment sexual harassment can pose conflicts with free speech. The AAUP, in its *History, Uses and Abuses of Title IX*, expresses concern that a broad definition of hostile environment sexual harassment will make it more difficult for faculty members to discuss sexual issues in class.[25] The faculty member who wants to discuss sexual deviance as part of an abnormal psychology course may be reluctant to do so for fear of being accused of creating a hostile environment.

Title IX may also prove to be an important tool in addressing gender inequities in higher education employment where wage gaps and underrepresentation exist, particularly in fields that are more traditionally male-dominated and in leadership positions. As previously discussed, the less desirable and prestigious parts of U.S. higher education remain predominantly filled by women. According to a Title IX information website, women make up more than 50 percent of the ranks of lecturers and instructors, less than 50 percent of assistant professors, 36 percent of associate professors, and 21 percent of full professors.[26] As compared to men, women earn less, hold positions of lower rank, and are less likely to be in a tenured position. Only 19 percent of colleges and universities are led by women. Title IX may undergird future challenges to such age-old higher education structures and disparities.

Mental Health Issues

More students are demanding that their colleges and universities help them deal with mental health issues. According to a 2015 report issued by the Center for Collegiate Mental Health, the student demand for mental health services has risen dramatically.[27] Based on our over four decades of experience in institutions of higher learning, we have learned that students whose mental health concerns in the past would have made it difficult for them to function on a college campus are now able to mask their symptoms to the point where they believe they can deal with the academic and social demands of college life. It is only after they arrive on campus that they realize they cannot cope with the pressures of being a full-time student. These pressures stem from leaving home and being on one's own for the first time, the demands of a seemingly endless and confusing array of academic and social obligations, substance abuse, indecision about the selection of a major and future career plans, traumatic events such as assaults or betrayals, and the backlash of broken romances. All of these issues have the potential to exacerbate psychological problems such as depression or personality disorders.

Colleges and universities are experiencing a strain on resources as they try to keep up with the demand for expensive mental health services. In addition to increasing the number of counselors, some colleges and universities are trying to enlist the support of faculty members to identify and refer problem students. Unfortunately, faculty members may lack the training and experience to help students in need. They may also fear lawsuits if they become too involved with a student experiencing severe mental health problems.

A Final Word on Risk Management

The many concerns discussed raise questions about the strategic alignment of college and university functions. How do institutions of higher learning manage to balance the many conflicting issues described here and in earlier chapters? Even simple problems can turn into difficult-to-handle issues in the hypersensitive world of higher education. The tenure denial of a popular faculty member can create a divisive culture in an academic unit. A misplaced word, phrase, or alleged microaggression can lead to the destruction of a faculty member's career. An irresponsible faculty member with a propensity to make careless and unsubstantiated remarks about almost any subject can generate embarrassing media coverage that can destroy the hard work of administrators and faculty who have built the reputation of an institution brick by brick through years—or even decades—of hard work.

To address these risks and concerns, colleges and universities may feel forced into hiring—and paying generous salaries to—administrative specialists to oversee (in no particular order) fund raising, media relations, grant activities, human resource management, the treatment of human subjects, student career counseling and placement, housing, the operation of fraternity and sororities, student welfare, campus safety, athletics, and more. The problem with so many disparate functions and entities is that it becomes next to impossible to coordinate and manage all of them efficiently. Each has its own agenda, which may lead to balkanization and turf battles, both of which create a financial drain on the institution and hinder its ability to create and disseminate knowledge.

Complex institutions generate complex problems. To protect the creation and dissemination of knowledge, and the faculty responsible for these basic institutional functions, those in leadership roles must heighten their awareness of and carefully identify, evaluate, and wisely manage the countless risks.

Notes

Introduction

1. Azvolinsky 2017.
2. See Pringle, Ryan, Hamilton, and Elmahrek 2017.
3. Pringle and Elmahrek 2017.
4. We will use the terms "faculty," "faculty member," and "professor" interchangeably; we will similarly treat the designations of "college," "university," "school," and "institution of higher learning" as interchangeable, as well as department "chair" or "chair person" and "department head."
5. Sabbaticals are usually granted to full-time tenure track and tenured academics with eligibility approximately every seven years. Pay arrangements vary, but professors are expected to "repay" their institution by returning to their job for a stipulated amount of time. Faculty who fail to honor their return agreement are subject to civil suit.
6. "Basic Classification Description," Carnegie Classification of Institutions of Higher Education, Carnegie Institution for the Advancement of Teaching, accessed March 31, 2018, http://carnegieclassifications.iu.edu/classification_descriptions/basic.php.
7. Lynn O'Shaughnessy, "12 Most Expensive College Textbooks in America," CBS MoneyWatch, May 10, 2010, http://www.cbsnews.com/news/12-most-expensive-college-text books-in-america/.
8. "Paying for College" 2015; "Better Ways to Pay for College" 2015.
9. See "Hillary Clinton's Student Loan Forgiveness Plan, Benefits for Massive Amount of Borrowers," Student Debt Relief website, November 15, 2017, https://www.studentdebtrelief. us/forgiveness/hillary-clinton-student-loan-forgiveness-plan/.

10. CollegeBoard, "Four-Year Graduation Rates for Four Year Colleges," 2013, http://media.collegeboard.com/digitalServices/pdf/professionals/four-year-graduation-rates-for-four-year-colleges.pdf.

11. Belkin 2015.

12. Sowell 1998.

13. Ung 2015.

14. Colleges and universities also encourage students to complete online evaluations of their courses. These evaluations are usually scheduled at the end of the academic semester (or quarter) when the coursework has been completed (or nearly completed), but before final grades are distributed. In a typical class, a majority of students fail to submit an evaluation form and, for those who do, their assessment of the professor and the course is often perfunctory.

15. Ginsberg 2011, 2.

16. Seery 2017, 61–71.

17. Woodhouse 2015.

18. Campos 2015.

19. Gladwell 2011.

20. People from outside the realm of higher education often believe that academic freedom and academic nonsense are one and the same. There is sometimes a perception that research performed under the protections afforded by academic freedom is of little or no practical consequence. While those in the academy believe that their research will have an impact, albeit sometimes in a delayed and roundabout way, the public often views academic research as trivial, esoteric, and nonsensical.

21. See Hinds 1993.

22. Hartocollis and Bidgood 2015.

23. Some comedians are afraid to bring their acts to campus for fear of creating a politically incorrect backlash. See Clark Conner, "It's No Laughing Matter: Campuses Have Become Intolerant" (blog post), John William Pope Center for Higher Education website, August 17, 2015, https://www.jamesgmartin.center/2015/08/its-no-laughing-matter-campuses-have-become-intolerant/.

24. "Bias-Free Language Guide," University of New Hampshire website, https://www.unh.edu/unhtoday/statement-unh-president-mark-huddleston-bias-free-language-guide. This page has since been removed by the university, but the guide can be viewed on the blog *Girard at Large*, accessed March 23, 2018, https://www.girardatlarge.com/wp-content/uploads/2015/07/Bias-Free-Language-Guide-Inclusive-Excellence-073015.pdf.

25. Wood 2015.

26. We recognize that MOOCs and other forms of online education have their drawbacks—most notably high attrition rates.

27. Neil Gross wrote in a 2016 op-ed, "Critics say the end result is that liberal political opinions now drown out other viewpoints in the classroom" (Gross 2016). Gross also commented that "only 14% of professors" in a 2006 survey he conducted with Solon Simmons "identified as Republican." For additional discussion, see Langbert, Quain, and Klein 2016, who investigated the voter registration of faculty at forty leading U.S. universities in the fields of economics, history, journalism/communications, law, and psychology and found an overall Democrat to Republican ratio of 11.5:1, which was an increase from 2004 and was expected in the future to be "even higher."

28. See, e.g., Trevor Griffey, "The Decline of Faculty Tenure: Less from an Oversupply of PhDs and More from the Systematic Devaluation of the PhD as a Credential for College

Teaching," Labor and Working Class History Association website, January 9, 2017, https://www.lawcha.org/2017/01/09/decline-faculty-tenure-less-oversupply-phds-systematic-devaluation-phd-credential-college-teaching/.

29. We direct readers looking for an in-depth discussion of non–tenure track faculty to the works of Adrianna Kezar. Kezar, a professor at the University of Southern California, has written several excellent books on the changing landscape of higher education in the United States.

30. U.S. House of Representatives, House Committee on Education and the Workforce, Democratic Staff, "The Just-In-Time Professor," 2014, http://democrats-edworkforce.house.gov/imo/media/doc/1.24.14-AdjunctEforumReport.pdf.

31. Gross 2017.

32. Gee 2017.

33. Furthermore, certain academic units must answer to more than one accrediting body; a university business school, for example, is held accountable by both a regional accreditation body and an accreditation agency devoted solely to business schools. For additional discussion about accreditation and considerations for institutional research leaders, see Flood and Roberts 2017, 73–84.

34. Baker and Moss 2009.

35. Walter Williams, "Fraud in Academia," Townhall.com, May 6, 2009, https://townhall.com/columnists/walterewilliams/2009/05/06/fraud-in-academia-n1119752.

36. Smith and Willingham 2015.

1. Establishing a Career in Academia

1. "Academic Job Search: The Hiring Process from the Other Side," University of California, Berkeley Career Center website, accessed March 14, 2018, https://career.berkeley.edu/PhDs/PhDhiring.

2. Cassuto 2013.

3. Application documents, such as a letter of interest and a vita, are usually submitted electronically. A candidate usually becomes an applicant when the electronic file is opened by a search committee member or administrative assistant.

4. CPS Human Resource Services, "Creating a Realistic Job Preview-Phases 1–5," accessed March 14, 2018, http://www.cpshr.us/workforceplanning/documents/GuidelinesRJPPhases1-5.pdf.

5. Gatewood, Feild, and Barrick 2016, 151–99.

6. Being articulate and well spoken can be major assets in the academic world. Glibness is also a hallmark characteristic of psychopathy, which explains why con artists can be so likeable and destructive. Bartol and Bartol 2014, 177–78.

7. Regression coefficients (R-square) range from −1.00 to +1.00. Reliability and validity measures approaching these limits are regarded as being more significant than measures approaching zero. A validity coefficient of 0.46 for a selection predictor such as a structured job interview, for example, indicates that 46 percent of the variation in a candidate's performance, if hired, would be predicted or explained by the structured job interview. Conversely, a validity coefficient of 0.46 also means that 54 percent of the variation remains unexplained by the structured job interview. The amount of explained variance can be increased (that is, the unexplained variance can be reduced) by using additional selection predictors such as background checks, job knowledge tests, or personality assessments. Unexplained variance can be reduced, but not eliminated. That is why the hiring process is sometimes full of surprises. We call these surprises "false positives" (the candidate looked good during the hiring process, but

turned out to be mediocre) and "false negatives" (the candidate did not look good during the hiring process, but turned out to be much better than expected). That is why we believe that using carefully designed hiring procedures reduces risk.

8. A perfect set of selection predictors would yield only correct decisions; the "true positives" that we hired who turned out to be successful and the "true negatives" that we did not hire and who later were proven to be inadequate at another school. Selection predictors are far from perfect, however, which means that we usually are going to encounter both false positives and false negatives.

9. Note that a faculty candidate's fit cannot be based on her race, gender, religion, color, national origin, age, or disability status.

10. See the average salary for "professor—accounting" on Salaries.com, accessed April 17, 2017, http://www1.salary.com/Professor-Accounting-Salary.html.

11. Maren L. Wood and Robert B. Townsend, "The Many Careers of History PhDs: A Study of Job Outcomes, Spring 2013. A Report to the American Historical Association," American Historical Society website, 2013, https://historians.org/Documents/Many_Careers_of_History_PhDs_Final.pdf.

12. See, e.g., Bohnet 2016.

13. Gatewood, Feild, and Barrick 2016, 471–83.

14. Mount, Ilies, and Johnson 2006, 591–622.

15. DeYoung, Quilty, and Peterson 2007, 880–96.

16. Judge, Van Vianen, and de Pater 2004, 325–46.

17. Gatewood, Feild, and Barrick 2016, 542–43.

18. Grossman and Leroux 1993.

19. Paul Gattis, "Judge Throws Out Wrongful Death Lawsuit Against Ex-UAH Provost in Amy Bishop Shooting,"*Al.com* (blog), January 15, http://blog.al.com/breaking/2014/01/judge_throws_out_wrongful_deat.html.

20. Rynes, Brown, and Colbert 2002, 95.

21. Werner and Bolino 1997, 1–24.

22. Zoffer 1978, 903.

2. Risk, Biases, and Logical Fallacies

1. Leap 1995, 211–33.

2. "Beta," Investopedia, accessed March 23, 2018, http://investopedia.com/terms/b/beta.asp.

3. Desai 2015.

4. See, e.g., Long, Bowers, Barnett, and White 1998, 704–14.

5. The FBI has developed profiling techniques—a form of risk analysis—that help investigators to narrow the list of likely perpetrators of a violent crime. Despite its scientific appearance, profiling is still regarded by forensic psychologists as more of an art than a science.

6. Hardy and Maguire 2016, 80–108.

7. Farnsworth 2007, 136–43.

8. Mark Little, "How to Measure and Manage Risk" (blog post), Berkman Solutions website, May 2, 2014, https://www.berkmansolutions.com/blog/item/how-to-measure-and-manage-legal-risk.

9. Little's terminology for risk management includes the terms "avoiding," "increasing," "removing," and "changing" instead of the more common terms of risk "assumption," "avoidance," "reduction," and "transfer." Both Little's list of terms and the more commonly used term include risk "sharing."

10. Mark Little, "6 Steps to Legal Risk Management" (blog post), Berkman Solutions website, July 17, 2014, https://www.berkmansolutions.com/blog/item/6-steps-to-legal-risk-management.

11. Association of Governing Boards and United Educators 2009, 2–3.

12. "Best Practices in Risk Management for Higher Education: Addressing 'What If' Scenarios," PMA Companies website, October 2010, https://www.pmacompanies.com/pdf/MarketingMaterial/PMA_Education_BestPractices_WhitePaper.pdf.

13. "Herbert Simon" 2009.

14. "Herbert Simon" 2009.

15. Julia Galef, "A Day Late and a Dollar Short: The Planning Fallacy Explained," *Big Think* (blog), http://bigthink.com/in-their-own-words/why-you-cant-plan, accessed March 23, 2018; Buehler, Griffin, and Ross 1994, 366–81.

16. Fischhoff, Slovic, and Lichtenstein 1977, 552–64.

17. See, e.g., Roese and Vohs 2012, 411–26.

18. Sukon Kanchanaraksa, "Bias and Confounding," Johns Hopkins University Bloomberg School of Public Health, 2008, http://ocw.jhsph.edu/courses/FundEpiII/PDFs/Lecture18.pdf.

19. Wittenbaum 2000, 379–401.

20. Kahneman 2011.

21. See "Three Things You Should Know about the Availability Heuristic" (blog post), Farnham Street website, 2011, https://www.farnamstreetblog.com/2011/08/mental-model-availability-bias/.

22. "Confirmation Bias," Science Daily, accessed March 14, 2018, https://www.science daily.com/terms/confirmation_bias.htm.

23. "Trait Ascription Bias," NLP Notes, accessed March 14, 2018, http://nlpnotes.com/trait-ascription-bias/.

24. Pronin, Lin, and Ross, 2002, 369–81; Rea 2015.

25. See Jost 2017.

26. James Gill, "Irrational Escalation," *Cognitive Bias Parade—An Illustrated Review of Misjudgments and Reconstructed Realities* (blog), May 28, 2014, http://www.cognitivebias parade.com/2014/05/irrational-escalation-sunk-cost-fallacy.html.

27. Schacter 2001.

28. David McRaney, "The Backfire Effect," *You Are Not So Smart: A Celebration of Self Deception* (blog), June 10, 2011, https://youarenotsosmart.com/2011/06/10/the-backfire-effect/.

29. DuCharme 1970, 66–74.

30. Birch and Bloom 2007, 382–86.

31. "Dunning-Kruger Effect," Rational Wiki, accessed March 14, 2018, http://rational wiki.org/wiki/Dunning-Kruger_effect.

32. Brown, Tamborski, Wang, Barnes, Mumford, Connelly, and Devenport 2011, 1–12.

33. "Self-Fulfilling Prophecy," Literary Devices, accessed March 14, 2018, https://liter arydevices.net/self-fulfilling-prophecy/.

34. Shermer 2014.

35. Colleen Sharen, "Contrast Effect—Learning About Our Own Biases," *Thinking is Hard Work* (blog), December 10, 2010, https://colleensharen.wordpress.com/2010/12/20/contrast-effect-learning-about-our-own-biases/.

36. Thayer Watkins, "Kahneman and Tversky's Prospect Theory," San Jose State University Department of Economics, faculty website, accessed March 14, 2018, http://www.sjsu.edu/faculty/watkins/prospect.htm.

37. Watkins, "Kahneman and Tversky's Prospect Theory."

38. Landau 2014.

39. C.W. 2013.

40. "Naïve Realism," Theory of Knowledge, accessed March 14, 2018, http://www.theoryofknowledge.info/theories-of-perception/naive-realism/.

41. "Groupthink," Psychologists for Social Responsibility website, Publications and Resources, accessed March 14, 2018, http://www.psysr.org/about/pubs_resources/group think%20overview.htm.

42. Claire Andre and Manuel Velasquez, "The Just World Theory," Markkula Center for Applied Ethics: Ethics Resources, 2015, https://www.scu.edu/ethics/ethics-resources/ ethical-decision-making/the-just-world-theory/.

43. Williams 2012.

44. "Clustering Illusion," *Changing Minds* (blog), accessed March 23, 2018, http:// changingminds.org/explanations/theories/clustering_illusion.htm.

45. Etchells 2015.

46. "Distinction Bias," Behavioral Diagnostics Toolkit: Social, BEWorks website, http:// beworks.com/Toolkit-Details/?id=12, accessed March 14, 2018.

47. Gary N. Curtis, "The Hot Hand Fallacy," *The Fallacy Files* (blog), accessed March 14, 2018.

48. Saravanan 2015; Norton, Mochon, and Ariely 2012, 453–60.

49. "Not Invented Here Syndrome," Technopedia, accessed March 14, 2018, https:// www.techopedia.com/definition/3848/not-invented-here-syndrome-nihs.

50. "Reactive Devaluation (Part 1)," Viaconflict, July 15, 2013, https://viaconflict.word press.com/2013/07/15/reactive-devaluation-part-1/.

51. Christian Jarrett, "The Social Comparison Bias—or Why We Recommend New Candidates Who Don't Compete With Our Own Strengths," *The British Psychological Society Research Digest*, October 28, 2010, http://bps-research-digest.blogspot.com/2010/10/ social-comparison-bias-or-why-we.html.

52. Marotta 2013.

53. Sinnott-Armstrong and Fogelin 2015, 275–349.

54. Sinnott-Armstrong and Fogelin 2015, 308.

3. Faculty Contracts

1. Kakes v. George Washington University, 683 A.2d 128, 129 (D.C. 1996).

2. Haegert v. University of Evansville, 977 N.E.2d 924 (Ind. 2012).

3. *Haegert*, 977 N.E.2d at 951.

4. In 2015, the flagship campus of Louisiana State University and other state-assisted schools in Louisiana were faced with the grim prospect of shutting down because of extreme budget shortages. Although it remains to be seen whether flagship campuses are too big to fail, Louisiana State University and other institutions of higher learning have continued to experience funding issues that are tied to tax reforms in the state. For additional information see Alexander 2017.

5. Lieberman v. Gant, 630 F.2d 60, 67 (2nd Cir. 1980) (citing Keddie v. Penn., 412 F.Supp. 1264, 1270 (M.D. Pa. 1976)).

6. See O'Neil 2010, 729.

7. *Lieberman*, 630 F.2d at 67–68.

8. *Lieberman*, 630 F.2d at 64.

9. See Craine v. Trinity College, 791 A.2d 518, 540 (2002). The court made clear that a "university cannot claim the benefit of the contract it drafts but be spared the inquiries designed to hold the institution to its bargain" and that "the principle of academic freedom [did] not preclude [the court] from vindicating the contractual rights of a plaintiff who has been denied tenure in breach of an employment contract." See also Kyriakopoulos v. George Washington University, 866 F.2d 438, 447 (D.C. Cir. 1989) ("This case does not involve a judicial recalculation of the University's evaluation of a professor's scholarly merit. The factfinder's

scrutiny need extend only far enough to ensure that the University perform its contractual duty. . . .").

10. See AAUP 2009.

11. Mayo v. N.C. State University, 608 S.E.2d 116 (N.C. App. 2005) *aff'd.* 360 N.C. 52 (2005) (*per curiam*).

12. *Mayo*, 608 S.E.2d at 121–22.

13. For instance, chapter 112, sections 112.311 to 112.326 of Florida's statutes establishes general provisions for the code of ethics for public officers and employees; chapter 105 of Missouri's statutes covers miscellaneous provisions for state officers and employees, such as how salaries will be adjusted and vacancies will be filled.

14. For a resource on handbook drafting, see Franke 2011.

15. Munsch and Verdi 2006, 889–900. See, e.g., Taggart v. Drake University, 549 N.W.2d 796, 800 (Iowa 1996). Three conditions under which a faculty handbook may give rise to an enforceable contract include: "(1) document must be sufficiently definite in its terms to create an offer; (2) document must be communicated to and accepted by employee so as to create acceptance; and (3) employee must continue working, so as to provide consideration."

16. *Craine*, 791 A.2d 518.

17. *Craine*, 791 A.2d at 527.

18. *Craine*, 791 A.2d at 528.

19. *Craine*, 791 A.2d at 528.

20. *Craine*, 791 A.2d at 541

21. *Craine*, 791 A.2d at 541.

22. *Craine*, 791 A.2d at 542.

23. *Craine*, 791 A.2d at 542.

24. Black v. Western Carolina University, 426 S.E.2d 733, 737 (N.C. App. 1993).

25. Stanton v. Tulane University, 777 So.2d 1242, 1250–51 (La. App. 2001), writ denied, No. 2001-C-0391, 2001 La. LEXIS 1410 (La. Apr. 12, 2001).

26. Holland v. Kennedy, 548 So.2d 982 (Miss. 1989).

27. *Holland*, 548 So.2d at 985.

28. Georgetown University, Faculty Handbook: Faculty Rights and Responsibilities, accessed November 25, 2017, https://facultyhandbook.georgetown.edu/toc/section3/c, Faculty Rights and Responsibilities.

29. Hillis v. Meister, 483 P.2d 1314, 1316 (N.M. App. 1971).

30. Clampitt v. American University, 957 A.2d 23 (D.C. 2008).

31. Maas v. Cornell University, 721 N.E.2d 966 (N.Y. 1999).

32. Knowles v. Unity College, 429 A.2d 220 (Me. Sup. 1981).

33. Ricioppo v. County of Suffolk, 2009 U.S. Dist. WL 4042877 (E.D.N.Y. March 4, 2009) (unpublished) (affirmed 353 Fed. Appx. 656, 657 (2nd Cir. 2009)).

34. Brown v. District of Columbia, U.S. District Court, DC, Civil Case No. 12–799 (RJL), Memorandum Opinion, January 28, 2013.

35. Brown, U.S. District Court, DC, Civil Case No. 12–799 (RJL), Memorandum Opinion, at 9–10.

36. Brown, U.S. District Court, DC, Civil Case No. 12–799 (RJL), Memorandum Opinion, at 15–17.

37. See AAUP 2009, 7.

38. Faculty Handbook, Baylor University website, last updated March 31, 2016, https://www.baylor.edu/provost/index.php?id=948247.

39. Faculty Handbook, Auburn University at Montgomery website, accessed March 24, 2018, http://www.aum.edu/about-aum/governance/university-policy/faculty-handbook.

40. Lim v. The Trustees of Indiana University, 2001 U.S. Dist. LEXIS 24822 (S.D. Ind. Dec. 4, 2001), aff'd, 297 F.3d 575 (7th Cir. 2002).

41. *Lim*, 297 F.3d at 575.

42. Fenn v. Yale University, 283 F.Supp. 2d 615 (D. Conn. 2003).

43. See "NC State University and Campbell Law School Partner on Law and Master of Public Administration Dual," Campbell University website, news, accessed November 25, 2017, https://news.campbell.edu/articles/nc-state-university-and-campbell-law-school-partner-on-law-and-master-of-public-administration-dual/; "Campbell Law, NC State Launch JD/MAC Dual Degree," NC State University, Poole College of Management website, accessed November 25, 2017, https://poole.ncsu.edu/news/2017/02/06/campbell-law-nc-state-launch-jdmac-dual-degree/.

44. Landrum v. Lindsey Wilson College, 2004 WL 362317 (Ky. App. Feb. 27, 2004) (unpublished; discretionary review denied June 9, 2004).

45. *Landrum*, 2004 WL 362317 at 3.

46. Tuomala v. Regent University, 477 S.E.2d 501, 502 (Va. 1996).

47. *Tuomala*, 477 S.E.2d at 506.

48. Branham v. Thomas M. Cooley Law School, 689 F.3d 558, 562–63 (6th Cir. 2012) (rehearing denied October 3, 2012).

49. *Branham*, 689 F.3d at 562–63.

50. *Branham*, 689 F.3d at 563.

51. See, e.g., Neal Hutchens, "Sixth Circuit Issues Worrisome Decision Regarding Legal Interpretation of Tenure," *Higher Education Law: Views, News, and Information about Higher Education Law* (blog), accessed November 25, 2017, http://higheredlaw.squarespace.com/url/author/higheredlaw?currentPage=17. This commentary labeled the decision "troublesome and sobering" and said the court's definition of the professor's employment arrangement "ignor[ed] years of academic custom and practice."

52. For a related discussion on the role of internal policies in protecting shared governance and furthering academic freedom, see Nugent and Flood 2014, 154–55.

53. See the website of the National Education Association (NEA), accessed November 25, 2017, https://www.nea.org/home/2580.htm?cpssessionid=SID-807A4E37-4B412722 (accessed 11.25.17).

54. See "Statement on Collective Bargaining," website of the American Association of University Professors (AAUP), reports and publications, accessed November 25, 2017, https://www.aaup.org/report/statement-collective-bargaining.

55. "Statement on Collective Bargaining."

56. National Labor Relations Board v. Yeshiva University, 444 U.S. 672 (1980).

57. *Yeshiva*, 444 U.S. at 680–86.

58. Point Park University v. Newspaper Guild of Pittsburgh/Communication Workers of America Local 38061, AFL-CIO, CLC, N.L.R.B. Case No.: 06-RC-012276 (Board Decision 2015).

59. Jaschik 2015.

60. See National Labor Relations Board v. Catholic Bishop of Chicago, 440 U.S. 490 (1979).

61. Weissmann 2013.

4. From Contracts to Constitutions

1. Shimshock 2017.

2. Nicholas Mikelionis, "Drexel Professor Who Called for 'White Genocide' Under Investigation as Donors and Students," Heatstreet, April 24, 2017, https://heatst.com/culture-

wars/drexel-professor-who-called-for-white-genocide-under-investigation-as-donors-and-students-flee/. Website no longer active.

3. Sweezy v. New Hampshire, 354 U.S. 234 (1957).

4. *Sweezy*, 354 U.S. at 250.

5. Rebecca Blank, "On Academic Freedom and Free Speech" (blog post), Office of the Chancellor website, University of Wisconsin, Madison, January 8, 2017, https://chancellor.wisc.edu/blog/on-academic-freedom-and-free-speech/.

6. West Virginia Board of Education v. Barnette, 319 U.S. 624, 642 (1943).

7. *Sweezy*, 354 U.S. at 263–64.

8. Keyishian v. Board of Regents, 385 U.S. 589 (1967).

9. *Keyishian*, 385 U.S. at 603. See also *Keyishian*, 385 U.S. at 606 (affirming Keyishian v. Board of Regents, 345 F.2d 236, 239 (1965), which rejected the idea that public employment may be subjected to any conditions, regardless of how unreasonable).

10. Tinker v. Des Moines (Iowa) Independent School District, 393 U.S. 503 (1969).

11. *Tinker*, 393 U.S. at 514. But see Morse v. Frederick, 551 U.S. 393 (2007), in which a banner supporting illegal drug use was confiscated by school officials. The court ruled that the public interest in stopping the use of illegal drug use outweighed the students' free speech rights.

12. Kurtz 2017.

13. Kurtz 2017.

14. Nelson 2010.

15. Pickering v. Board of Education, 391 U.S. 563 (1968); Garcetti v. Ceballos, 547 U.S. 410 (2006).

16. *Pickering*, 391 U.S. at 578.

17. *Pickering*, 391 U.S. at 578–83.

18. Arnett v. Kennedy, 416 U.S. 134 (1974).

19. *Arnett*, 416 U.S. at 162–64.

20. Connick v. Myers, 461 U.S. 138 (1983).

21. *Connick*, 461 U.S. at 153–54.

22. See Abcarian v. McDonald, 617 F.3d 931 (7th Cir 2010) (rehearing denied, unpublished).

23. Kerr v. Hurd, 694 F Supp 2d 817 (S.D. Ohio 2010).

24. Garcetti v. Ceballos, 547 U.S. 410, 414-16 (2006).

25. *Garcetti*, 547 U.S. at 413. See also "Garcetti v. Ceballos," *Oyez*, accessed March 15, 2018, https://www.oyez.org/cases/2005/04-473, which frames the question as: "Should a public employee's purely job-related speech, expressed strictly pursuant to the duties of employment, be protected by the First Amendment simply because it touched on a matter of public concern, or must the speech also be engaged in 'as a citizen?'"

26. *Garcetti*, 547 U.S. at 425–26.

27. Waters v. Churchill, 511 U.S. 661 (1994).

28. *Waters*, 511 U.S. at 681–82.

29. Isenalumhe v. McDuffie, 697 F.Supp. 2d 367 (E.D.N.Y. 2010).

30. Fox v. Traverse City Area Public Schools Board of Education, 605 F.3d 345 (6th Cir 2010).

31. Lane v. Franks, 134 S.Ct. 2369, 2383 (2014).

32. *Lane*, 134 S.Ct. at 2378–80.

33. *Lane*, 134 S.Ct. at 2380.

34. Whitfield v. Chartiers Valley School District, 707 F.Supp.2d 561 (W.D. Pa. 2010).

35. Gary Gauthier, "The Pickering-Connick Balancing Test" (blog post), LandMark Publications website, January 22, 2016, http://www.landmark-publications.com/2016/01/the-pickering-connick-balancing-test.html.

36. *Whitfield*, 707 F.Supp. at 596–97.

37. See Demers v. Austin, 746 F.3d 402 (9th Cir. 2014) (superseding and withdrawing Demers v. Austin, 729 F.3d 1011 (9th Cir. 2013), on denial of rehearing).

38. *Demers*, 746 F.3d at 406 (quoting *Garcetti*, 547 U.S. 410 (2006)).

39. *Demers*, 746 F.3d at 406.

40. *Demers*, 746 F.3d at 412. See also Arthur Willner, "Ninth Circuit Upholds Professor's First Amendment Claim in Demers v. Austin," The Federalist Society, July 29, 2014, http://www.fed-soc.org/publications/detail/ninth-circuit-upholds-professors-first-amendment-claim-in-demers-v-austin.

41. *Demers*, 746 F.3d at 411.

42. *Demers*, 746 F.3d at 406. For additional discussion see also Employment Law 2014.

43. See generally Ruane 2014.

44. Owens 2014.

45. Reed 2005.

46. Reed 2005.

47. Elliott 2007.

48. Adams v. University of North Carolina-Wilmington, 640 F.3d 550 (4th Cir. 2011).

49. *Adams*, 640 F.3d at 561–62.

50. Strauss 2017.

51. Strauss 2017.

52. Strauss 2017.

53. Strauss 2017.

54. Strauss 2017.

55. Van Heerden v. Board of Supervisors of Louisiana State University, No. 3:2010cv00 155—Document 60 (M.D. La. 2011).

56. *Van Heerden*, No. 3:2010cv00155—Document 60 (M.D. La. 2011).

57. Hustler Magazine, Inc. v. Falwell, 485 U.S. 46, 57 (1988).

58. See Axson-Flynn v. Johnson, 356 F.3d 1277 (10th Cir. 2004) and Edwards v. California University of Pennsylvania, 156 F.3d 488 (3rd Cir. 1998) cert. denied, 525 U.S. 1143 (1999).

59. See Yacovelli v. Moeser, Case No. 02-CV-596 (M.D.M.C. August 15, 2002) and Savage v. Gee, 665 F.3d 732 (6th Cir. 2012).

60. See Parate v. Isibor, 868 F.2d 821 (6th Cir. 1989) and Brown v. Armenti, 247 F.3d 69 (3rd Cir. 2001).

61. "Breaking Free" 2017, 10, 12.

62. See Martin v. Parrish, 805 F.2d 583 (5th Cir. 1986).

63. Rankin v. McPherson, 483 U.S. 378, 380 (1987).

64. *Rankin*, 483 U.S. at 380.

65. United Press International 1988.

66. Sullivan 2017.

5. Collegiality

1. Zirkel 1984, 231.

2. AAUP 2016b.

3. *American Heritage Dictionary of the English Language*, s.v. "collegiality," accessed March 30, 2018, https://www.ahdictionary.com/word/search.html?q=collegiality.

4. Wikipedia, s.v. "Collegiality," last modified April 8, 2018, https://en.wikipedia.org/wiki/Collegiality.

5. "Collegiality and Public Life," call for papers, *Public Policy* special issue, Society for Phenomenology and Existential Philosophy, accessed March 30, 2018, http://www.spep.org/papers/collegiality-and-public-life/.

6. Cipriano 2011, 163; see "What is Collegiality," North Dakota State University website, October 2013, https://www.ndsu.edu/fileadmin/forward/climate_workshops/20131106_Collegiality_Defined_Oct._2013.pdf.

7. Organ 1990, 43–72.

8. Barding v. Board of Curators of Lincoln University, 497 F.Supp. 1013 (W.D. Mo., 1980).

9. *Barding*, 497 F.Supp. at 1018.

10. *Barding*, 497 F.Supp. at n. 17 and 1021.

11. We recognize, of course, that personality and behavior are linked. The AAUP also prefers to define collegiality in behavioral terms instead of by personality traits.

12. AAUP 2016b.

13. Braxton, Proper, and Bayer 2011.

14. Professor Pompous and Professor Reticent are pseudonyms for colleagues that we have worked with during our careers.

15. See generally Tierney and Rhoads 1994.

16. Van Maanen and Schein 1979, 1–80.

17. See Antony 2002.

18. AAUP 2016b.

19. AAUP 2016b.

20. Seigel 2004, 406–41.

21. Connell and Savage 2001, 37–40.

22. Gross 2016; Cohen, 2010.

23. Johnson 2014.

24. Cho 2006, 805–57.

25. Christina Hynes Mesco, "Can Using an Emoji Land You in Court?" (blog post), Prinz Law Firm website, October 17, 2017, http://www.prinz-lawfirm.com/blog/2017/october/can-using-an-emoji-land-you-in-court/.

26. Volokh 2016.

27. See Roy Baroff's blog post about this on the North Carolina State University website, "Microaggressions: Can We Shift the Landscape to Microaffirmations?" June 29, 2016, https://facultyombuds.ncsu.edu/microaggressions-can-we-shift-the-landscape-to-microaffirmations/. The blog post explains further that the tool was "adapted from Sue, Dearly Wing, Micro aggressions in Everyday Life: Race, Gender and Sexual orientation, Wiley & Sons, 2010." An editor's note clarified that the "'Microaggression Tool' included in this post was provided as part of a workshop and was not developed by the Faculty Ombuds." It was provided, instead, "to allow exploration of comments and actions taken that can negatively impact people."

28. Baroff, "Microagressions."

29. Baroff, "Microagressions."

30. Baroff, "Microagressions."

31. Baroff, "Microagressions."

32. Romer v. Board of Trustees of Hobart and William Smith Colleges, 842 F.Supp. 703 (W.D.N.Y. 1994).

33. *Romer*, 842 F.Supp. at 705.

34. Mayberry v. Dees, 663 F.2d 502, 513 (4th Cir. 1981).

35. *Mayberry*, 663 F.2d at 514.

36. Connell, Melear, and Savage 2011, 529–87.

37. Rousseau 1995, 37.

38. Muhl 2001, 7–9.

39. Nelson v. University of Maine System, 944 F.Supp. 44 (D. Me. 1996).

40. Kaplan v. State University of New York at Geneseo, No. 93-CV-61 49T, slip op. at 28–29 W.D.N.Y. Sept. 24, 1998 (unpublished).

41. *Kaplan*, No. 93-CV-61 at 49T.

42. *Kaplan*, No. 93-CV-61 at 49T.

43. Watts v. Board of Curators, University of Missouri, 363 F.Supp. 883, 890 (W.D. Mo. 1973), aff'd, 495 F.2d 384 (8th Cir. 1974).

44. *Watts*, 363 F.Supp. at 890 (quoting Chitwood v. Feaster, 468 F.2d 359, 361 [4th Cir. 1972]).

45. *Watts*, 363 F.Supp at 890.

46. Mabey v. Reagan, 537 F.2d 1036 (9th Cir.1976) (reh'g denied June 24, 1976).

47. *Mabey*, 537 F.2d at 1040.

48. *Mabey*, 537 F.2d at 1046.

49. *Mabey*, 537 F.2d at 1048, 1050.

50. *Mabey*, 537 F.2d at 1050–51.

51. Yackshaw v. John Carroll University, 624 N.E.2nd 225 (Ohio App. 1993).

52. *Yackshaw*, 624 N.E.2nd at 230.

53. Bresnick v. Manhattanville College, 864 F.Supp. 327 (S.D.N.Y. 1994).

54. *Bresnick*, 864 F.Supp. at 328.

55. *Bresnick*, 864 F.Supp. at 328.

56. *Bresnick*, 864 F.Supp. (citing AAUP 1990a).

57. University of Baltimore v. Iz, 123 Md. App. 135 (1997).

58. *Iz*, 123 Md. App. at 135.

59. *Iz*, 123 Md. App. at 135.

60. *Iz*, 123 Md. App. at 135.

61. See Fisher v. Vassar College, 70 F.3d 1420 (2nd Cir. 1995) (Decided Sept. 7, 1995, Amended Dec. 14, 1995).

62. *Fisher*, 70 F.3d at 1428.

63. *Fisher*, 70 F.3d at 1429.

64. *Fisher*, 70 F.3d at 1429.

65. Stein v. Kent State University Board of Trustees, 994 F.Supp. 898, 909 (N.D. Ohio 1998).

66. Schalow v. Loyola University, 646 So.2d 502, 505 (La. App.1994).

67. Baker v. Lafayette College, 504 A.2d 247 (Pa. 1986), aff'd, 532 A.2d 399 (Pa. 1987).

68. Beitzell v. Jeffrey, 643 F.2d 870, 875 (1st Cir.1981).

69. See Paul Caron, "University of Arkansas to Permit Firing of Tenured Faculty for Lack of Collegiality," *TaxProf Blog*, November 23, 2017, http://taxprof.typepad.com/taxprof_blog/2017/11/university-of-arkansas-to-change-tenure-policy-to-permit-firing-of-faculty-for-lack-of-collegiality.html.

70. See Lewin 2002.

71. Arenson 2002.

72. Arenson 2002.

73. See "Essay on Collegiality," USM News, accessed March 30, 2018, http://www.usmnews.net/On_Collegiality%201%20.pdf.

74. Johnston, Schimmel, and O'Hara 2010, 1–13.

75. Zirkel 1984, 224–44.

76. Heiser 2004, 385–428.

77. Heiser 2004, 385–428.

Conclusion

1. Hanson 2017.

2. Stranger 2017.

3. William Jacobsen, "Smear Campaign Against Cornell Prof Who Opposed Grad Student Unionization" (blog post), *Legal Insurrection*, April 27, 2017, http://legalinsurrection.com/2017/04/smear-campaign-againt-cornell-prof-who-opposed-grad-student-unionization/.

4. North Carolina House Bill 527/Senate Bill 507.

5. Locker 2016.

6. See "Diversity at Tennessee," The University of Tennessee, Knoxville, Faculty Senate website, accessed March 31, 2016, https://senate.utk.edu/diversity-at-tennessee/.

7. Kristina Cowan, "High Education's Higher Accountability" (blog post), American Council on Education website, December 15, 2013, http://www.acenet.edu/the-presidency/columns-and-features/Pages/Higher-Education's-Higher-Accountability.aspx.

8. "Why the U. of Chicago is the University of Common Sense" 2016.

9. Vivanco and Rhodes 2016.

10. Rudgers and Peterson 2017.

11. Woodhouse 2015.

12. Abby Jackson, "ITT Tech's Closure is One of the Largest in U.S. History—and it was 'Long Overdue,'" *Business Insider*, September 6, 2016, http://www.businessinsider.com/itt-techs-closure-was-one-of-the-largest-in-us-history-2016-9.

13. Seltzer 2017.

14. See, e.g., Ward 2017, reporting on financial challenges, declining enrollment, a vote of the board of directors to suspend admissions for 2018, and the possibility that the school could close.

15. Kim D. Chanbonpin, "The Legal Writing Institute" (press release, March 8, 2017), https://www.saltlaw.org/wp-content/uploads/2017/03/Press-Release-Citizenship-Project-FINAL.pdf. See also Paul Caron, " 'Full Citizenship for All Law Faculty' Launched to Correct Gender Disparities Among Law Profs," *TaxProf Blog*, March 8, 2017, http://taxprof.typepad.com/taxprof_blog/2017/03/full-citizenship-project-for-all-law-faculty-launched-to-correct-gender-disparities-among-law-profs.html, for additional information about the project and further discussion as to challenges facing many of the faculty who teach in skills-based positions. Additional status-related advocacy information is available at the Legal Writing Institute, https://www.lwionline.org/resources/status-related-advocacy.

16. Chanbonpin, 1.

17. Chanbonpin, 1.

18. Lubet 2017.

19. Caleb Park, "Drexel Professor Booted After Blaming Vegas Massacre on 'Trumpism' Threatens Legal Action," Fox News website, October 10, 2017, http://www.foxnews.com/us/2017/10/10/drexel-professor-who-tweeted-about-white-supremacist-patriarchy-threatens-legal-action.html.

20. AAUP 1990b.

21. See, e.g., Cash, Rae, Steel, and Winkler 2012, 292–98.

22. "Fact Sheet," U.S. Department of Education, Office of Civil Rights, April 4, 2011, https://www2.ed.gov/about/offices/list/ocr/docs/dcl-factsheet-201104.html.

23. Von Spakovsky and Slattery 2017.

24. Von Spakovsky and Slattery 2017.

25. AAUP 2016a.

26. "Employment," Title IX, accessed March 31, 2018, http://www.titleix.info/10-Key-Areas-of-Title-IX/Employment.aspx.

27. Simon 2017.

REFERENCES

AAUP. 1990a. *Policy Documents and Reports*. 7th ed. Washington, DC: AAUP.

——. 1990b. *Statement on Government of Colleges and Universities*. 1966, rev. 1990. https://www.aaup.org/report/statement-government-colleges-and-universities.

——. 2009. *Faculty Handbooks as Enforceable Contracts: A State Guide*. Washington, DC: American Association of University Professors. https://www.aaup.org/sites/default/files/files/Faculty%20Handbooks%20as%20Contracts%20Complete.pdf.

——. 2016a. *The History, Uses and Abuses of Title IX*. https://www.aaup.org/report/history-uses-and-abuses-title-ix.

——. 2016b. *On Collegiality as a Criterion for Faculty Evaluation*. 1999, rev. 2016. https://www.aaup.org/report/collegiality-criterion-faculty-evaluation.

Alexander, F. King. 2017. "Tax Reform Should Not Come on the Backs of Students and Universities." *Greater Baton Rouge Business Report*, November 21. https://www.businessreport.com/politics/tax-reform-lsu-king-alexander-column.

Antony, James Soto. 2002. "Reexamining Doctoral Student Socialization and Professional Development: Moving Beyond the Congruence and Assimilation Orientation." In *Higher Education: Handbook of Theory and Research*, vol. 17, edited by J. C. Smart and William G. Tierney, 349–80. New York: Agathon Press.

Arenson, Karen W. 2002. "Star Scholar Fights for His Life at Brooklyn." *New York Times*, December 18. http://www.nytimes.com/2002/12/18/nyregion/star-scholar-fights-for-his-future-at-brooklyn-college.html.

Azvolinsky, Anna. 2017, "Dealing with Unethical or Illegal Conduct in Higher Education." *The Scientist*, November 1, 2017. https://www.the-scientist.com/?articles. view/articleNo/50651/title/Dealing-with-Unethical-or-Illegal-Conduct-in-Higher-Education/.

Association of Governing Boards and United Educators. 2009. *The State of Enterprise Risk Management at Colleges and Universities Today*. Washington, DC: Association of Governing Boards of Universities and Colleges. http://www.vsu.edu/files/docs/ internal-audit/the-state-of-enterprise-risk-manangement-at-colleges-and-universities-today.pdf.

Baker, Tom, and David Moss. 2009. "Government as Risk Manager." In *New Perspectives on Regulation*, edited by David Moss and John Cisternino, 87–109. Cambridge, MA: Tobin Project.

Bartol, Curt R., and Anne M. Bartol. 2014. *Criminal Behavior: Psychological Approach*. 10th ed. Boston: Pearson, 2014.

Belkin, Douglas. 2015. "Test Finds College Graduates Lack Skill for White-Collar Jobs." *Wall Street Journal*, January 16. https://www.wsj.com/articles/test-finds-many-students-ill-prepared-to-enter-work-force-1421432744.

"Better Ways to Pay for College." 2015. *Economist*, August 22. http://www.econo mist.com/news/leaders/21661663-hillary-clinton-and-especially-marco-rubio-have-promising-ideas-how-finance-university.

Birch, Susan A. J., and Paul Bloom. 2007. "The Curse of Knowledge in Reasoning About False Beliefs." *Psychological Science* 18, no. 5: 382–86.

Bok, Derek. 2013. *Higher Education in America*. Princeton, NJ: Princeton University Press.

Bohnet, Iris. "How to Take the Bias Out of Interviews." 2016. *Harvard Business Review*, April 18. https://hbr.org/2016/04/how-to-take-the-bias-out-of-interviews.

Braxton, John M., Eve Proper, and Alan E. Bayer. 2011. *Professors Behaving Badly: Faculty Misconduct in Graduate Education*. Baltimore: The Johns Hopkins University Press.

"Breaking Free." 2017. *Economist*, March 25–31.

Brown, Ryan P., Michael Tamborski, XiaoQian Wang, Collin D. Barnes, Michael D. Mumford, Shane Connelly, and Lynn D. Devenport. 2011. "Moral Credentialing and the Rationalization of Misconduct." *Ethics and Behavior* 21, no. 1 (February 2): 1–12.

Buehler, Roger, Dale Griffin, and Michael Ross. 1994. "Exploring the Planning Fallacy: Why People Underestimate Their Task Completion Times." *Journal of Personality and Social Psychology* 67, no. 3 (September): 366–81.

Campos, Paul F. 2015. "The Real Reason College Tuition Costs So Much." *New York Times*, April 4. https://www.nytimes.com/2015/04/05/opinion/sunday/the-real-reason-college-tuition-costs-so-much.html?mcubz=1.

Cash, Hilarie, Cosette D. Rae, Ann H. Steel, and Alexander Winkler. 2012. "Internet Addiction: A Brief Summary of Research and Practice." *Current Psychiatry Reviews* 8, no. 4: 292–98.

Cassuto, Leonard. 2013. "Ph.D. Attrition: How Much is Too Much?" *Chronicle of Higher Education*, July 1. http://www.chronicle.com/article/PhD-Attrition-How-Much-Is/ 140045/.

Cho, Sumi. 2006. " 'Unwise,' 'Untimely,' and 'Extreme': Redefining Collegial Culture in the Workplace and Revaluing the Role of Social Change." *University of California Davis Law Review* 39: 805–57.

Cipriano, Robert E. 2011. *Facilitating a Collegial Department in Higher Education: Strategies for Success.* San Francisco: CA: Jossey-Bass.

Cohen, Patricia. 2010. "Professor is a Label That Leans to the Left." *New York Times*, January 17. http://www.nytimes.com/2010/01/18/arts/18liberal.html.

Connell, Mary Ann, Kerry Brian Melear, and Frederick Savage. 2011. "Collegiality in Higher Education Employment Decisions: The Evolving Law." *Journal of College and University Law* 37, no. 3: 529–87.

Connell, Mary Ann, and Frederick Savage. 2001. "Does Collegiality Count?" *Academe* 87, no. 6: 37–40.

C. W. 2013. "Prospect Theory and Economics." *Economist*, August 5. https://www.economist.com/blogs/freeexchange/2013/08/prospect-theory-and-economics.

Desai, Meghnad. 2015. *Hubris: Why Economists Failed to Predict the Crisis and How to Avoid the Next One.* New Haven: Yale University Press.

DeYoung, Colin G., Lena C. Quilty, and Jordan B. Peterson. 2007. "Between Facets and Domains: 10 Aspects of the Big Five." *Journal of Personality and Social Psychology* 93, no. 5, 880–96.

DuCharme, Wesley. 1970. "A Response Bias Explanation of Conservatism in Human Inference." *Journal of Experimental Psychology* 85, no. 1 (July): 66–74.

Elliott, Dan. 2007. "Colorado Prof Fired After 9/11 Remarks." *Washington Post*, July 24. http://www.washingtonpost.com/wp-dyn/content/article/2007/07/24/AR2007072402000.html.

"Employment Law—Free Speech Rights—Ninth Circuit Finds Garcetti Official Duty Rule Inapplicable to Professorial Speech in Public-University Context.—Demers v. Austin, No. 11-35558, 2014 WL 306321 (9th Cir. Jan. 29, 2014)." 2014. *Harvard Law Review* 127, no. 6: 1823–30.

Etchells, Pete. 2015. "Declinism: Is the World Actually Getting Worse?" *The Guardian*, January 16. https://www.theguardian.com/science/head-quarters/2015/jan/16/declinism-is-the-world-actually-getting-worse.

Farnsworth, Ward. 2007. *The Legal Analyst: A Toolkit for Thinking About the Law.* Chicago: University of Chicago Press.

Fischoff, Baruch, Paul Slovic, and Sarah Lichtenstein. 1977. "Knowing With Certainty: The Appropriateness of Extreme Confidence." *Journal of Experimental Psychology: Human Perception and Performance* 3, no. 4: 552–64.

Flood, Julee T., and Jeffrey Roberts. 2017. "The Evolving Nature of Higher Education Accreditation: Considerations for Institutional Research Leaders." In *Legal Considerations for Assessment and Institutional Research Leaders*, edited by Matthew B. Fuller, 73–84. New Directions for Institutional Research, vol. 172. New York: John Wiley and Sons.

Franke, Ann H. 2011. "Faculty Handbooks: Their Legal Significance, What They Should Contain and How to Draft Them." Paper presented at the 21st Annual Legal Issues in Higher Education Conference, Washington, DC, October 16–18.

Fried, Charles. 2015. *Contracts as Promise: A Theory of Contractual Obligation.* 2nd ed. New York: Oxford University Press.

Gatewood, Robert, Hubert S. Feild, and Murray Barrick. 2016. *Human Resource Selection*. 8th ed. Boston: Cengage.

Gee, Alastair. 2017. "Outside in America: Facing Poverty, Academicians Turn to Sex Work and Sleeping in Cars." *Guardian*, September 28. https://www.theguardian.com/us-news/2017/sep/28/adjunct-professors-homeless-sex-work-academia-poverty.

Ginsberg, Benjamin. 2011. *The Fall of the Faculty: The Rise of the All-Administrative University and Why It Matters*. New York: Oxford.

Gladwell. Malcolm. 2011. "The Order of Things: What College Rankings Really Tell Us." *New Yorker*, February 14. http://www.newyorker.com/magazine/2011/02/14/the-order-of-things.

Gross, Neil. 2016. "Professors Are Overwhelmingly Liberal. Do Universities Need to Change Hiring Practices?" *Los Angeles Times*, May 20. http://www.latimes.com/opinion/op-ed/la-oe-gross-academia-conservatives-hiring-20160520-snap-story.html.

——. 2017. "Professors Behaving Badly." *New York Times*, September 30. https://www.nytimes.com/2017/09/30/opinion/sunday/adjunct-professors-politics.html.

Grossman, Ron, and Charles Leroux. 1993. "The Absent Professor: Scholar Two-Timed 2 Universities, But That May Not Have Been His Worst Sin." *Chicago Tribune*, January 29. http://articles.chicagotribune.com/1993-01-29/features/9303173848_1_tzvee-zahavy-professors-academic-affairs.

Hanson, Victor Davis. 2017. "Behind the Facades, Universities Have Broken Faith with a Once-Noble Legacy of Free Inquiry." *National Review*, May 4. http://www.nationalreview.com/article/447323/berkeley-claremont-free-speech-violations-result-losing-university-principles?u.

Hardy, Cynthia, and Steve Maguire. 2016. "Organizing Risk: Discourse, Power, and Riskification." *Academy of Management Review* 4, no. 1: 80–108.

Hartocollis, Anemona, and Jess Bidgood. 2015. "Racial Discrimination Protests Ignite at Colleges Across the U.S." *New York Times*, November 11. https://www.nytimes.com/2015/11/12/us/racial-discrimination-protests-ignite-at-colleges-across-the-us.html?_r=0.

Heiser, Gregory M. 2004. " 'Because the Stakes are So Small': Collegiality, Polemic, and Professionalism in Academic Employment Decisions." *University of Kansas Law Review* 52: 385–428.

"Herbert Simon." 2009. *Economist*, March 20. http://www.economist.com/node/13350892.

Hinds, Michael de Courcy. 1993. "A Campus Case: Speech or Harassment?" *New York Times*, May 15. http://www.nytimes.com/1993/05/15/us/a-campus-case-speech-or-harassment.html?pagewanted=all.

Jaschik, Scott. 2015. "A Weaker 'Yeshiva' "? *Inside Higher Ed*, July 21. https://www.insidehighered.com/news/2015/07/21/point-park-recognizes-faculty-union-possible-sign-nlrb-has-weakened-yeshiva-decision.

Johnson, Jeffrey A. 2014. "The Happy Hour Test." *Inside Higher Ed*, April 25. https://www.insidehighered.com/advice/2014/04/25/essay-defending-idea-collegiality-matters-hiring.

Johnston, Pattie C., Tammy Schimmel, and Hunter O'Hara. 2010. "Revisiting the AAUP Recommendation: Initial Validation of a University Faculty Model of Collegiality." *College Quarterly* 13, no. 2 (Jan 10): 1–13.

Jost, John T. 2017. "A Theory of System Justification." *Psychological Science Agenda*, June. http://www.apa.org/science/about/psa/2017/06/system-justification.aspx.

Judge, Timothy, E. M. Annelies van Vianen, and Irene de Pater. 2004. "Emotional Stability, Core Self-Evaluations, and Job Outcomes: A Review of the Evidence and an Agenda for Future Research." *Human Performance* 17, no. 3: 325–46.

Kahneman, Daniel. 2011. "Don't Blink! The Hazards of Confidence." *New York Times Magazine*, October 19. http://www.nytimes.com/2011/10/23/magazine/dont-blink-the-hazards-of-confidence.html?pagewanted=all.

Kurtz, Stanley. 2017. "Federal Funding and Campus Free Speech: A Proposal." *National Review*, February 21. http://www.nationalreview.com/corner/445102/federal-funding-and-campus-free-speech-proposal.

Landau, Joel. 2014. "Crocodile Hunter Steve Irwin's Final Moments before Death Revealed by Cameraman." *Daily News*, March 10. http://www.nydailynews.com/news/world/steve-irwins-final-moments-death-revealed-article-1.1716587.

Langbert, Mitchell, Anthony J. Quain, and Daniel B. Klein. 2016. "Faculty Voter Registration in Economics, History, Journalism, Law, and Psychology." *Econ Journal Watch* 13, no. 3: 422–51.

Leap, Terry L. 1995. *Tenure, Discrimination, and the Courts*. 2nd ed. Ithaca, NY: Cornell University Press.

Lewin, Tamar. 2002. "'Collegiality' as a Tenure Battleground." *New York Times*, July 12.

Locker, Richard. 2016. "University of Tennessee Diversity Funding Bill Allowed to Become Law." *The Tennessean*, May 20. http://www.tennessean.com/story/news/politics/2016/05/20/university-tennessee-diversity-funding-bill-allowed-become-law/84650208/.

Long, Rebecca G., William P. Bowers, Tim Barnett, and Michael C. White. 1998. "Research Productivity of Graduates of Management: Effects of Academic Origin and Academic Affiliation." *Academy of Management Journal* 4, no. 6, 704–14.

Lubet, Steven. 2017. "Steven Salaita's Exile from Academia: 'I Refuse to Tolerate the Indignities of a Blacklist.'" *Chicago Tribune*, July 27. http://www.chicagotribune.com/news/opinion/commentary/ct-steve-salaita-academia-exit-perspec-0728-jm-20170727-story.html.

Marotta, David John. 2013. "What is Rent-Seeking Behavior?" *Forbes*, February 24. https://www.forbes.com/sites/davidmarotta/2013/02/24/what-is-rent-seeking-behavior/#7526128f658a.

Mount, Michael, Remus Ilies, and Erin Johnson. 2006. "Relationship of Personality Traits and Counterproductive Work Behaviors: The Mediating Effects of Job Satisfaction." *Personnel Psychology* 59, no. 3 (August 17): 591–622.

Muhl, Charles J. 2001. "The Employment-at-Will Doctrine: Three Major Exceptions." *Monthly Labor Review*, January: 3–11. https://www.bls.gov/opub/mlr/2001/01/art1full.pdf.

Munsch, M. H., and J. D. Verdi. 2006. "Administration of Tenure Policies." In *Academic Freedom and Tenure: A Legal Compendium*, edited by S. G. Olswang and C. A. Cameron, 889–900. Washington, DC: National Association of College and University Attorneys.

Nelson, Cary. 2010. "Defining Academic Freedom." *Inside Higher Ed*, December 21. https://www.insidehighered.com/views/2010/12/21/defining-academic-freedom.

Norton, Michael I., Daniel Mochon, and Dan Ariely. 2012. "The IKEA Effect: When Labor Leads to Love." *Journal of Consumer Psychology* 22, no. 3 (July 3): 453–60.

Nugent, Bridget, and Julee Flood. 2014. "Rescuing Academic Freedom from Garcetti v. Ceballos: An Evaluation of Current Case Law and a Proposal for the Protection of Core Academic, Administrative, and Advisory Speech." *Journal of College and University Law* 40, no. 1: 116–31.

O'Neil, Robert M. 2010. "Judicial Deference to Academic Decisions: An Outmoded Concept?" *Journal of College and University Law* 36, no. 3: 729–47.

Organ, Dennis W. 1990. "The Motivational Basis of Organizational Citizenship Behavior." In *Research in Organizational Behavior*, vol. 12, edited by Barry M. Staw and Larry L. Cummings, 43–72. Greenwich, CT: JAI Press.

Owens, Mike 2014. "Former UVa Associate Dean Sentenced to 8 Years for Child Pornography Charges." *Daily Progress*, July 15. http://www.dailyprogress.com/news/former-uva-associate-dean-sentenced-to-years-for-child-pornography/article_3b8df468-0bd9-11e4-8d3c-001a4bcf6878.html.

"Paying for College: A Teaspoon of Sugar." 2015. *Economist*, June 20. http://www.economist.com/news/united-states/21654669-very-old-solution-new-problem-teaspoon-sugar.

Pringle, Paul, and Adam Elmahrek. 2017. "USC Had Many Warnings about Medical Dean's Behavior but Took Little Action." *Los Angeles Times*, November 14. http://www.latimes.com/local/lanow/la-me-usc-dean-20171114-story.html.

Pringle, Paul, Harriet Ryan, Matt Hamilton, and Adam Elmarek. 2017. "Investigators Seek Photos and Videos of Former USC Medical School Dean With Drugs." *Los Angeles Times*, August 31. http://www.latimes.com/local/lanow/la-me-usc-dean-photos-drugs-20170831-story.html.

Pronin, Emily, David Y. Lin, and Lee Ross. 2002. "The Bias Blindspot: Perceptions of Bias in Self Versus Others." *Personality and Social Psychology Bulletin* 28, no. 3 (March 1): 369–81.

Rea, Shilo. 2015. "Researchers Find Everyone Has Bias Blind Spot." *Piper: Campus and Community News*, June 8. https://www.cmu.edu/news/stories/archives/2015/june/bias-blind-spot.html.

Reed, T. R. 2005. "Professor Under Fire For 9/11 Comments." *Washington Post*, February 5. http://www.washingtonpost.com/wp-dyn/articles/A76-2005Feb4.html.

Roese, Neal, and Kathleen D. Vohs. 2012. "Hindsight Bias." *Perspectives on Psychological Science* 7, no. 5 (September 5): 411–26.

Rousseau, Denise M. 1995. *Psychological Contracts in Organizations: Understanding Written and Unwritten Agreements*. Thousand Oaks, CA: Sage Publications.

Ruane, Kathleen Ann. 2014. "Freedom of Speech and Press: Exceptions to the First Amendment." Congressional Research Service 7-5700, September 8.

Rudgers Lisa M., and Julie A. Peterson. 2017. "Coming in 2017." *Inside Higher Ed*, January 13. https://www.insidehighered.com/views/2017/01/13/upcoming-trends-2017-colleges-should-prepare-essay.

Rynes, Sarah L., Kenneth G. Brown, and Amy E. Colbert. 2002. "Seven Common Misconceptions About Human Resource Practices: Research Findings Versus Practitioner Beliefs." *Academy of Management Executive*, 16, no. 3: 92–102.

Saravanan, P. 2015. "How to Avoid Loss Aversion Trap, Few Techniques Which Can Help." *The Financial Express*, December 1. http://www.financialexpress.com/industry/banking-finance/staying-put-how-to-stop-loss/172476/.

Schacter, Daniel. 2001. *The Seven Sins of Memory: How the Mind Forgets and Remembers*. Boston, MA: Houghton Mifflin.

Seery, John E. 2017. "Somewhere Between a Jeremiad and a Eulogy." *Modern Age 59*, no. 3 (Summer): 61–71. https://home.isi.org/sites/default/files/MA59.3_Seery_Symposium Essay.pdf.

Seigel, Michael L. 2004. "On Collegiality." *Journal of Legal Education 54*, no. 3: 406–41.

Seltzer, Rick. 2017. "What Comes After Whittier Shutdown?" *Inside Higher Ed*, April 25. https://www.insidehighered.com/news/2017/04/25/whittier-law-school-shutdown-raises-prospect-future-closures-and-access.

Shermer, Michael. 2014. "How the Survivor Bias Distorts Reality." *Scientific American*, September 1. https://www.scientificamerican.com/article/how-the-survivor-bias-distorts-reality/.

Shimshock, Rob. 2017. "Professor: 'Trump Must Hang': Republicans Should be Executed for Each Immigrant Deported." *Daily Caller*, April 7. http://dailycaller.com/2017/04/07/professor-trump-must-hang-republicans-should-be-executed-for-each-immigrant-deported/.

Simon, Caroline. 2017. "More and More Students Need Mental Health Services. But Colleges Struggle to Keep Up." *USA Today*, May 4. http://college.usatoday.com/2017/05/04/more-and-more-students-need-mental-health-services-but-colleges-struggle-to-keep-up/.

Sinnott-Armstrong, Walter, and Robert J. Fogelin. 2015. *Understanding Arguments: An Introduction*. 9th ed. concise. Stamford, CT: Cengage Learning.

Smith, Jay M., and Mary Willingham. 2015. *Cheated: The UNC Scandal, the Education of Athletes, and the Future of Big-Time College Sports*. Lincoln, NE: Potomac Books.

Sowell, Thomas. 1998. "Abolish Adolescence." *Jewish World Review*, May 1. http://www.jewishworldreview.com/cols/sowell050198.html.

Stranger, Allison. 2017. "Understanding the Angry Mob at Middlebury that Gave Me a Concussion." *New York Times*, March 13. https://www.nytimes.com/2017/03/13/opinion/understanding-the-angry-mob-that-gave-me-a-concussion.html.

Strauss, Valerie. 2017. "Georgetown Professor Under Fire for Lecture About Slavery and Islam." *Washington Post*, February 17. https://www.washingtonpost.com/news/answer-sheet/wp/2017/02/17/georgetown-professor-under-fire-by-conservatives-for-lecture-about-slavery-and-islam/?utm_term=.0a401d3632b8.

Sullivan, Tim. 2017. "UK Fans Could Face Felonies, Lawsuits." *Courier Journal*, April 8. http://www.courier-journal.com/story/sports/tim-sullivan/2017/04/07/sullivan-uk-fans-could-face-felonies-lawsuits/100165482/.

Tierney, William G., and Robert A. Rhoads. 1994. "Faculty Socialization as a Cultural Process: A Mirror of Institutional Commitment." ASHE-ERIC Higher Educational Report No. 93-6. Washington DC: George Washington University, School of Education and Human Development.

Ung, Jenny. 2015. "International Students Earn More than Half of Advanced Degrees STEM Degrees in the U.S." *USA Today College*, July 8. http://college.usatoday.com/2015/07/08/international-students-stem-degrees/.

United Press International. 1988. "Fired Over Reagan Barb, Clerk Wins Job, Back Pay." *Los Angeles Times*, April 29. http://articles.latimes.com/1988-04-29/news/mn-2575_1_back-pay.

Van Maanen, John, and Schein, Edgar H. 1979. "Toward a Theory of Organizational Socialization." In *Research in Organizational Behavior: An Annual Series of Analytic Essays and Critical Reviews*, edited by Barry M. Staw, 209–64. Greenwich, CT: JAI Press, Inc.

Vivanco, Lenor, and Dawn Rhodes. 2016. "U. of C. Tells Incoming Freshmen It Does not Support 'Trigger Warnings' or 'Safe Spaces.'" *Chicago Tribune*, August 25. http://chicagotribune.com/news/local/breaking/ct-university-of-chicago-safe-spaces-letter-met-20160825-story.html.

Volokh, Eugene. 2016. "UC Teaching Faculty Members Not to Criticize Race-Based Affirmative Action, Call America 'Melting Pot,' and More." *Washington Post*, June 15.

Von Spakovsky, Hans, and Elizabeth Slattery. 2017. "Betsy DeVos Stands Up for Due Process Rights in Campus Sexual Assault Cases." *Daily Signal*, September 8. http://dailysignal.com//print?post_id=355364.

Ward, Stephanie F. 2018. "Valparaiso Law School Told by Board to Not Admit First-year Students in 2018." *ABA Journal*, November 16. http://www.abajournal.com/news/article/valparaiso_law_school_told_by_board_to_not_admit_first-year_students_in_201.

Weissmann, Jordan. 2013. "The Ever-Shrinking Role of Tenured College Professors (in 1 Chart)." *The Atlantic*, April 10. https://www.theatlantic.com/business/archive/2013/04/the-ever-shrinking-role-of-tenured-college-professors-in-1-chart/274849/.

Werner, Jon M., and Mark C. Bolino. 1997. "Explaining U.S. Courts of Appeals Decisions Involving Performance Appraisal: Accuracy, Fairness, and Validation." *Personnel Psychology* 50, no. 1 (March): 1–24.

"Why the U. of Chicago is the University of Common Sense." 2016. *Chicago Tribune*, August 25. http://www.chicagotribune.com/news/opinion/editorials/ct-university-chicago-safe-spaces-trigger-warnings-edit-20160825-story.html.

Williams, Walter E. 2012. "Schools of Education." *The Patriot Post*, January 25. https://patriotpost.us/opinion/12397.

Wittenbaum, Gwen M. 2000. "The Bias Toward Discussing Shared Information: Why Are High Status Group Members Immune?" *Communication Research* 27, no. 3 (June): 379–401.

Wood, Melody. 2015. "One College's War Against 'Mothering' and 'Fathering.'" *Daily Signal*, July 31. http://dailysignal.com/2015/07/31/one-colleges-war-against-terms-mothering-and-fathering/.

Woodhouse, Kellie. 2015. "Does Compliance Cost $11K per Student?" *Inside Higher Ed*, August 3. https://www.insidehighered.com/news/2015/08/03/vanderbilt-university-weighs-its-controversial-compliance-costs-report.

Zirkel, Perry A. 1984. "Personality as a Criterion for Faculty Tenure: The Enemy It Is Us." *Cleveland State Law Review* 33, no. 1: 224–44.

Zoffer, H. J. 1978. "The Consummate Faculty Person." *The Academy of Management Review* 3, no. 4 (October): 901–6.

INDEX

CPSIA information can be obtained
at www.ICGtesting.com
Printed in the USA
LVHW090544071118
596285LV00002B/457/P

9 781501 728952